DONOR-CENTERED FUNDRAISING

US EDITION

DONOR-CENTERED FUNDRAISING

How to hold on to your donors and raise much more money

PENELOPE BURK

BURK & ASSOCIATES LTD. / CYGNUS APPLIED RESEARCH, INC.
UNITED STATES—CANADA—UNITED KINGDOM

Donor-Centered Fundraising
Penelope Burk

Director, Research and Data Analysis: Jeff Dubberley, B.A., M.A.
Associate Researcher: Brian Twohey
Contributing Researcher: Annabelle Bennetts
Editor: Marion K. Ringe, M.A., CFRE
Design: Mark Narsansky, RBA Advertising Ltd., Toronto
Publisher: Burk & Associates Ltd.
Printer: Friesens Corporation
Printed in Canada

ISBN: 0–9687978–1-4

To order direct from the publisher please contact Burk & Associates Ltd.

in the United States
211 East Ontario Street
Suite 1800
Chicago, IL 60611
t. (800) 263 0267

in Canada
3240 Twin Oaks Cres.
Burlington, ON
L7M 3A2
t. (800) 263 0267

email: j.dubberley@donorcentered.com
www.donorcentered.com

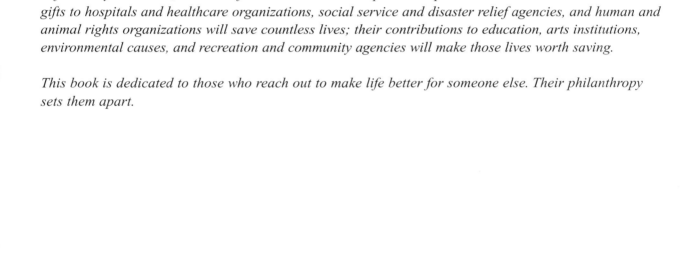

Before the year is over, millions of Americans will make philanthropic contributions to charities. Their gifts to hospitals and healthcare organizations, social service and disaster relief agencies, and human and animal rights organizations will save countless lives; their contributions to education, arts institutions, environmental causes, and recreation and community agencies will make those lives worth saving.

This book is dedicated to those who reach out to make life better for someone else. Their philanthropy sets them apart.

TABLE OF CONTENTS

Part I   Donor-Centered Fundraising

Part II   Making Donor-Centered Fundraising Work

PART I
Donor-Centered Fundraising

1

Defining a New Fundraising Standard

In the first place, I advise you to apply to all those who you know will give something;
next to those of whom you are uncertain whether they will give anything or not, and show
them the list of those who have given; and lastly, do not neglect those who you are sure
will give nothing; for in some of them you may be mistaken.[1]

—Benjamin Franklin

Most professional fundraisers can recite this famous eighteenth century quotation by Benjamin Franklin in which the widely acknowledged father of American fundraising describes his winning strategy for raising money. These few words illuminate Franklin's approach and reflect his innate understanding of the connection between influence and fundraising success. Franklin's perfunctory description still captures the essence of fundraising practice today—or at least the part of fundraising practice that raises most of the money.

"Most of the money" does not mean most of the contributions, though. In fact, in 2000, 89% of American households gave over $160 billion in cash, real property or other in-kind donations to charitable organizations.[2] This is a laudably high rate of participation in philanthropy. But, an earlier study by HNW and Harris Interactive, Inc. (1995) found that 20% of American households make 71% of the charitable contributions.[3] As wealth has become concentrated in even fewer hands since then, it is likely that philanthropy has followed the same pattern. Is it just a fact of life that the few must shoulder most of the load or could the imbalance be attributable, in part, to fundraising methodology?

[1] Franklin, Benjamin *The Autobiography of Benjamin Franklin* ed. Leonard W. Labaree, (Yale University Press) 1964

[2] Toppe, Christopher et al. *Giving and Volunteering in the United States: Findings from a national survey* (Independent Sector: Washington, DC) 2001, p 28

[3] AAFRC Trust for Philanthropy *Giving USA 2002: The Annual Report on Philanthropy for the year 2001.* (AAFRC: Indianapolis, IN) 2002

If a rising tide floats all ships, then a buoyant economy carries along with it a prosperous fundraising industry. But the fundraising industry's real test comes when the economic engine slows down . . . or when a national crisis drains support from charities in favor of a single issue . . . or when some of the big players in business and philanthropy fall from grace.

Philanthropy is not simply a factor of the economy. Every fundraising practitioner can recount stories about the reclusive senior, who after working as a secretary and living a thrifty life, leaves a million dollars to the local university . . . which she never attended. Philanthropy is a funny thing. It can grab hold of people and make them do joyful, wonderful things, often well beyond what appears to be their financial capability. Yet for all the strides that the fundraising business has made, it is too often on the sidelines marvelling at these happy surprises when it should be on the front lines making them happen.

Though the fundraising industry has grown in the last forty years from a largely volunteer force to an industry of hundreds of thousands of professionals, charitable giving as a percentage of GDP has remained the same. When looking at the relationship between philanthropy and income, giving actually fell from 2.1% of personal income in 1967 to 1.8% in 2001.[4] But fundraising is capable of establishing a much higher standard of performance, first because philanthropic potential is nowhere near capacity and second because fundraising methodology can be significantly improved. Transforming untapped giving potential into real dollars, however, will require examining long held beliefs about who is a philanthropist and how money should be raised. The things that are not working for donors need to be put on the table for discussion; then they need to be dealt with.

The prophetic Ben Franklin knew all about barriers to success in fundraising. Though this paragraph doesn't tend to get quoted by people in the fundraising business, here's what else he said when he was asked to assist in raising money for a new venture:

> *It was about this time that . . . the Reverend Gilbert Tennent came to me with a request that I would assist him in procuring a subscription for erecting a new meeting-house.... Unwilling to make myself disagreeable to my fellow-citizens by too frequently soliciting their contributions, I absolutely refused. He then desired I would furnish him with a list of the names of persons I knew by experience to be generous and public-spirited. I thought it would be unbecoming in me, after their kind compliance with my solicitations, to mark them out to be worried by other beggars, and therefore refused to give such a list.*

Instead, Franklin gave the Reverend the advice that introduces this chapter, after which Tennent . . .

> *. . . laughed and thanked me, and said he would take my advice. He did so, for he asked of everybody; and he obtained a much larger sum than he expected, with which he erected the capacious and elegant meeting-house that stands in Arch Street.*

[4] *ibid*

The genius of Franklin's fundraising philosophy is that it focused not on the money but on the people behind the money. By not exposing his donors to over-solicitation and by respecting their privacy, he established parameters for Reverend Tennent's own fundraising efforts. Far from being restrictive, they worked. Fundraising practice today, however, focuses on the gift, relegating the donor to the role of means to an end. Nowhere is this more evident than in the direct marketing programs which now control the business of fundraising and through which most donors give. Though very adept at acquiring donors, direct marketing is much less successful at retaining them. Franklin warned against over-solicitation, but a growing charitable sector did not hear that part of the message. Now over-solicitation is donors' number one complaint. It is also among their top three reasons for discontinuing support.

There is a disturbing complacency in the charitable sector about fundraising performance, especially in donor retention and in the movement of donors into more sophisticated forms of giving. A 1987 study on planned giving conducted by Decima Research noted that 34% of respondents would be willing to include a bequest to a charity in their will if asked to do so, but only 7% had actually been asked or had decided to commit a bequest on their own. More recent data on the same subject (2000) has revealed that bequests account for only 8% of total giving nationwide,[5] a figure that has increased by less than 1% in more than a decade. Since the fundraising industry has placed a great deal of emphasis on the growth of planned giving, why is performance in this most important of all fundraising programs not showing dramatic improvement?

Why, too, is a 50% renewal rate after the first gift considered to be the "industry standard" in direct marketing programs? If people have made an effort to support a charity in the first place, then what is happening in fundraising that causes half of them to say "no" the very next time they are asked to give, and almost 90% of them to disappear within five renewal campaigns?

Where are these donors going? Since the annual participation rate in giving remains fairly stable year to year, most disheartened donors seem to move on to support another charity. Limited by the strategies employed in mass acquisition and more cautious than they were before, donors keep giving but their contributions stall at the introductory level. A cycle ensues: giving, seeking but not finding satisfaction, moving on to another charity. However, a growing number of donors is looking for another way to give that circumvents the fundraising business entirely and, interestingly, the private sector is stepping up to the plate to satisfy that desire. Donor-directed funds available through private trust companies like Fidelity Trust have seen huge growth in only a few years. As more companies realize that they can increase their market share by facilitating customers' charitable giving, the minimum dollar requirement will drop[6] and that will attract an even greater share of the philanthropic market. In the highly competitive financial services business, donor-directed funds may become the industry's strategic loss leader.

If donors are finding another way to give, does it matter as long as they keep on giving? The answer to that question can be found at the top of the fundraising pyramid where truly skilled relationship specialists

[5] *Planned Giving in the United States 2000: A Survey of Donors*, National Committee on Planned Giving, October, 2000

[6] currently $10,000

provide good information to donors, advocate on their behalf, and interact with them in ways that are meaningful, respectful, and judicious. By cultivating sincere relationships and stewarding those relationships effectively, senior fundraisers negotiate more generous gifts than donors would otherwise offer themselves. The work that planned and major gifts professionals do and, more important, the way they do that work is the example of what *all* fundraising should be and *could* be. Even direct marketing programs can be designed and executed in ways that are palatable to donors and which minimize donor attrition.

To adequately support America's 865,000 charities, the fundraising industry needs to adopt these priorities:

- increase the value of gifts contributed by currently active donors. The average gift value of American households that participated in charitable giving in 2000 was $1,620. This includes 0.00085% of the giving population who contributed 10.5% of all charitable dollars raised.[7]
- improve donor loyalty. In other words, keep donors giving more often and over a longer period of time. Fundraisers know that average gift value increases with donor longevity, so the most productive use of professional and volunteer time in fundraising is spent giving donors what they need to stay loyal to the cause.
- take a more progressive, industry-wide approach to developing the skills of professional fundraisers and volunteer leaders, giving them the human and financial resources they need to get the job done.

Can this happen? Yes. Modern-day fundraising practice may have its flaws, but it can boast huge advantages like sophisticated technology for tracking donor relationships, influential associations, dedicated leadership volunteers and, of course, committed and energetic fundraising professionals. A dramatic increase in charitable giving is possible if all these advantages are used to their fullest extent while less effective practices give way to **donor-centered fundraising and communication.**

This book is the culmination of six years of research and two national studies on the effect of communication and recognition on donor retention and gift value. Its findings and recommendations will help charities raise more money while showcasing fundraising as the respectful and respectable business that Ben Franklin championed.

[7] Gifts with a value of one million dollars or more were identified in the *Million Dollar List,* published quarterly by the Center on Philanthropy at Indiana University. Because the list is compiled only from publicly available reports in national and local press, the average household gift is likely to be somewhat smaller than estimated above.

2
Looking for Something and Finding Something More

Email posted to Stewardship Listserv

Dear friends:

I have been asked to develop, distribute, and evaluate a customer service survey dealing with all aspects of our development process, but probably keying on the issues of fund updates, gift acknowledgment, recognition, and the information we distribute in general. Has anyone out there had experience with this?

Reply:

That's interesting. I've just been asked by my boss to conduct a similar assignment and I have to admit I'm stumped. Actually, what I am supposed to do is develop objective performance evaluation criteria (or OPEC, as I lovingly refer to them). In thinking this through, I initially thought, "Well, we produce X number of endowment reports and X number of acknowledgment letters." But that's not what the assignment is. Rather, I'm supposed to come up with some way of measuring how effective my department is at what it's doing—not how many letters we send out, but how much donors appreciate them.

I think I'll switch to brain surgery — it's gotta be easier!

These two emails triggered this national research study on the relationship between donor relations and fundraising success. At the time I saw this email exchange, I had just published the results of several years' work studying donor communication and recognition practices in Canada. That initial project was launched with a fairly narrow focus but took on a life of its own as I became more intrigued with the subject. As so often happens in this kind of research, I set out looking for one thing and turned up something else in the process—something much better.

Profile of Charities in the Study

education **26%**

social service **22%**

hospitals/health care **16%**

arts **12%**

environment **7%**

advocacy/animal rights **7%**

religious **3%**

non-governmental organization **2%**

volunteer/community **2%**

sport/recreation **2%**

disaster/emergency relief **1%**

Geographic Scope
regional **39%**

national **23%**

local **23%**

state-wide **15%**

Budget
under $500,000 **15%**

$500,001 to $1,000,000 **13%**

$1,000,001 to $2,500,000 **18%**

$2,500,001 to $5,000,000 **12%**

$5,000,001 to $10,000,000 **17%**

$10,000,001 to $25,000,000 **10%**

$25,000,001 to $50,000,000 **7%**

$50,000,001 to $100,000,000 **1%**

over $100,000,000 **7%**

FTE (full time equivalency) of paid staff in fundraising
< 1 **5%**

1 **27%**

2 **16%**

3-4 **16%**

5-7 **15%**

8-10 **4%**

11-15 **4%**

16-20 **3%**

> 20 **10%**

The objective of the original study was to learn more about the work that charities were doing in donor recognition so that my associates and I could use this information to add more depth to our firm's fundraising planning work. Donor recognition had always been the "add on"—a thin chapter at the end of an otherwise in-depth fundraising plan, or a passing reference in a report. I sensed that donor recognition was more important than the attention being given to the subject, but everywhere I turned for information I came up empty. Publications, booklets, and articles (and even that list was short) focused on the "formal" or "tangible" aspects of donor recognition like donor walls, gifts, and donor recognition events. Designed for high profile capital campaigns, they seemed somewhat "over the top" for donors to the annual fund. More important, I had always felt uncomfortable about what charities and the fundraising industry tended to do with and for annual fund donors between one gift and the next request. Considering their gestures of support, donors received too little, and what they did get was often detached and contrived. I was sure that there must be a wealth of information and innovative ideas out there. I just had to unearth it.

Charity respondents completed a lengthy questionnaire investigating their practices in donor recognition and communication. The body of information they offered provided the project with considerable data and memorable anecdotes. However, even more significant was that many respondent charities took part in the study, not because they felt they had particularly innovative ideas to share but because they wanted to see what other participants were doing. Study respondents were concerned about the content, tone, and effectiveness of their own efforts and instinctively felt that a greater emphasis should be placed on donor recognition and on that nebulous thing called "donor communication." They cautioned, however, that they had neither the budget nor the time to increase their workload. In short, the study raised more new questions than it answered.

The project would have ended there but a chance remark during an interview with a donor piqued my curiosity once more. This individual and her family had been very active donors for more than fifty years. As I came to the end of my prepared questions, I felt compelled to ask:

"Given your family's long-term commitment to philanthropy, can you recall an instance when a charity did something memorable to acknowledge a gift you made or to communicate with you about your gift at work?"

There followed a prolonged silence during which I became increasingly uncomfortable.

"No," she eventually said, "I can't think of anything."

After an awkward pause, I started to pack up my papers and thank my gracious donor for her time.

"Wait, I remember something," she said.

"Wonderful," I replied, imagining a lovely tea held in her honor or a citizen's award for her philanthropy. I looked at her, smiled, and waited for the heartwarming story.

"Somebody sent me a fridge magnet once," she said.

This conversation was the catalyst to a parallel national study of Canadian donors, the results of which were as informative and belief-shattering as the first study was predictable and inconclusive. In short, when the data from both studies was compared, charities and donors seemed like two ships passing in the night.

The Canadian study was published in late 2000 in a book called, *Thanks, a Guide to Donor-Centred Fundraising*. In May, 2001 I saw the two emails that introduced this chapter and responded with information on the research I had done. That simple exchange led to a larger and more in-depth study with American charities and donors, the results of which are featured in this book.

THE AMERICAN RESEARCH STUDY ON DONOR COMMUNICATION

Over 400 charities and donors from 49 states and representing every not for profit discipline participated in a national study on donor relations between August, 2002 and March, 2003.

267 charities completed an on-line survey of more than 200 questions about their donor communication and recognition practices. The survey gathered statistical information and anecdotal experiences concerning all aspects of charities' donor communication and recognition practices, including budget-related issues. Charities from every state responded, with the exception of Alaska. Charities of all types and sizes are included in the study, representing every not for profit discipline.

Over 150 individual and corporate donors and charitable foundations participated in interviews that were tailored to the category of the respondent. Interviews were conducted by phone, averaging forty-five minutes in length, and gathered statistical and anecdotal information through almost one hundred questions. Selection of respondents was based on philanthropic experience including a history of giving that extended back several years.

While the respondent groups in both the charity and donor studies were not in and of themselves sufficiently large in number to draw conclusions with

---

Fundraising Programs Employed by Respondent Charities

direct mail **90%**
foundations **87%**
major gifts—individual **80%**
fundraising events **76%**
corporate sponsorship **66%**
in memoriam gifts **65%**
board/staff/volunteer gifts **64%**
planned giving **62%**
government grants **57%**
major gifts—corporate **56%**
united way **37%**
capital campaign **36%**
membership **35%**
corporate campaign **30%**
employee funds **30%**
telemarketing **17%**
telethons **10%**
service clubs **9%**
canvassing **2%**
online/internet giving **1%**

Our 267 respondent charities had 2,843,056 active donors and 1,749,735 lapsed donors at the time the study was conducted.

88% of charities store donor records in a specialized fundraising database; **68%** have records that go back at least five years.

Profile of Individual Donors in the Study

Individual donors have been contributing to charitable causes for an average of 32 years.

72% of individual donors can remember the first time they gave a charitable gift.

What prompted respondents to become donors?
parents' influence **42%**
a particular cause became important **18%**
religious upbringing **11%**
wanting to give back to community **9%**
feeling privileged/fortunate **7%**
feeling obligated to give **5%**
influenced to give through volunteering **4%**

Most common ways of giving
direct mail **47%**
in-person "asks" **38%**
personal letters from someone known to the donor **31%**
fundraising events **15%**
telephone solicitations **9%**
automatic payroll deduction **6%**

When donors make their charitable contributions
once a year, at a specific time **23%**
more than once a year, but on a set schedule **12%**
on no particular schedule **65%**

90% of individual donors single out one particular charity for special or unusual support.

mathematical certainty, they did offer strikingly similar and very demonstrative opinions. The decision to concentrate on a more in-depth exploration of the subject with a smaller number of respondents was a conscious one, made from the outset of this project in order to create a more comprehensive and multi-layered understanding of the issues.

Findings from the American study generally echoed those in the original study conducted with Canadian charities and donors. Charities felt that more personal and meaningful communication with donors is warranted but that current fundraising structure and tight budgets prevent them from doing what they think would be effective. Even though there has been a marked increase in the number of charities who employ someone full time or part time in donor relations between the first and second studies, the same concerns about under-servicing donors exist. Due to the size of this current project, though, and the format which allowed for unlimited comments, American charities had the opportunity to express their views more fully. And, they did so on every issue, one of the more revealing being the value they place on creating close relationships with donors.

Donor respondents contributed to many charities but they also tended to give gifts of significant value to some of the charities they supported. They were a representative sample of the kind of donor who is most often singled out for special recognition and who is more likely to receive meaningful communication. Any concerns, then, that this select group had about charities' communication practices and donor recognition would pale by comparison with concerns of donors who make more modest or less frequent contributions as they receive less communication, if at all, and inferior recognition.

Although some study donors could describe very meaningful relationships with charities they supported, a common theme emerged that definitely contradicts charities' assumptions about donor recognition and challenges their priorities concerning donor communication. The vast majority of donors said that although recognition is appreciated, what they really wanted was more meaningful information and, if they got it, they would continue to give and they would make increasingly generous contributions. This is what they said they needed:

- prompt, personalized acknowledgment of their gifts
- confirmation that their gifts have been set to work as intended
- measurable results on their gifts at work prior to being asked for another contribution

So consistent were donors' views on the positive impact of these three considerations, that I gave them a name —"donor-centered fundraising." This simple and logical definition of good customer service as it relates to fundraising is seen as obvious for donors but quite difficult to achieve for charities. Fundraising is designed on a volume-driven model and charities are cost-conscious to the extreme. So, adjusting current practice to meet donors' expectations, even if it means a lucrative payoff, is a big challenge for the fundraising industry.

The research statistics and anecdotal comments in this study advocate change in the ways we acknowledge and recognize donors and communicate with them about their gifts at work. Also described in this book is a controlled test which generated a 39% increase in giving among subjects who received just the first thing that donors said they wanted — prompt, personalized gift acknowledgment.

Through their thoughtful comments and fascinating insights, donors in this study have clearly articulated what it will take to raise much more money. In turn, fundraisers have identified current deficiencies while reinforcing their desire to bring more money to the table for their deserving charities. All that remains is to act on their collective advice.

Profile of Corporate Donors in the Study

Geographic Scope
national **47%**
state-wide **29%**
local **24%**

Corporate donors tend to support these kinds of organizations as a priority (by percentage of donors who do so)
education **77%**
welfare/social service **54%**
environment **39%**
arts **30%**
hospitals/health care **23%**
children's charities **23%**
sport/recreation **15%**
United Way **8%**

Prime motivations for giving
to give back to community **46%**
the President/Founder believes in philanthropy **19%**
to send a message to customers **12%**
to stand out from the competition **12%**
to support causes important to our employees **8%**
religion/faith **3%**

75% of respondent companies give preferential treatment to charities for which their employees volunteer

3

Donors Are People

GENEROSITY WITHIN ONE'S OWN MEANS

I had recently been transferred from the other end of the country and didn't know anyone socially in my new city. So, I decided to volunteer on the Board of Directors of a local organization. To be honest, it was pretty evident from my initial offer of service that I didn't fit in with the rest of the group. First, I offered my service which, it seems, is rare in itself. Until then, members of the Board had been used to calling up others within their business and social circles when they were looking for new members. They didn't quite know what to do with me, having no idea of my background. I was also the only single parent who had ever applied for a Board position in that organization.

But I did have something they wanted. I had fundraising experience and the organization was about to launch its first capital campaign. So, after a brief debate, I was invited to become a member.

Now, given my previous volunteer experience in campaigns, I was well aware that Board members should give and give first. I had been thinking about this for some time because I also believe that members of the Board should make a strong statement through the level of their generosity as well as by being 100% committed to the campaign. This was going to be tough. I had four young children and was just starting my own business—in a new city where I knew it would take me several years to build the contacts and turn a profit. The lowest gift amount in the major gift category was $5,000. I felt that with very strict controls on the family spending, we might be able to manage that over two years.

I waited to be asked. Three board meetings later, no one had approached me. So, at the end of the fourth meeting, I took the Chair of the Board aside and said that I would like to make a gift to the campaign. I went on to say that I would like to give more but with a large family, one income and a new business, $5,000 would be what I could do at this time. I knew the Chair had pledged $150,000 to the campaign. I was afraid he would say that $5,000 wasn't enough or, worse, that as a single mother, he never expected me to be able *to afford anything, but he didn't. Without hesitation, he thanked me for my generous gift and said how important both it and I would be to the success of the campaign.*

It was important. To be able to fulfill my commitment, I had to give the campaign post-dated checks for $200 each month, and there were times when I really needed that money. Now many years later, my children have grown, my business is a success, and I have given several larger gifts to charitable organizations. But that $5,000 contribution will always be the most generous gift I have ever made.

MONEY OR DONORS: IT'S NOT THE SAME THING

Philanthropy is simply a way of sharing one's good fortune. The more you have, the more you want to give to others. It's kind of like paying your way in a civilized society.

It's the emotional connection that ties me to a charity for a long time. For example, I had a friend in high school. We were both cheerleaders and very close. My friend developed MS and died twenty years later. I've been supporting the MS Society for all that time and will continue to do so because the issue is so personal.

I see philanthropy as a form of investment, albeit investing in community instead of investing for one's own benefit. As in any investment there is a return, but one that benefits all of society instead of just oneself.

If you have conducted a donor acquisition program in the last six months, you probably have some important data at your fingertips. Like a good fundraiser on top of his game, you know your acquisition or renewal rate, your average gift value, and of course, the amount of money you raised and whether that was up or down from your last campaign. But, do you know the first and last names of ten of those donors you just acquired . . . OK, five . . . one?

Statistics are vital in fundraising, but fundraising is not just a numbers game. Heavy focus in the development industry on volume of donors and dollars raised is often at the expense of creating relationships with the very people that fundraising programs are trying to capture and keep. When only the money matters, we lose the donor pretty quickly and, along with it, that donor's *future* potential.

Considering fundraising revenue without the donor information that generated it is deceiving. For instance, you can compensate for low donor retention in renewal campaigns by increasing the volume of prospects and/or frequency of solicitations in acquisition programs. As long as you reach your target, you can be pretty sure that there will be no objection from the Development Director or CEO. But, when you fail to renew a donor who had been previously acquired, you lose both the immediate gift and that person's future potential, an amount which is simply incalculable. A charity that opts for increasing volume over improving retention soon finds itself with an even higher attrition rate. With more of the budget now dedicated to soliciting a higher volume of prospects in acquisition campaigns, and with margins falling as good prospects diminish, there is neither the budget nor the time to put measures in place that would retain existing donors. The only option charities think they have at this point is to increase the number of campaigns in an attempt to find even more new donors and squeeze every possible dollar out of existing supporters. Though it can work for awhile, over-solicitation soon becomes the reason for donor attrition, and the downward slide begins.

Donor attrition is not yet on the radar screen of the fundraising industry, even though it is the number one problem in the business. If it were, industry research on giving trends would be asking different questions. Surveying why people don't give in the first place is interesting, but their reasons have less to do with fundraising and more to do with a charity's brand awareness and the competing priorities for potential donors' disposable income. The question that should really matter to the fundraising industry is: "Why do you *stop* giving?" for in the answers to that question lie all the information that charities need to overcome this serious problem.

When we asked our study donors that question, we found that 46% would stop giving to a charity they once supported for reasons that are tied to insufficient or poor quality information concerning their gifts at work. Some of their reasons were based on outright experience, such as "receiving no information about program achievements." Others were assumptions based on what charities did or failed to do to keep them properly informed. These included "discontinuing support because charities failed to fulfill their mandate" or "believing that charities no longer needed their support." Charities may feel that these are misunderstandings, but left to their own devices, donors draw their own conclusions.

Research in the fundraising industry has provided valuable insight on the question "why do donors give?" but to better understand how to build relationships with donors, it is also important to know how they *feel* when they give. Though donors in this study averaged thirty-two years of giving to charitable causes, many could remember the first time they gave and what it felt like. And, all those years later, it still feels the same. Giving is a rush. It is an emotional act as well as an intellectual decision that may be the culmination of many years of thinking about giving. When a donor sits down to write a check, her heart may be racing, she may be imagining how you will react when you open the envelope, and she is certainly wondering whether her gift will have a positive impact on your work.

Being conscious of how donors feel when they give makes it easy to respond in kind. A gift given eagerly in the anticipation of achieving something worthwhile should be matched by an equally enthusiastic response from the solicitor or the charity. However, in the rush to deal quickly and fairly with large numbers of donors, organizations produce generalized communications, the tenor and content of which leave donors cold. A charity's first post-gift contact with a donor can either be reassuring or it can be the beginning of a nagging doubt in the donor's mind about whether he has done the right thing.

93% of individual donors in the study serve as volunteers and 95% give to organizations for which they volunteer.

I was just a child the first time I made a charitable gift. I was a girl scout and my mother was the Troup Leader. We went to seniors centers and made things for the underprivileged. I grew up in a very comfortable situation and this was what we were taught to do. Having an organized way to give through the Girl Scouts had a demonstrable impact on developing my philanthropic spirit.

Number of charities supported by individual donors in a
single year (by percentage of
donors supporting that number)
2-5 **23%**
6-10 **20%**
11-20 **23%**
over 20 **34%**

20% of individual donors make
all their giving decisions inde-
pendently; **13%** respond to
requests that charities make of
them; **67%** do both.

*I wouldn't be 'me' without philan-
thropy. I'm always doing something useful for some group or
other, regardless of whether I have
an official connection with it or
not. Giving and volunteering
means obeying the call to feed
the hungry, to visit those in prison,
to "give water to those dying of
thirst." Ever since I've had my own
income, I've given to charitable
causes every week.*

Fundraising methodologies have become more sophisticated in order to handle larger and larger numbers of donors without expanding development staff proportionately. This seems commendable on the surface but it has forced fundraisers into an increasingly systematic approach to donor recognition and communication which, in turn, has prevented them from developing meaningful relationships. Fundraising practitioners have become less and less focused on the single donor in an attempt to deal with the numbers instead of the people that those numbers represent.

DOES FUNDRAISING NEED FUNDRAISERS OR MARKETERS?

Who is really a donor? I term someone who gives for the first time (regardless of the size of the gift and regardless of how it was secured) as a potential donor at a stage of "intense cultivation." That's because the largest number of donors is lost between that first gift and the second ask than at any other time. Once a donor reinforces her commitment to an organization with a second gift, the likelihood of her continuing loyalty grows. What happens between the first gift and the second ask, then, makes or breaks the relationship and determines real fundraising potential. And, since an investment of 70% to 100% or more of the value of the donor's first gift is made in simply acquiring her, there is a lot riding on the choices that charities make concerning post-gift communication.

One of the strongest reasons for giving is the wish to support a particular cause. It stands to reason, then, that the better known causes are likely to attract the most new donors. So, are fundraisers required for effective donor acquisition or are marketers the better choice? Most development departments include donor acquisition as a fundraising program; however, that may be contributing to the industry's poor performance in acquisition, and it is most definitely putting a huge strain on fundraising budgets. A 1% or less success rate in direct mail acquisition, for instance, is hardly a commendable fundraising performance. However, as a marketing program, direct mail acquisition is part of a strategic array of devices that get the message out and position a charity against its competition. Acquisition is the initial call to action and the end function in the marketing mix. Fundraising, which is relationship building, begins the moment a new donor's first gift is received.

If receipt of and not the request for the first gift were to mark the beginning of the fundraising process, several of today's more serious problems in raising money would subside. First, as marketing and not fundraising is required to capture a first time donor, then marketing expertise is required for donor acquisition. As long as the industry considers it to be a fundraising role, donor acquisition will be handled by people who are not trained for the job.

Second, by entrenching donor acquisition (marketing) costs in the fundraising budget, expenses become attached to fundraising that don't belong there, significantly increasing the cost per dollar raised in the process. The statistical performance of acquisition programs actually tells us where these costs really belong. A 1% return in a direct mail acquisition campaign means a 1% success rate for fundraising. But in marketing terms, success is measured much differently. The marketing objective of brand awareness or reinforcement is met when the recipient sees the charity's name on the envelope; the goal of information dissemination is achieved with those who go on to open the envelope and read the letter. The fact that 1% or less of the list actually responds with a gift is icing on the cake for marketers, and the beginning of the money-raising process for fundraisers. As brand awareness and communication are also essential to the fundraising process, I'd want as much marketing talent attached to my direct mail acquisition programs as possible. The same goes for telemarketing and canvassing. Costs of an activity whose primary effect is market awareness should be charged against the marketing budget, with the reply device and envelope and apportioned mailing cost only charged against fundraising. Fundraising is really quite a cost-effective process, but not when it has to carry the marketing budget as well.

Third, by incorporating marketing costs and activities into fundraising, charities convince themselves that they don't really need discrete marketing at all. Nothing could be further from the truth. For instance, a study of donor expectations by the Better Business Bureau found that more than two thirds of Americans look for information or ask questions before deciding to make a charitable contribution. 73% felt it is very important that charities' advertising and promotion clearly describe who they are and what they do.[8] Furthering name recognition, reinforcing brand image, and communicating the mission and purpose of a charity are very important. You simply cannot do the whole job of turning an uninformed prospect into a committed donor by relying solely on fundraising appeals.

Most corporations spend more money on marketing than on anything else. Today, it is likely that a marketing and communication professional will be promoted to the President's job over the Finance VP. Companies know that their products are only as good as the advertising and marketing programs that get

77% of donors contribute to a cause that personally affects them or someone in their family.

70% of corporations in the study rate their charitable giving as very important or extremely important to their companies.

Philanthropy is definitely an emotional thing for our family. We are very involved in looking at our community and identifying where the need is. What makes it even better is knowing that the people who administer the funds we donate are just as impassioned as we are. It's also about those they serve—helping people is what it's really all about. That's why we focus our giving on a small number of charities, so we can have a significant impact.

---

[8] *Princeton Survey Research Associates, Inc*. BBB Wise Giving Alliance Donor Expectations Survey, September, 2001

85% of individual donors in the study have a personal policy or philosophy about organizations to which they would not contribute financial support. **69%** of corporate donors have a policy about charities who would not qualify for support.

Our relationship is different with every charity we support. I'm more involved with some, especially those for which I volunteer. The emotional attachment to college, however, is the strongest and it is a bond that has grown over thirty-five years. We now have our own foundation and we become close to the charities we support because we assess them in advance.

them to market. The corporate sector is also starting to learn that marketing to sell product plus customer service is essential in a highly competitive world. I now commonly get a hand-written thank you note from the person who sells me a car or a suit. They want my new business of course, but they want my repeat business even more. Why? Because it costs less to keep me as a loyal customer than it does to find someone else to replace me, and because there is a higher probability of "upselling" me if they treat me right. The same thing applies in fundraising.

Fundraisers and marketers are both vitally important, but for different reasons. Charities need marketers to acquire donors and fundraisers to keep them, and they need adequate budgets to support them both.

A FAILURE TO COMMUNICATE

Last year we traded membership lists with another local organization. After our letters went out, one was returned to us in its original envelope. The letter had a note at the top that read, "What did we do to deserve this? This doesn't make us feel like valued members of the team. You won't lose us, but others may be less committed."

This came from a fifteen-year donor who had recently given us a $20,000 gift. We phoned this donor immediately and followed up with a handwritten note explaining that our mail house had not adequately purged the list of existing supporters.

The donor responded favorably and attended our next fundraising event. We now spend many hours checking and double-checking these lists so that we don't inadvertently include our major donors in our direct marketing solicitations.

Why do some donors give more with each successive ask while others hold the line? Why do some donors reduce the size of their gifts while still others stop giving altogether? If all receive similar solicitations and relatively equitable treatment, what then are the reasons behind their significantly different patterns of response? The individual donors in our study all have two things in common; they have been giving for a substantial amount of time and they contribute to many different causes. By any measure, they are loyal, dedicated philanthropists. These are the people who occupy "most coveted" status in fundraising programs; they are representative of donors who can be counted on to remain loyal to the cause and to increase their giving over time. Yet 84% of individual donors in the study and 83% of corporate donors voiced dissatisfaction about the quality of information they receive from charities they support concerning their gifts at work. Though this is a key reason why less experienced donors stop giving, it does not have the same impact on more loyal, long term donors. And that makes sense. Experienced donors are already well informed about the charities they support. They make it their business to acquire the information they need to guide their giving decisions. They are proactive. These experienced donors, most of whom learned about philanthropy from their parents, have developed a resilience that enables them to maintain their fundamental belief in charitable giving in spite of charities' varying communication skills. When they stop giving to a charity, it is most often because of mismanagement of funds, disagreement with the charity's change in policy or philosophy, or failure of the charity to fulfill its mandate.

If loyal donors keep giving, often in spite of poor communication from the charities they support, then it stands to reason that donors who stop giving or give less than they could, do not have the same *philanthropic resiliency* that more experienced donors exhibit. Within the population at large, about 89% of American households contribute to charitable causes.[9] According to the fundraising industry's own information, however, about 50% of donors do not renew their gifts after making a first contribution and, by the fifth renewal campaign, about 90% have stopped giving to the charities that once elicited their support. Worthwhile charities and clever direct marketing methodology can claim responsibility for the impressive participation rate in philanthropy but they must also take responsibility for rampant donor attrition. Driving home the same message of "give, give, give" without satisfying donors' need for information on the effectiveness of their giving, keeps donor attrition high and prevents charities from raising so much more money.

Professional and volunteer fundraisers need to turn their considerable skill to the majority of donors who give and then either stop giving, reduce their giving, or choose not to increase the amount of money they give. Time and resources should not be focused on acquisition but on reinforcing existing donors' support. Special attention must be paid, as well, to donors recently acquired and to donors whose giving is tenuous so that they, too, can become resilient philanthropists.

Meaningful information on their gifts at work is the key to donors' repeat and increased giving. Communication is the process by which information is delivered. Fundraising under-performance, therefore, is actually a failure to communicate.

53% of study donors could recall an instance when a charity did something unexpected or out of the ordinary to acknowledge their philanthropy.

Philanthropy is a natural part of my upbringing. I know what goes around comes around, and the world is a village. I rate giving and volunteering very highly as personal values.

[9] *Giving and Volunteering in the United States*, pg 28, Table 1.i

*My grandfather was a philan-
thropist, and up until he died at
the age of 84, I thought that all
philanthropists were "rich old
people." One day I looked up
the definition of philanthropist
in the dictionary and discovered,
to my surprise, that the word
means "lover of mankind."*

*I came from a philanthropic family.
When I was ten, my grandparents
encouraged me to start giving to
Save the Children. I adopted an
overseas child and sent 10% of
my allowance to them every
month. I watched that child grow
up and get married while I was
still in high school. It was an
amazing experience.*

Why We Lose Our Donors

Saying thank you and providing donors with information on their gifts at work is simply the right thing to do, but just because it's right doesn't mean it's done consistently or well. There are many reasons why charities delay or mass-produce thanks and take shortcuts with the provision of information. They usually have something to do with time and cost.

This study found that development departments with staff dedicated to donor relations spend about 30% of their time in donor communication; 25% for departments without dedicated donor relations staff. Board and committee members in all charities in the study devote about 20% of their volunteer time to donor relations. However, it actually takes more time to keep donors informed about what their money is achieving than it does to ask them for it. As you read more about this study's findings and conclusions, you will learn that the key to sustained and increased giving is communication and not fundraising. It stands to reason, then, that charities should rethink their priorities when it comes to the allocation of paid and volunteer time.

Understanding how and when donors make decisions about renewing their support and how stewardship affects donor psychology makes it easier to consider devoting more staff and volunteer time to donor communication. Here are two scenarios to consider:

A donor who becomes eager to renew her support

- Donor is in the right frame of mind to consider a charitable gift.
- Donor considers requests from several charities.
- Donor focuses on your charity because . . . (your brand awareness or marketing plus the key selling features of your solicitation).
- Donor makes a commitment to give and writes the check.
- Donor imagines what you will think when you get it.
- Donor hears from you promptly.
- Donor's possible hesitancy about whether she supported the right charity dissolves when she hears the delight in your voice or feels your genuine gratitude in the letter you wrote.
- Donor learns in the call or letter how her gift will be used; she can picture her gift at work in a tangible way.

- Donor hears from you again sometime later and learns that the program to which her gift was designated has had some effect or has progressed in some tangible way.
- Donor is now sure she supported the right charity and decides then and there to give you another gift . . . if you ask for it.
- Sometime later, you ask her to consider another gift.
- Donor says "yes" with no hesitation because she knows it will be money well spent and that she is part of your team.
- You ask if she'll consider a larger gift and again she says yes.

Through this entire process, you are a big part of every decision the donor makes and the reason that she is satisfied with your charity's performance. The combination of the charitable cause, the effect of her giving, and the relationship with the solicitor make the decision to give again and give more an easy one.

The cycle continues. As long as the donor remains confident that her gifts have been set to work as intended, and that her contributions combined with other donors' gifts are achieving what you intended, the likelihood is very high that she will continue to give.

A donor who loses interest in a charity he once supported
- Donor is in the right frame of mind to consider a charitable gift.
- Donor considers requests from several charities.
- Donor focuses on your charity because . . . .(your brand awareness or marketing plus the key selling features of your solicitation).
- Donor makes a commitment to give and writes the check.
- Donor imagines what you will think when you get it.
- Time goes by. Donor hasn't heard from you. He starts to worry that perhaps you didn't get the check.
- More time goes by. He sees from his bank statement that the check has been cashed. He is relieved, but a bit disappointed, too.
- Donor receives an acknowledgment for his gift— a pre-printed postcard with his name misspelled.

86% of individual donors will not knowingly support a charity that sells or trades their names with others.

I get a lot of personal satisfaction from sharing. It started with the feeling I would get when I gave Christmas presents to other people. That feeling spread to an interest in giving in a wider way. Eventually, the desire to give became an ingrained part of my being.

Someone I know and respect who volunteered for another charity asked me directly to give seven years ago. I've been giving ever since because the approach was so personal.

I remember distinctly the first time I gave. It was during my first job and I was managing a small department. I gave to the Salvation Army because they helped one of the employees in my department who was in need.

- Donor soon gets a letter from the same charity asking for another gift. It's addressed, "Dear Friend." It doesn't reference his previous giving.
- Donor ignores the letter.
- Donor wonders whether all charities are like that.
- Donor decides to give philanthropy another try. He chooses another charity but this time makes a smaller gift. They'll have to prove themselves first.

Participation in giving is high among Americans but attrition is high as well. So, it seems that a disillusioned donor is likely to keep on giving, but moves from charity to charity searching for one that will give him what he needs. Until that happens, he is in a perpetual state of acquisition.

THE TRIPLE BENEFIT OF DONOR-CENTERED FUNDRAISING

Donor-centered fundraising is an approach to raising money and interacting with donors that acknowledges what donors really need and puts those needs first. Donor-centered fundraising impacts fundraising success in three ways. First, it retains more donors longer, giving them time to develop their own philanthropic resiliency; second, it causes more donors to offer increasingly generous gifts; and third, it raises the performance of even the most active and loyal donors to a new standard. Donor-centered fundraising aims its sights at our two worst enemies in fundraising: attrition and stagnation.

The Compound Catastrophe of Donor Attrition

If a donor gives to do something worthwhile for a cause or because of a compassionate feeling toward people in need, and if it feels good to give, then why would he ever stop? Maybe it's because soon after giving, it doesn't feel so good anymore. Perhaps he never finds out whether he made a difference to a cause or helped someone in need. Or maybe he feels that the charity wasn't all that excited about getting his money. No charity would ever intentionally make a donor feel unimportant, but could there be a communication gap between charities and their donors? And could that gap be translating into a measurable decline in fundraising revenue?

Our study with donors suggests that there could be. We found that 46% of donors decide to stop giving for reasons that are tied to lack of meaningful information or to a feeling that their giving is not appreciated.[10] But we also looked at the same issue from a more positive perspective, asking donors what would influence them to give again. An amazing 93% of respondents said they would definitely or probably give again the next time they were asked to a charity that provided them with meaningful information on their gifts at work; 64% would definitely or probably give more; and 74% would continue to give indefinitely as long they received meaningful information. We cannot expect to retain every donor who comes our way. Some donors encounter serious situations that force them to stop giving or to reduce their contributions. All donors die eventually. But this research is saying that a significant percentage of donors stop giving because of circumstances that are entirely within the control of charities and fundraisers to change.

The "revenue gap" in fundraising is the difference between what charities are raising now and what they could be raising if they did things differently — not if they acquired more donors, but if they interacted with their existing donors in a more effective manner. Calculating the revenue gap in charities' fundraising operations requires the courage to first look at donor attrition in the cold light of day. Though there seem to be no published industry standards on attrition rates after first and subsequent gifts in direct marketing programs, fundraisers and service providers supplied consistent information. Attrition rates after the first gift are most commonly around 50%, though this figure can certainly fluctuate depending on the quality of the initial acquisition program and post-gift communication. A 30% attrition rate after the second gift is commonplace, followed by a further 20% loss of donors with each subsequent appeal. When extended over five renewal campaigns this attrition pattern is alarming, especially considering that the period of time for five consecutive solicitations can be as little as eighteen months and is never more than five years. Consider the calculation in Table 1 for a charity with 1,000 newly acquired donors, with gifts averaging $100 each, and what happens to both the number of donors and gross revenue in only five renewal campaigns. Average gift increase for renewing donors has been calculated at 15% for each campaign, a target that most organizations can reach with donors in their first few renewal solicitations.

---

[10] While we were unable to locate any other research that studied donor attrition in the United States, a study by the Canadian Centre for Philanthropy produced similar results. This study found that when donors decide to stop giving or give less than they could, 40–49% do so for reasons that are tied to lack of meaningful information or to a feeling that the gift is not appreciated. (Canadian Centre for Philanthropy, *Caring Canadians, Involved Canadians: Highlights from the 1997 Survey of Giving, Volunteering and Participating*, Ottawa, 1998)

Giving is definitely both an emotional and an intellectual experience. The emotional need hits you first; then you decide objectively whether the cause is worthy or not.

When I was unemployed I was given career transition assistance from someone in a not for profit organization. As soon as I found a new position, I began making contributions to this charity. My first gift was offered in honor of the staff person who had been so helpful to me.

When we first contributed to public radio, we gave a large gift that qualified for a premium. It was a CD player which we had to pick up at a local store. When we went there to get it we were treated very rudely. Then the station switched to that horrible jazz all evening long, claiming it was America's serious music. I don't think so! They took off all the classical music so we stopped giving. Too bad—otherwise we'd be a major donor by now.

Table 1

Campaign #	Attrition Rate	# Retained Donors	Average Gift	Campaign Revenue	Accumulated Revenue
0 - Acquisition	n/a	1,000	$100.00	$100,000	$100,000
1	50%	500	$115.00	$57,500	$157,500
2	30%	350	$132.25	$46,287	$203,787
3	20%	280	$152.09	$42,585	$246,372
4	20%	224	$174.90	$39,177	$285,549
5	20%	179	$201.14	$36,004	$321,553

In only five campaigns, the number of still active donors fell from 1,000 to 179, a loss of 82%. Even though gift averages of the remaining donors increased by 101% between acquisition and the fifth campaign, total revenue in the final campaign was a mere 36% of the amount raised in the acquisition program.

Now, without altering average gift values, consider what the impact would be if the charity found a way to retain 46%–93% more donors instead of losing them through attrition. (This range incorporates the low and high end percentage responses from study donors when asked why they stop giving and whether they would continue giving if communication improved.) Table 2 illustrates.

Table 2

Campaign #	Attrition Rate	# Retained Donors	Average Gift	Campaign Revenue	Accumulated Revenue
0–Acquisition	n/a	1,000	$100.00	$100,000	$100,000
1	3.5-27%	730-965	$115.00	$83,950-110,975	$183,950-210,975
2	2.1-16.2%	612-945	$132.25	$80,903-124,941	$264,853-335,916
3	1.4-10.8%	546-932	$152.09	$82,990-141,671	$347,843-477,587
4	1.4-10.8%	487-918	$174.90	$85,131-160,641	$432,974-638,228
5	1.4-10.8%	434-906	$201.14	$87,327-182,150	$520,301-820,378

Table 2 shows that the charity was able to raise between $198,748 and $498,825 more in as little as eighteen months by instituting donor-centered communication practices. The organization also retained between 255 and 727 more people as active donors, the future long term giving potential of whom is simply immeasurable.

Stagnant or Declining Gifts: Sending a Message with Every Contribution

Donors who increase their giving in successive campaigns are sending a message that they approve of the charity's activities. If they are not being provided with meaningful information on their gifts at work, some may continue to give because their positive view of the cause outweighs the poor quality of post-gift communication. These donors' faith in their chosen charities' reputations, history, or public image can support their loyalty for some time. Some donors may be determined contributors to a cause because of first hand experience; others may have access to the information they need from their work as leadership volunteers; still others may simply be hoping and trusting that their money will be well used.

Donors who decide to give the same amount or give less, even when fundraising solicitations ask them to give more, are also sending a message. Their message is a warning. They have not yet taken the extreme step of refusing to give, but they are not fully satisfied either. The cause may still be compelling enough to generate another gift but the charity has failed to reassure these donors that their previous contributions have achieved beneficial results.

Even if a donor increases her previous gift by as little as a dollar, she is demonstrating her growing generosity within her own means. It is important to remember that all donors, whether they give more, the same or less than they gave the last time, supported the cause to begin with. Charities cannot blame the donor, therefore, for becoming disenchanted with the cause or for having other priorities. Responsibility rests with the charity and specifically with the development office for giving her the information that would facilitate a different decision.

The following tables illustrate the impact that stagnant and declining giving can have on a single fundraising campaign. Table 3 brings forward information from Table 1 that showed the number of donors still active after Campaign #1 and their average gift value.

Now that I am giving a lot more to my university, I am becoming much more proactive as my interest grows. As a donor, I keep an eye on what I want to achieve through my affiliation with the charities I support. Recently I narrowed my focus so I could become more involved with a smaller number of charities and so I could monitor their effectiveness. I'm looking for results.

I don't give to any charities that bombard me with solicitations. If they can afford to send me a request about every three weeks, then they obviously don't need my money.

Some organizations seem to be duplicating services, such as several who say they work in cancer or arthritis research, for instance. I don't know which ones to support.

Table 3

Campaign #	Attrition Rate	# Retained Donors	Average Gift	Campaign Revenue	Accumulated Revenue
0 - Acquisition	n/a	1000	$100.00	$100,000	$100,000
1	50%	500	$115.00	$ 57,500	$157,500

Table 4 shows how the giving patterns of the 500 retained donors breaks down, expressed as average gift values for all donors who gave more money, for those who gave the same amount, and for those whose giving decreased.

Table 4
Breakdown of Gifts Contributed by 500 Retained Donors in Campaign #1

Donors Whose Giving Increased			Donors Whose Giving Stayed the Same			Donors Whose Giving Declined		
# GIFTS	AVERAGE	TOTAL	# GIFTS	AVERAGE	TOTAL	# GIFTS	AVERAGE	TOTAL
200	$150.00	$30,000	155	$100.00	$15,000	145	$82.75	$12,000

The average gift value for all donors who gave in Campaign #1 is $115; but the group of donors whose giving increased gave an average of $150. These are the most responsive donors, the ones who are particularly dedicated to the cause and who are expressing confidence in the charity's work. If all donors who gave in Campaign #1 did so at an average gift of $150, the charity would have raised $75,000 instead of $57,500, a 30% improvement.

Industry standards on attrition and renewal are derived from the collective performance of thousands of charities. These organizations raise money for different types of causes, with or without marketing support, under widely varying budgets, and under the direction of fundraisers with differing levels of expertise. A standard based on this many variables is of little use to a single organization. A much more valuable indicator of performance for a charity is its own *high performance standard*, indicated by those donors who remain loyal and increase their giving over time, as reflected in Table 4. It is this standard that charities should be reaching for with all their donors.

THE CURRENT REVENUE GAP

The *current revenue gap* is the amount of money your charity is failing to raise now due to the absence of donor-centered fundraising and communication. Calculating the current revenue gap in your organization is a necessary and valuable first step toward raising more money.

Every organization is different and, therefore, every organization's fundraising potential is also different. Nature of service, name recognition, longevity, experience in fundraising, types of fundraising programs—all these things and more impact donor retention and overall fundraising success.

Regardless of a charity's donor profile or fundraising programs portfolio, every organization can estimate its own revenue gap.

Measuring Attrition in Fundraising Programs

Attrition in direct marketing programs—direct mail, telemarketing, canvassing, corporate campaign—can be analyzed by following the examples in Tables 1 and 2.

Fundraising events also experience donor or participant attrition. Even though contribution levels are often fixed amounts and not donor-determined (such as the price of admission to the annual ball), analyzing attrition will be revealing. If the annual attrition rate of event attendees and sponsors is high, and/or if attendees are not moving up into higher level giving programs, then event donors are not getting the information they need that directly ties the achievements of the charity to their continuing support.

Major and planned gifts fundraising are the examples to the industry of the beneficial effect of meaningful communication on donor retention. Attrition in these programs is exceptionally low *because* donors are well informed and satisfied. However, fundraising potential in these most important of all programs is severely compromised by donor attrition at the bottom of the giving pyramid and by insufficient communication. Obviously, one cannot secure a major gift from a donor who has already stopped giving. And a donor who is disillusioned with a charity is also less likely to name it in his will. Better to have loved and lost than never to have loved at all? Not in fundraising!

Results in planned and major giving are tied to both the number of available prospects and the degree to which those prospects have been "cultivated" at the time they are passed along to the major gifts officer. Few charities support their planned giving offices sufficiently in order to fully capitalize on potential. Most charities make do with as few staff as possible, even in their most sophisticated program areas. So, in an under-resourced department, the speed at which a prospect can be turned into a major or planned gift donor is critical. In a donor-centered environment, donors are always informed and satisfied from the moment they are acquired. Once they are in the major/planned gifts prospect group, they need less time to become acquainted with the charity's long term goals, dreams, and options for giving, and they need no time to be convinced that the charity is dependable and uses donors' money wisely.

39% of charities have established recognition awards specifically for donors. The most common criteria for qualifying for these awards are cumulative giving over time (**36%**), significant value of a single gift (**25%**), recommendation by a board or staff member (**27%**).

46% of charities distribute awards to donors at donor recognition events; **28%** at an annual general meeting; another **28%** at fundraising events.

My father was a fire fighter and every year he was involved in the Jerry Lewis Telethon. Together he and I would go around the neighborhood and collect for the telethon. I was only six or seven years old.

Calculating the Gap

By using your own organization's standard period of attrition,[11] you can determine your current revenue gap. For instance, in a direct mail program with an eighteen-month attrition period, it will only be necessary to go back three years from your most recent campaign, comparing the performance of your donors in the first eighteen-month period with the performance of the same donors in the most recent eighteen months.

Measuring Under-Performance in Fundraising Programs

Tables 3 and 4 demonstrate how to calculate your high performance standard and to use that as your benchmark for estimating the negative financial impact of declining or stagnant giving by some donors.

PROJECTING THE REVENUE GAP OVER THE LONG TERM

When you total the lost revenue from stagnant and declining giving plus attrition, you have a figure that represents your organization's *current revenue gap.* This is the amount of money you are losing today due to an absence of donor-centered fundraising and communication. This is important information for fundraisers, CEOs, and Boards. But by projecting the aggregate loss of donors and money ahead ten years, you see an even more important picture of the serious consequences of long term inaction. In ten years, donors and money dwindle to a negligible amount, a vivid reminder of both the tragic loss of these once earnest supporters and the frustrating need to replace them through aggressive and expensive donor acquisition. A ten-year projection gives you your *future revenue gap,* an alarming calculation that tells decision-makers what they can expect to be dealing with in the future if action is not taken now. Combined with a pragmatic plan to solve the problem, you will have a compelling case for the adoption of a donor-centered approach to raising money.

---

[11] Many organizations determine that a donor has become lapsed (no longer active) after 18 months without giving, but attrition periods vary with types of fundraising programs and solicitation frequency.

Much More Is Possible

Arresting donor attrition and overcoming gift stagnation is only the beginning. The real amount of money that charities are failing to raise is actually much higher than depicted in the above examples. The most dramatic evidence of the potential impact of donor-centered fundraising and communication came from a test which extended from our first study, and which has been replicated by many charities, always with positive results. The test and its implications are explored in detail in Chapters 6 and 7.

Combining significantly reduced attrition with dramatically increased average gift levels through donor-centered fundraising will yield a new standard in fundraising success, one that we have not yet dared to imagine.

The flip side of the current fundraising gap is the enormous fundraising potential just waiting to be unleashed. Donors want to give and they are ready to fulfill their philanthropic ambitions now. The charitable sector needs to seize this opportunity.

Whether a million dollar donor or small contributor, philanthropy is giving a little back of what you have been gifted with. You don't have to give a lot to be a donor; it's the spirit of giving and sharing one's own personal success with others that is important.

4

Three Simple Steps to Raising More Money

Dillon International has a fund called the Building Families Fund, which was established to provide grants to adoptive families. These families need financial assistance in order to adopt a waiting child with moderate to severe special needs. One family adopted two of these very special children who needed surgery and special care, and grants from our fund helped them with both adoptions.

They lived in another city but one day the whole family stopped by our agency on their way across the country. Upon their arrival, I called the Building Family Fund's major donor and invited him to come to our office to meet the family who had been helped through his contributions. He left work immediately and was in our office within a few minutes. The encounter was very meaningful for both the donor and the family. They thanked him and told him spontaneously and emotionally that without his help they would not have their wonderful children. The donor talked and laughed with the older boy and then held the new baby girl. He received hugs from the entire family and they all shed a number of tears.

As he left, our donor told me that seeing first hand how his donation had helped was truly a joy for him. I know we can count on his support for many years to come.

A DONOR NEEDS TO KNOW:
1. that the gift was received . . . and you were pleased to get it
2. that the gift was "set to work" as intended
3. that the project or program to which the gift was directed had/is having the desired effect

By simply saying thank you, organizations can satisfy a donor's first two needs immediately. All it takes is a prompt acknowledgment letter that includes confirmation of the intended use of funds and is a pleasure to read. The third need can only be addressed over time, and the length of time depends on how the gift is being applied. For instance, measurable progress in medical research takes longer to realize than does premiering a new play. Happily, donors are very generous as long as they are given satisfactory information in a timely manner. Even if a program has not been successful, most donors will continue to support a charity that analyzes what went wrong and puts controls in place to minimize the likelihood of repeat failure. They will be forgiving and generous if the new program is designed to learn from past mistakes. Donors are familiar with failure and disappointment themselves. Like good business leaders or good parents, donors will not punish a charity for making a mistake, only for failing to learn.

If information on gifts at work is the critical third requirement of donors, then the pattern of receiving a gift, acknowledging it, and then asking for another gift (no matter how much time passes between the acknowledgment and the next ask) doesn't work for donors. And, if recognition is offered as a substitute for information, it can actually interfere with donors' commitment to do good by focusing attention on donors themselves before they are satisfied that their giving has been worthwhile. This may contribute to the reasons why most donors say they don't want to be recognized and why sometimes they become quite agitated with organizations' attempts to showcase them publicly. Charities genuinely believe that they create a climate for future giving by offering recognition when what donors are really looking for is information.

Providing meaningful information is not easy, however. Organizations running large direct marketing programs are challenged to handle data input and record-keeping in a way that connects the donor to the program and to the claims that won his support in the first place. That's why most appeals are non-specific, referring to individual programs only as examples of the work that charities do, while being careful not to pin themselves down to a commitment to designated giving. But this distances donors, especially new ones. It is hard for them to see how they are going to make a difference when they cannot visualize where their money has gone. It also makes it impossible for charities to report meaningfully on their gifts at work. (See Chapter 8.)

Running multiple acquisition and renewal programs within a single calendar year only adds to the problem. How do you keep track of which donors are giving to which programs? That's where your sophisticated database is indispensable. And what do you tell them? In a social service agency where human need always outstrips an organization's ability to alleviate that need, how do you demonstrate measurable progress to donors who want to see tangible results before they give again? The answer is found not in the fundraising office but at the Board table. Strategic planning is the key to successful designated giving programs, the key to satisfied donors, and the key to your organization's ultimate success.

THE EVIDENCE IS THERE

The evidence already exists that prompt gift acknowledgment, designated giving, and meaningful reporting on gifts at work equals fundraising success. It can be found in capital campaigns.

A successful capital campaign has a defined, achievable objective, a concurrent marketing program, detailed planning, and committed volunteer leadership; but the fifth critical element to success is a donor-centered approach to fundraising. When contributing to a capital campaign, donors know what and why they are supporting and what their gifts will achieve. This is clearly laid out in the Case for Support. Gifts to capital campaigns are acknowledged promptly, donors are given progress reports throughout the campaign period, and they are appropriately recognized for their contributions.

If there is any weakness in this fundraising methodology, it comes at the end. Feeling a combination of relief and exhaustion, the solicitation team folds its tent and disappears. With staff now concentrating on building the annual fund, communication with campaign donors either diminishes drastically at this point or ceases altogether. Five or ten years later when the organization is ready to embark on another capital project, past donors need to be cultivated all over again because the information flow has been interrupted.

Many universities are in a perpetual capital campaign mode and their fundraising goals are continually escalating. Universities, more than other charitable organizations, have seen the importance and benefits of a highly structured and strategic approach to fundraising and have applied a capital fundraising model to their annual fund operations. It's not so much that they are running a continuous capital campaign; it's just that they've altered their fundraising methodology to give donors what they really need, and in so doing they have reaped the rewards.

On one level, donor-centered fundraising is simply the obvious and the right thing to do; on another level, it is the guarantee of a future with your donors and the vital ingredient to raising much more money than you are raising now.

How charities communicate with donors during capital campaigns (apart from solicitations)
through correspondence **79%**
personal visits to donors to update them on campaign progress **64%**
calling donors to thank them for gifts **55%**
calling donors to update them on campaign progress **48%**

59% of charities running capital campaigns agreed that communication with campaign donors tends to fall off between one campaign and the next, and that this increases the time and effort required to cultivate these donors when the next campaign begins.

Communication can be more of a negative thing. If you don't get it, it's a turnoff. When I think about why people stop giving or give less than they could, it's because of the lack of two-way communication. Donors' sustained giving might improve if charities paid more attention to that.

5

Saying Thank You

Our small school for children with emotional disabilities has a vocational program which includes a culinary arts class. When I learned that one of our donors was an expert in Italian cooking, we invited him to the school to cook with our students. Our donor agreed—and brought with him all the required ingredients and much of the equipment. Five students, two teachers and our donor/chef spent two hours in the kitchen, and ate all the fruits of their labor—literally. Everyone had a fabulous time.

Now, this donor is a high profile contributor to some of the biggest arts organizations in the city and many times he has been publicly acknowledged for his generosity. We could in no way compete with that level of recognition, so I simply had the students all contribute to a hand-made thank you card. A few days later I followed up with a handwritten note of my own in which I described the effect he had had on our students. I told our donor that his willingness to spend time with these children showed them they were valued, which is something that could never be bought with money.

Soon after, I saw him at our annual fundraising event. During the evening he spent more than any other donor at our auction, thanked me twice for the students' card and my handwritten note and, as I learned later, mentioned these letters to several other guests. Then, at the end of the year, he sent us the largest gift our school has ever received.

WHAT'S IN A GREAT THANK YOU LETTER?

There are many ways to say "thank you," but the most common one in fundraising is saying it by letter. A simple thank you letter has the power to assure a donor that he has done the right thing or sow that first seed of doubt.

We think a thank you letter should be an acknowledgment, not just of the donation, but of the connection between the donor and the success of our organization, both currently and in the future.

The thank you letters from my boarding school are simply the best. Their letters are very informative so that I know where my money is going. I am informed about what it means to give to the annual fund as opposed to the campaign so that it is clear why I am being asked to give twice a year instead of once.

After reviewing almost two hundred sample thank you letters submitted by charities in this study, we identified these twenty attributes of a great thank you letter:

1. The letter is a real letter, not a pre-printed card.
2. It is personally addressed.
3. It has a personal salutation (no "dear donor" or "dear friend").
4. It is personally signed.
5. It is personally signed by someone from the highest ranks of the organization.
6. It makes specific reference to the intended use of funds.
7. It indicates approximately when the donor will receive an update on the program being funded.
8. It includes the name and phone number of a staff person whom the donor can contact at any time or an invitation to contact the writer directly.
9. It does not ask for another gift.
10. It does not ask the donor to do anything (like complete an enclosed survey, for example).
11. It acknowledges the donor's past giving, where applicable.
12. It contains no spelling or grammatical errors.
13. It has an overall "can do," positive tone as opposed to a hand wringing one.
14. It communicates the excitement, gratitude, and inner warmth of the writer.
15. It grabs the reader's attention in the opening sentence.
16. It speaks directly to the donor.
17. It does not continue to "sell."
18. It is concise—no more than two short paragraphs.
19. It is received by the donor promptly.
20. Plus, in some circumstances, the letter is handwritten.

All but three of the two hundred thank you letters reviewed were original correspondence, not pre-printed form letters, which was very good to see. Over 95% were personally addressed and referred to the donor by name in the salutation. Only one otherwise creative letter included a reply device at the bottom that asked for another gift. Spelling and grammar were excellent in every letter.

For all but five, however, the good news ends there. Charities' thank you letters generally fell short of "communicating the excitement, gratitude, and inner warmth of the writer." Overly cautious in their construction, they seemed to have been purged of any hint of emotion and, consequently, forfeited the opportunity to be memorable. I suspect that many of these letters didn't look like this in the first draft; they are probably the remnants of several levels of internal approval.

When creating a thank you letter, it helps to think about the role that philanthropy plays in donors' lives and to understand how they feel about their charitable giving. We asked donors in our study to rate the importance of their charitable giving against the other things in their lives that are meaningful. 34% of respondents rated it important or very important. Donors also told us what philanthropy means to them, and comments like this were typical:

> *For me, philanthropy is simply a way of sharing my good fortune. The more you have, the more you want to give to others.*

Considering the very personal and emotional connection that donors have with charitable giving, it is only appropriate that the passion be reciprocal. You can be sure that at the moment a donor is opening the envelope, she is experiencing a feeling of happy anticipation. Don't let her down with this kind of response . . .

> *On behalf of. . . I would like to sincerely thank you for your generous contribution of $X.*

28% of the letters we reviewed started with "On behalf of . . ." 43% began with "Thank you for . . ." Not only are these phrases predictable, but they put the writer in a literary straight jacket. When composing thank you letters, let your writing style soar. Try to recapture the spirit of what the donor was feeling when he wrote the check.

As you read the twenty attributes of a great thank you letter, you may have thought it would be difficult to achieve some or even many of them. Implementing any new way of communicating with your donors requires planning and resources and affects all your other fundraising work. It will be a challenge for most organizations to take a more personalized approach to acknowledging donors' gifts, but it is a question of setting priorities. If you prioritize donor communication (which includes gift acknowledgment), you will soon see how it affects donor loyalty and gift size; then allocating time to create personalized thank you letters will rise to the top of your priority list.

When you communicate, you send a message on two levels: what you actually say, and what you also say through how you deliver the message.

What donors feel makes a thank you letter superior

personalized in some way **51%**
acknowledges how the gift will be used **30%**
handwritten **16%**
signed by a member of the board **13%**

Prompt acknowledgment reaffirms that I made the right decision.

Form letters are not appropriate and can cause all kinds of problems with donors who are already very close to the charities they support.

39% of donors say they always receive a thank you letter after making a charitable gift; **41%** do most of the time; **19%** receive a thank you letter sometimes.

I gave a large gift to a big charity recently who sent a letter back to 'Dear Dick.' The gift was not from my husband, it was from me. That was very irritating. It is not smart to automatically assume that it is the man in the family who is making the gift.

Understanding that second level message more fully will help you determine whether improving your thank you correspondence is warranted.

1. A real letter, not a pre-printed card

Some charities use pre-printed cards to thank large numbers of donors quickly, to save money, and to "send a message" to donors who have made smaller gifts.

Pre-printed cards do not reference the donor personally; they are more distant and impersonal than letters and they send several messages that you may not be intending to communicate. They tell the donor that his gift is not significant enough to warrant a personal letter. Mass produced, these cards may have been printed long before the donation was ever made, so the donor knows that no one at the organization ever paused for a moment to consider his generosity.

You can be sure that donors do pay attention to the content of thank you letters. 51% of study respondents said that the thing that makes a thank you letter superior is that it is personalized in some way. Using pre-printed cards or fill-in-the-blanks style thank you letters also has a direct impact on future giving. 67% of individual donors in the study said that their first gift is purposefully smaller than they could have given. Before committing a more generous gift, they want to see how the organization will communicate with them about their work. Satisfied donors give again and give more the next time they are asked.

People don't like to feel that they are just a number in a system and they certainly don't want to think that you've pre-judged their worth as a donor. Pre-printed cards say you just don't care.

2/3. Personally addressed with a personal salutation

A letter without a personal address is assumed to be (and usually is) a form letter. Again, it leaves the donor feeling that the charity is conscious of the gift but not the individual behind the contribution. With word processing and fundraising technology as sophisticated as they are, there is no reason not to personally address every thank you letter.

4. Personally signed

Viewed by donors as both a sign of respect and an indication that the writer was thinking about that donor in particular as he signed the letter, a personal signature on thank you correspondence is essential. It is particularly vital on typed or word processed form thank you letters as this is often the only personalized aspect of the correspondence.

5. Signed by someone from the highest ranks of the organization

A letter of thanks from a member of the Board of Directors is a demonstration of the highest possible respect for and acknowledgment of the donor. For a leadership volunteer to even be aware that a donor has given, information about the gift would have had to travel up the chain of command. Nothing could be better. A select few paid staff are also appropriate signatories on gift acknowledgment correspondence. In arts organizations, this means the Artistic Director, Conductor, or Prima Ballerina, for example. In hospitals or universities, it could be the physician who heads the research project to which the donor's gift was designated.

An exception to this preferred course of action concerns gifts contributed by donors with whom the Development Director or other staff member has built a strong relationship. If the donor would expect to receive immediate thanks from someone other than a Board or Committee volunteer, then of course this is what should happen. However, a second letter from the Board volunteer may help cement the donor's connection to the organization even more strongly.

And then, of course, there are letters that are composed and signed by the people that the charity serves. 76% of study donors said getting personal letters from someone who has benefitted from the charity's work is very meaningful. This wonderful story is an example of the power of such meaningful communication:

The One Million Dollar Thank You Letter

An advancement officer in one of our schools needed our help urgently. In one week, his Dean would be traveling to meet with one of their major donors, planning to solicit him for a million dollar-level gift. The Dean needed ammunition. He wanted current information on the donor's endowed funds and thank you letters from his scholarship recipients. The school's advancement officer panicked as there were no thank you letters ready to share. With less than a week until the anticipated meeting, the University's Development office was called upon to contact all of the recently awarded scholarship recipients and ask them to kindly write a letter to the donor.

The timing wasn't very good. It was last minute notice for everyone. The students were surprised that they were

The CEO or Artistic Director is by far the most likely person to sign thank you letters to donors (**61%**)

Our organization recently instituted handwritten thank you notes from board members to donors. We supply the board with stationery and any non-confidential information about the donor/donation that would be helpful to the author of the note. We're not sure of the effectiveness yet but we do know that the Board truly enjoys this project and it has helped us to become more conscious of our contributors.

given less than a couple days to return their letters to us, and to top it off, it was exam week. For some, it was an even bigger shock, as they were hearing for the first time that they had been selected as a beneficiary of the fund!

As soon as the donor read one of the letters—which was from a student who had suffered many hardships in her life and who expressed such sincere gratitude for the scholarship—he pledged $500,000 more and another $500,000 through a bequest expectancy. Needless to say, the Dean was thrilled . . . and our Development Department didn't look bad, either!

6. Makes specific reference to the intended use of funds

This has far-reaching implications. The positive reputation of your organization and its appealing mandate may have won the donor initially, but if you want to keep her, you need to focus her attention on something that can demonstrate measurable results. You are in business to achieve something and the programs, projects, and services that you deliver are the vehicles through which achievement can be measured. Overcoming resistance to designating gifts to specific programs is one of the greatest challenges your organization will face. (See Chapter 8.)

Thank you letters tend to include either no explanation at all about where the money is going or a comprehensive list of the organization's programs and services. Neither approach is helpful to the donor who is trying to create a picture in his mind about what his gift might achieve. By being specific, you can help the donor focus on a goal while reducing or eliminating any concern about the gift disappearing into the general operating budget.

Confirming where the money is going is essential, but this is not the time for lengthy explanations of your organization's varied services. Save the longer narrative until later when you communicate your progress. In a single paragraph, PCC Farmland Fund (Seattle) did a good job of explaining where the donor's money had been put to work:

Thank you for your gift to the PCC Farmland Fund. You are part of a growing community (in all senses) of progressive businesses who understand the importance of protecting our food at its source. Your gift will go directly to help protect the Shipley Fields.

7. Indicates when a program update will be sent

This is the donor's evidence that his gift has been put to work and that it has started to yield some results. Results are measured in many ways, but all programs or initiatives for which funds are raised can be measured.

Assuring your donor in the thank you letter that this information will be forthcoming establishes you as the guardian of his gift. The donor knows you are working with him to make sure that his contribution is being maximized. Later, when he gets that update and it does not include a request for another gift, he will be doubly impressed. Expect to receive unsolicited gifts at this time from donors who have decided for themselves that you have now met their stewardship criteria.

8. Includes the name and phone number of someone the donor can contact

Always appreciated and seldom abused, this information lights a clear path directly to someone who can answer questions, provide information, and deal with concerns. It also redirects the donor away from the volunteer who signed the letter and who is not as readily accessible.

When the thank you letter comes from someone at the top of the charity and includes the name and contact information of a staff person, it acts as a high level referral. This important introduction makes it easy and appropriate for development staff to follow up and establish an early working relationship. And, in the most discreet and appropriate manner, it suggests that staff are better equipped to handle the donor's day-to-day needs.

9. Does not ask for another gift

This is simply a matter of good manners, but some organizations ask outright or in an indirect way for more money in thank you correspondence. Comments such as "though we are gratified by our donors' response to this Campaign, we still have such a long way to go . . ." are viewed as veiled solicitations and they imply that you are not satisfied with what the donor has just done. This is not the time to put your hand out.

10. Does not ask the donor to do anything

Some organizations use thank you correspondence as an opportunity to gather statistical data or other information through surveys of some kind. They may be trying to be cost effective or to leave the impression that they are interested in learning more about the donor. Thank you letters with enclosures requiring action are actually interpreted as thank you letters with ulterior motives. Just at

According to charities, only **7%** ask for another gift within the body of thank you letters, but **21%** include a pledge form and/or return envelope with the thank you letter (hint, hint)!

66% of individual donors say they have received requests for another gift within the body of thank you letters. **53%** say that this is rude; an additional **8%** stop giving if this happens.

86% of charities include some kind of enclosure in thank you letters such as surveys, newsletters, invitations, gifts.

We vary the text of thank you letters monthly and always try to have something current to say about our work.

the moment when you should be simply expressing your gratitude, you are asking the donor to do one more thing. Convenience is not what matters at this sensitive moment. To avoid leaving the impression that you are already gathering information that will help you plan the next solicitation, it is preferable to leave space between a thank you and any other request.

11. Acknowledges the donor's previous giving
If the recipient is a former donor, making reference to her past giving is a sign that you are paying attention. Many donors in the study said that acknowledging their previous support (which might include reminding a long-time donor that she has been giving for X years) helps make a thank you letter superior.

12. Contains no spelling or grammatical errors
Poorly constructed correspondence makes donors wonder whether they have supported the right organization, so charities should make every effort not to give someone an easy reason to give to a different charity the next time.

13. Written in a "can-do," positive tone
There are times when organizations should focus on the seriousness of the issue they are trying to address and times when they should emphasize the solution. The donor's gift is his contribution to the solution. This is a time for rejoicing, not hand wringing.

Avoid starting thank you letters with an apology. If you feel the urge to do that, you are probably trying to compensate for something that could have been avoided in the first place. The most common reason for an apology is late issuing of thank you letters. (See point 18 below.) Verbosity cannot overcome tardiness, so don't try to compensate for slow gift acknowledgment with long letters of explanation.

14. Communicates the excitement, gratitude, and inner warmth of the writer
This is your opportunity to help the donor feel good about what he has done and about the people behind the organization, as represented by the person who writes the letter. In keeping with the fundraising truth that "people give to people," your ability to communicate how you feel about receiving the donor's contribution will be remembered fondly when the donor considers another gift to your organization in the future.

Thank you letters for in memoriam gifts are particularly sensitive. Hesitancy in communicating with the grief-stricken can elicit some of the coldest and most impersonal correspondence at the very moment when warmth and sincerity are vital and would be so appreciated. This is a typical example:

> *Dear Mrs. X:*
>
> *On behalf of (organization), I would like to thank you for the donations made in memory of Mr. X. These funds will help to enhance health services in our community. Enclosed please find a list of the names and addresses of those who sent donations in memory of Mr. X. Each of the donors has been individually thanked for their gift.*
>
> *Sincerely . . .*

Hospice organizations, who deal with death and dying as a natural part of life, are often more adept at this kind of communication. Here is the best example provided to us by the Dorothy Ley Hospice. It captures the spirit of thank you correspondence beautifully:

> *At a time when you were remembering someone very dear to you, you also thought of others now living with terminal illness and extended your hand of support to them. On their behalf and from us . . . thank you.*

A winning letter is one that is a pleasure to read. It should leave the donor with the wonderful feeling that comes from knowing she has done the right thing. It is personal, touches the heart, and expresses the writer's real depth of feeling.

15. Speaks directly to the donor

The phrase, "without the generous support of people like you," or something similar, is common in thank you letters but unappealing. Thank you letters should not be acknowledging the generosity of others who are similar, but the generosity of the specific donor to whom you are writing. ". . . without your support" is much more powerful and much more satisfying to read.

Compelling thank you letters to corporations make reference not only to the companies but also to their employees, whose indirect generosity has made the gifts possible. If your corporate acknowledgment letters thank employees directly, they are more likely to be displayed or distributed internally. One of

Don't just communicate when you are fundraising; do it after you get the gift as well. Really focus on developing the relationship, not just securing the revenue.

Tailor communications specifically to the donor. This would let us see that the charity is not simply sending out form letters. Demonstrate that you're aware of OUR mission and goals as well as your own.

the challenges that philanthropic corporations face is keeping their employees informed of and engaged in their community support. Automatic payroll deductions, participation in company charity events, and volunteering are all influenced by donor recognition and communication. Even the thank you letter can play a part in reinforcing employees' charitable giving.

16. Grabs the reader's attention

A great letter starts with a great opening sentence that grabs the reader's attention. Your first sentence should convey your excitement about receiving the gift or your passion about your organization. If you don't allow yourself to start a letter with "Thank you for . . ." or "On behalf of . . ." you will find your composition becomes much more creative. Here are introductions for two of the best letters received from study respondents.

> *"Good stewardship is a precious commodity on an academic board and you have just enhanced our supply with your recent gift. Many thanks for your contribution."*

> *"Music nourishes and enriches our lives. We are proud to be the only professional orchestra in the city to offer a principal series of high caliber concerts to the public free of charge. But we would be unable to do so without . . ."*

Note that the first sentence in each of these letters does not say thank you at all. These are unconventional yet very successful letters.

Several thank you letters we reviewed had that great opening line . . . buried further down in the letter. When you review your current correspondence, you may find that it just needs rearranging. In this example, the sentence that could be such a beautiful introduction is in bold type:

> *The XX Charity wishes to thank you for your charitable gift of $X. We are deeply grateful for your continued support and your willingness to share your resources with (program.) Your gift will allow us to continue. . . .* **When the Sisters say their daily prayers in the sacredness of the monastery chapel, you will be remembered.** *God bless you.*

17. Does not continue to "sell"

Fundraisers are so geared to getting the message across that sometimes they don't recognize when they have succeeded and can stop . . . for the moment. Often because they don't quite know what to say or in the attempt to provide worthwhile information to the donor, writers fill up thank you correspondence with lengthy explanations about programs and services, sometimes drawing from the same copy used in solicitation pieces. This is not necessary and it is counter-productive. A simple acknowledgment that the donation has been assigned to the intended program is all that is required.

18. Is concise

Brevity is a decided advantage. If you want your thank you letter to make a memorable impact on your donor, make it concise and say thank you in a way that makes your letter stand out. Brevity does not eliminate sincerity or creativity. For many reasons, including its brevity, this letter from Woodmere Art Museum in Philadelphia was hands down the best thank you letter of all that we reviewed from charities in this study:

> *You must have heard the cheers from Donna Karfunkle this morning when we told her that you are funding "Music, Art and Math." Her excitement was matched by our own deep appreciation for your belief in and support of our work. Donna, an extraordinary Woodmere docent who works with children, will be coordinating the project with A.M.Y.6 and is, indeed, the mastermind behind the entire concept.*
>
> *We look forward to being able to share the program's success with you next year. In the meantime, our regards and sincere thanks.*
>
> *Sincerely yours,*
> *Michael W. Schantz, Ph.D.*
> *The Patricia Van Burgh Allison Director and CEO*

Do not try to achieve too much in gift acknowledgment correspondence. Readers will absorb the first one or two paragraphs after which everything is just blah, blah, blah. So, save your valuable time for other things. Keep your thank you letters short!

Communicating with donors must be a permanent commitment. Donors use information to make decisions about their next gift. Communication must be short, concise, factual, and void of biases. Charities' communications often include subtle comments that assume everyone agrees with a charity's political or religious views. Be factual and straightforward.

The things that inspire me to give a larger gift to a charity the next time are information, results, and prompt acknowledgement—in other words, a personalized approach.

Prompt acknowledgment, meaningful feedback/information on outcomes and just a general sense that they are trying to keep in touch with me—that's what would get me to increase the value of my gifts.

Whether I give a larger gift the next time is directly related to how well the charity keeps in touch with me.

19. Received by the donor promptly

38% of respondents said they generally get a thank you letter within two weeks; 55% within a month. Only 8% felt that they had to wait longer than a month to have a gift acknowledged. This is significant since 44% of study donors said that prompt gift acknowledgment influences their decision regarding future support. And, when considered as part of an overall communication strategy that includes personal contact and meaningful information on gifts at work, prompt acknowledgment would influence 93% of respondents to give again, 64% of them to give more, and 74% of them to give indefinitely. It takes more than a timely thank you letter to influence future giving, but prompt gift acknowledgment definitely plays a part in the decision.

Donors are satisfied and impressed if they receive a thank you letter within two weeks of making the gift. 95% of charities in the study said that they are able to meet this timeframe with an amazing 45% saying that they turn around the thank you letter within two working days. Bravo! The following information is for charities who may be having a difficult time meeting this expectation:

With a two-week timeframe as your benchmark, you may have only two to four days to turn around your acknowledgment letters, allowing for delivery time in each direction and taking weekends and holidays into account. Guaranteeing prompt gift acknowledgment requires the commitment of many staff, both inside and outside the development office, plus a well thought out system for handling donations from the minute they arrive. For instance, if gift recording is done in the development office but gift receipting happens in the finance office, there is probably a delay of days or weeks in the processing of thank you letters. Though prompt communication with donors is a priority for fundraisers, accountants may not see the urgency.

Unless you work in an organization with a small number of donors, you are about to face your first hurdle in implementing donor-centered fundraising. Getting the support and cooperation of your colleagues and employers will be difficult because you will be asking others to change the way they do things while you make changes within your own office or department. (See Chapter 13.)

Here are some of the things you need to do or take into account if you want to improve turn-around time for thank you correspondence:

- Assess your current procedure: chart the movement of a donation from the moment it arrives in the mail to the time your thank you letter leaves your premises. Note the number of steps involved in getting from A to Z; the number of departments that the gift travels through; the names or titles of individual staff members who deal with the gift at some point; the time it takes to move the gift from one step to the next; the methodology for recording gift and donor information; the process for creating and signing thank you letters.

- Observe the same sequence with a broader sample of gifts received on different days and under different circumstances. Take a look during peak activity times as well as during slower periods.
- Analyze the information you have gathered. At what point(s) does an incoming gift get caught in a backlog or languish in someone's in-basket?
- What is the average processing time in your organization from beginning to end? If longer than three or four days, what functions can be streamlined, what steps eliminated, what movement in and out of your department minimized to shorten that period of time?
- How will employer, staff, and colleagues be affected by the changes you want to make? Whose co-operation do you need to gain so that this can happen as smoothly as possible?

One other thing . . . look to see how long it takes to deposit the check. If that can happen with the speed of light, so too can thanking donors. It's simply a matter of improving internal procedures, backed by an understanding of why prompt gift acknowledgment is important and how it affects future income.

20. The thank you letter is handwritten . . . in certain cases

A handwritten letter is the ultimate in personal recognition because it proves that someone in your organization spent at least a few moments thinking specifically about that donor.

In some situations, a handwritten letter might be interpreted by the donor as excessive or overly familiar. Handwritten letters make a statement of particular gratitude or they reflect a special relationship between the letter's author and the donor. You are the best judge about when to write a thank you letter by hand. When the circumstances are right, though, handwritten letters are very meaningful.

Charities compose hand-written thank you letters when...

the donor is well known to the writer **70%**

the gift is of exceptional value **68%**

the donor is also a leadership volunteer **42%**

the donor has been giving for a long time **39%**

the donor is prominent in the community **30%**

Handwritten notes with personal references apart from the gift are very effective in maintaining close ties with donors.

Write handwritten letters: I had a clumsy phone call with someone I'd never met who attended my school and who I was trying to interest in a gift. After that poor phone call, I decided to write a two-page handwritten letter to tell her all that I couldn't seem to say well enough over the phone. As soon as she received my letter, she called me and offered a significant gift. She also said that after the phone call she had no intention of giving but the personal style and handwritten letter changed her mind.

AN EXAMPLE OF AN ACKNOWLEDGMENT THAT INCLUDES ALL THE ATTRIBUTES OF A GREAT THANK YOU LETTER

Incorporating all or most of the twenty points that make your thank you correspondence superior is completely achievable. It only requires re-thinking what you say and how you say it. Real letters will cost a little more and will take a bit more time to produce. Think back to the calculation you did earlier to determine the revenue gap in your organization. If you want to close that gap, you'll need to communicate with your donors as individual supporters. Your personal touch will first be felt in the thank you correspondence you compose.

Except for the handwritten aspect, this simple letter incorporates all the attributes of a great thank you letter:

Mrs. Elizabeth Hamilton
211 Oak Street West
Chicago, Il 60698

Dear Mrs. Hamilton:

We needed you and you were there.

We are so grateful for your donation which has been allocated to our new literacy program for street youth. A report on the growth and impact of this program will be sent to you in January, but if you want to speak with us anytime before then, please contact our Development Director, Joyce Bird, at (555) 455-9825.

Thank you for your generosity and your confidence in our work.

Sincerely,
Robert Sable
Board of Directors

Additional Tips on Composing Thank You Letters . . .

A picture can be worth a thousand words. If you are in the midst of a capital campaign and receiving pledge payments during construction, slipping a current photo of the capital project in with your thank you letter is a way to keep your correspondence fresh and interesting each time you thank a donor for a pledge installment.

It is more difficult to write compelling thank you letters when you are a third party organization like the United Way who thanks donors for gifts which are put to work by their grantees. The same rules apply, though, when thank you letters are penned by fundraising organizations that raise money for a number of causes—but the scale is bigger and the logistics of gathering meaningful information are more challenging.

Oooh, that IRS wording . . .

> *"Thank you for your cash contribution of $X that (organization's name) received on (date). No goods or services were provided in exchange for your contribution."*[12]

Nothing can break the mood in an otherwise great letter better than the suggested IRS wording. Though many of the letters we reviewed made admirable attempts to incorporate the standard IRS references into thank you letters, the result was always jarring.

My preference would be to put the IRS acknowledgment wording in a separate attachment. If this is prohibitive, then definitely move this information below the signature. The letter should focus on your appreciation of the *donor;* the IRS addendum deals with the gift.

GETTING APPROVAL

When I do speaking engagements and seminars on donor-centered fundraising, I like to see delegates try their hand at writing compelling thank you letters. The courageous ones will sometimes read them to the group. At a recent seminar, someone composed and read out loud one of the most creative letters I have ever heard. After she finished, everyone in the room gave her an enthusiastic and well deserved round of applause.

The seminar continued but occasionally I caught a glimpse of this delegate out of the corner of my eye, and she looked concerned. At the break, I asked her if something was wrong. She told me that she had only been in her donor

Thank you's are the lifeblood of fundraising!

From my experience, our donors don't want anything other than a "thank you" when they make a gift. In fact, many of them shun our suggestion of a donor recognition luncheon or dinner.

---

[12] Suggested wording as it appears in IRS Publication 1771, Charitable Contributions—Substantiation and Disclosure Requirements

The cause is still the most important thing when I am considering
whether or not to increase the
size of my gift; but what they are
planning to do with my money
is a big issue as well.

At times I have received attention
that I thought was very kind and
thoughtful. A phone call or a
personal letter was very surprising
and always appreciated. That's
all that it took for me to offer a
larger gift.

relations position for six months. Soon after starting her new job, she had rewritten the staid and predictable gift acknowledgment letter that had been used by her organization for many years. When she was really happy with the new draft, she took it to her boss for approval and was quite taken aback when told, "We couldn't possibly send a letter like this to our donors. This is not how we do things here." She was instructed to resurrect the old letter and not to veer from accepted practice again.

Any change, even something as simple as improving the content of correspondence, might be met with hesitancy or resistance—even from senior fundraising practitioners. It is important to be realistic and to expect to justify your reasons for wanting to do things differently. The recommendations in this book are research-based so that you can refer to objective data to support the change in direction you may wish to take. Even armed with the facts, however, advocating innovation in a conservative industry is challenging.

I know that donors save and savor exceptional thank you letters. I have been shown many examples which held special meaning for them. Often kept under the blotter or in the back of a drawer for safekeeping, many are ripped at the crease marks from being opened, read, and refolded so often. In every case these letters were marvelous, beautifully composed, and they communicated a real sense of appreciation for both the gift and for the relationship between the charity and the donor.

Do not be afraid to be your best.

If you issue thank you correspondence promptly and make your communication as personal as possible, giving and receiving thanks will be more rewarding for both you and your donor. You might consider composing your letter as if you had just received the gift and were reaching for the phone to convey your appreciation. Better yet, why don't you do just that . . .

6

Saying Thank You the Donor-Centered Way

THE CORPORATE CAMPAIGN REACHES GOAL

We had been struggling with our corporate direct mail campaign since January, and it was now December 21st. A promising response from former donors early in the year had fueled our optimism, but by April giving had slowed to a trickle. To add to our anxiety, the acquisition campaign was also not performing well. Aiming for an ambitious goal, however, we sent reminder letters in mid-September and added many new prospects. We really worked this campaign. By early December I was insisting there was a "mathematical possibility" that we might reach goal, and on December 21st it happened when we received a significant gift from a first time donor.

The entire development office was congratulating each other. I was so excited myself that, on impulse, I picked up the phone and called the president of the company whose donation we had just received. I was put through to his assistant. "Would you please let Mr. Urquhart know that we just received your company's most generous gift and, as a result, we have reached our corporate campaign goal." I could barely contain my excitement. "Hold the line a moment, please. I think Mr. Urquhart would like to hear this himself." A few moments passed and then I was connected. When the president picked up his line, I could hear a lot of voices and laughter in the background.

"Excuse the noise," he said, "but you're on speaker phone and we're in the middle of our company Christmas party. I hear you have something you want to tell us. Go ahead." I repeated what I had said and a loud cheer went up from everyone in the president's office. "Great work," Mr. Urquhart said. "It's a fine organization and we're happy to support you. Thanks so much for calling. You've made our day."

"What a wonderful thing to say," I thought to myself as I hung up the phone. "I thought they had made our day."

The company gave again the next year—doubling the value of their gift; and, to this day, they continue to be a loyal supporter of our annual corporate campaign.

Have you ever said something nice to someone and regretted it? Probably not. As a fundraiser, do you think that personal contact with donors is a good thing? Probably. Why, then, is it not automatic for us to pick up the phone and call our donors to say thank you as soon as we receive their gifts? What is it that holds us back from responding to donors' generosity in such a natural way?

Personal contact really works and stories like the one above are commonplace. If strong bonds can be established through something as simple as a one-minute phone call, why is this activity not a priority in fundraising departments?

Here are ten real and, perhaps, familiar objections to communicating personally with donors, along with information that will help to overcome the hesitancy:

1. We are not sure whether donors want to hear from us.

This study demonstrated that donors would like to hear from the charities they support and are disappointed when they do not. Most individual donors in the study give to dozens of charities each year; corporate donors support hundreds or thousands, and the majority of respondents are leading or major donors with many of the charities they support. When asked to indicate the number of charities they support that call them just to keep in touch, 94% of individual donor respondents and 95% of corporate donors said "none" or "hardly any." When asked how many charities drop by to visit or take them out for coffee to update them on their progress, 99% of individual donors and 100% of corporate donors said "none" or "hardly any."

These statistics underscore donors' disappointment concerning the lack of meaningful contact with the charities they support. Not a single individual donor in the study said that he would prefer not to hear from a charity to which he contributes and 93% said that personal contact influences their future giving.

2. We feel awkward about speaking with people we don't know.

Even fundraisers with many years' experience hesitate to pick up the phone to talk to a donor for the first time. Whether this is as natural as brushing your teeth or the cause of recurring nightmares, your worth as a professional or volunteer fundraiser is not defined by your ability to "boldly go where no one has gone before." For those of you who feel the butterflies by just imagining that you are reaching for the phone, take lots of comfort in the reactions of donors in this study and in a special test on the impact of personal thanks which is outlined in the next chapter.

3. We are uncomfortable about contacting donors who have been giving for a long time and with whom we have never communicated in person for fear they will interpret our gesture of appreciation as a "set up" for another gift.

It all depends on when you make the call. A true gesture of thanks is one that happens immediately after the gift has been received. To avoid having to explain to the donor that you are not attempting to solicit another gift, make that call right away—within no more than forty-eight hours.

Calling donors to thank them for their continuing loyalty long after their most recent gift has been received can also be effective, but it requires more careful scripting and timing. A call placed four weeks after you receive the gift is too late to be a considerate and timely thank you but close enough to the original ask to be interpreted as over-solicitation. You will not have to explain yourself or run the risk of causing a negative rather than a positive reaction by making the call at the right time.

4. We don't know what will result from personalized contact with donors.

In other words, will it be worth it? It will.

When study donors were asked: "Would you give again to a charity that contacted you personally to thank you for your gift, sent a prompt acknowledgment letter, and followed up sometime later with a meaningful update on the program you funded," 93% of individual donors said "definitely" or "probably." 84% said that they would "definitely" or "probably" increase the size of their next gift, and 74% would "definitely" or "most likely" continue to support the charity for longer than they normally would have considered or indefinitely.

5. We are overwhelmed by the numbers and feel that if we make personal contact with one donor, we will be obliged to do the same with every donor within the same period, something that might be logistically impossible.

The desire to communicate personally with all donors is laudable, but for organizations with a large number of contributors, adopting a philosophy of equitable treatment is likely to result in no contact at all.

It is not in the best interests of a charitable organization to launch a program of personal communication with all donors prior to first testing a strategy with a limited number of contributors. The statistical and financial information you gather in the test will enable you to plan a larger scale communication program

---

What charities feel are the 5 most effective means of communicating with donors

calling donors to thank them for gifts **64%**

corresponding with donors apart from solicitations **56%**

making personal visits to donors **46%**

inviting donors to charities' functions **44%**

calling donors to update them on activities **40%**

We feel that personal phone calls and visits to donors are really important in our stewardship of them as ongoing, annual contributors. We also believe that our mission is what compels people to give and this is why we invite donors to tour our place so they know how their donations have helped our children. It also helps us get to know our donors better.

If charities improved the quality of their communication with individual donors so that they were demonstrably more satisfied, **47%** would definitely expand their overall philanthropy and an additional **23%** might do so.

Major gifts fundraising is all about relationships. Time spent with donors out of the office or in meaningful communication via e-mail, on the telephone, or in writing personal letters will create much more value for your organization than will direct mail.

that works for both the development office and donors. Without information from testing, you will be implementing blind and running a much greater risk of becoming overwhelmed or being unsuccessful.

The number of active donors in an organization is likely to increase over time, especially if the charity is relatively new to private sector fundraising and in a building phase. However, one of the main benefits of donor-centered fundraising is that it influences repeat giving and more generous gifts from *current* donors. Donors who renew their support are more cost-effective than new donors, so dependency on broad-based acquisition will diminish over time. A charity can still expect its net number of donors to rise, but at a more controlled and manageable rate.

Priority will shift from searching for new donors to keeping existing ones and increasing their average contributions. As well, cost-per-dollar raised will decrease while overall revenues rise, a doubly beneficial outcome.

If you can't communicate with your donors because you have so many of them, you will lose most of them *because* you can't communicate with them. But, trying to introduce something new while managing a large donor base is an important consideration. Chapter 7 advocates a gradual transition starting with testing and includes a detailed process for conducting a test of personal thank you calls.

6. Our donors may expect personal contact after every gift, something that we may not be able to sustain as our numbers grow.

Donors do not need to be called after every gift in order to maintain their loyalty. Our test, explained later in this chapter, followed a group of donors through several campaigns over a two-year span. Though they were called only once after making their initial contributions, they continued to give more generously for as long as we tracked them in our study.

7. Spending time making personal thank you calls will take time away from the other important work we have to do in our development office.

The purpose of the development office is to make money. Prompt, personal thanks is one of the things that influences donors to keep giving and to increase the value of subsequent gifts. Donor communication, therefore, is not an add-on; it is a core fundraising function that produces long term income security. If you want to make more money, make meaningful communication with donors your development department's top priority.

8. Changing the way in which we thank donors will require the cooperation of others outside the development office, and they may not see the value of altering their routines to suit fundraising.

The cooperation of non-fundraising personnel will be vital. For example:

- the Board of Directors may need to approve an initial investment in improved communication with donors. However, that outlay will soon be covered by the revenue that is generated from this activity. Board members will also be asked to become directly involved in thanking donors for their gifts;
- the CEO will most likely be responsible for "selling" the concept to the Board;
- development staff will need to interact with donors differently and document new information in donor files;
- even the person who opens the mail will be affected.

This is why testing is so important. It not only produces reliable information for future planning but it serves as a dry run for the real thing, giving everyone a taste of what donor-centered fundraising will involve and how people inside and outside the development office will be affected.

In Part II: Making Donor-Centered Fundraising Work, you will find practical information on gaining support and cooperation for donor-centered fundraising.

9. We are under pressure from our employers to produce revenue now and have to relegate anything other than asking for money to a lower priority.

The unfortunate belief that a fundraiser can produce revenue without sufficient time or investment is largely responsible for the high turnover of professionals and the related supply and demand problem in the industry today.

There is no such thing as short term fundraising, a fact that is understood well by fundraisers who have learned that lesson the hard way, but resisted by many Executive Directors and Boards. Current fundraising productivity is the result of what was done six months to two years ago to set the stage for success. Conversely, poor performance in fundraising today can be traced back to inaction or error six months to two years before. Just as in any other business, cause and effect are separated by time.

94% of study donors say that charities they support never or hardly ever call them up without asking for another gift. **98%** say that charities never or hardly ever pay them a visit without asking for money.

Donors validate their belief in your work by making a contribution. A follow up call to thank the donor or, better yet, to share information about the growth of a program that their gift made possible, reconfirms his original decision to support your cause.

Data from interviews with donors in this study and the test of personal thanks (later in this chapter) show that raising money beyond an organization's current level of performance requires a cycle that includes providing information, asking, thanking, and providing information again. **Contrary to the popular adage, fundraising is not the art of asking but the art of communicating that includes asking.**

Depending upon how much time elapses between one ask and the next, a charity can expect to begin reaping the benefits of donor-centered fundraising in the fundraising campaign that follows the initial test. No reasonable employer could ask for more.

10. Solicitation monopolizes our human resources; we do not have the personnel available for personalized communication.

As a charity adopts a donor-centered fundraising philosophy, the definition of fundraising as simply asking for money will give way to a more accurate definition of fundraising as a spectrum of varied and continuous communication. Time spent thanking donors and providing them with information will be recognized as equally essential to time spent asking for money. The issue, then, is not really the re-allocation of staff time but the redefinition of the fundraising process.

Many development offices are understaffed for even their current fundraising operation. The initial objective, however, is to execute a test so that future potential can be forecast. Armed with that crucial information, fundraising personnel will be able to create a long term plan which justifies increased or re-allocated staff time in light of predictable and higher net revenue.

THE CONTROLLED TEST OF PERSONAL THANKS

A few years ago, I met with a branch of the Canadian Paraplegic Association concerning their direct mail campaign. Performance in this long standing acquisition and renewal program had stalled, and excessive donor attrition after the first gift had been identified as the main reason for poor performance. By both the Paraplegic Association's and the direct marketing industry's standards, conversion of newly acquired to renewing donors was below par.

After reviewing letter content, drop dates, and doing some year-to-year comparisons, it seemed that the solicitation program was running according to plan. But when we looked at the speed and quality of gift acknowledgment and the provision of information to donors, performance was evidently inadequate.

The Paraplegic Association felt that a more satisfying recognition program might be warranted; one that included publishing donors' names by gift level, sending donors token gifts like cards or fridge magnets, and perhaps even adding a donor recognition event for more generous contributors. I was doubtful. As I had just completed a study with Canadian donors who were decidedly negative about these things,[13] I felt that the Paraplegic Association had nothing to lose and possibly much to gain by testing a new way of communicating with their donors. "Why don't you just pick up the phone and call a few donors or, better yet, have your board members call them," I suggested. "Maybe they will appreciate this more than getting a pin, and maybe you'll learn a few things about them in the process."

Much to my surprise and delight, that's what they did.

THE TEST

With the cooperation of their Board of Directors, the Paraplegic Association executed a controlled test of the effect of personal thank you calls on future giving. This was the procedure:

During their next scheduled direct mail acquisition campaign, every tenth donor was captured in a test group (a total of 224 donors) and called by a member of the Board of Directors within 24 hours of the receipt of the gift. The volunteer callers' only job was to thank donors for choosing to give to their organization. Where callers were unable to reach donors in person after two or three attempts, they left messages on answering machines or voicemail. There was no other variable in the test. (All 2,240 donors acquired in the campaign, including test donors, received the same solicitation mailing at the same time, and all donors received the same thank you letter within the same period of time after giving.)

The test and control group donors were re-solicited approximately four months later. Again, there were no differences in letter content, timing, etc. between the control and test groups. These were the results:

- The test group gave, on average, 39% more than did the control group.
- After 14 months, the average gift level of the test group was 42% higher than the control group. (Note that test group donors were never called again during this period, nor was there any other variation between control and test groups.)

95% of all study donors said that they would be very appreciative if a member of the board of directors called them just to say thank you within a day or two or receiving their gifts. **85%** of individual donors and **100%** of corporate donors said that this would influence them to give again to the charities that made this gesture. **84%** of individual donors and **88%** of corporate donors would definitely or probably give a larger gift the next time under these circumstances.

When you get a gift, call right away to say thank you, we got it, and a letter will follow. Don't leave it hanging because we then start wondering whether the gift got lost in the mail, especially when the check isn't cashed immediately.

[13] Results of this Canadian study were published in *Thanks! . . . A Guide to Donor-Centred Fundraising, 2000*

We're a small organization with a relatively small number of donors, so in our minds there is no excuse for not making personal calls and visits. I look forward to the day when we have so many donors that it becomes an issue.

Keep it informative. Communication to existing donors should never appear to be an additional fundraising effort. That is irritable. A phone call from an individual that the donor knows is effective and appreciated. The more personal the relationship, the better. Never let the donor feel that he is being taken for granted, being ignored, or only a source of money. Your rate of success will increase, you'll increase your number of donors, and you'll make more money.

Both directly and indirectly, this new information substantiated my belief that donors are influenced by personal contact. It also served to shape the definition of donor-centered fundraising.

The Value of Research and Controlled Testing

I am an impassioned advocate of research and testing because good research answers the original question and almost always offers something more. The only requirement for getting more out of research than you ask for is a willingness to accept what the data is trying to say. The personal thanks test of the Paraplegic Association's new donors was no exception, offering the following additional information that was equally, if not more, important than the gift value data itself:

1. Where Board members were able to reach donors in person, sometimes the conversation moved beyond a simple expression of thanks. Impressed not only by the call but by the fact that the caller was a member of the Board, many donors offered valuable information about why they decided to give. Any professional fundraiser knows how meaningful this is for strategizing future asks and how unusual it is to obtain such vital information at the time the donor is first acquired.

2. Nine of the two hundred twenty-four test donors (4%) expressed an interest during the phone call in contributing a major gift or at least in "doing something more." If you think about how long donors languish in direct marketing programs, and that 90% of them will stop giving before being asked for a major gift, you will understand how valuable this early contact is.

3. Until now, the Paraplegic Association's Board of Directors had not found a way to contribute consistently to fundraising in ways that they would define as meaningful and productive. As is the case with many not for profit Boards, this association's leadership volunteers were hesitant about fundraising though they knew they had a responsibility in this area. They performed at their best, however, in this test. The Board was directly responsible for a 39% increase in giving among test group donors and they found the experience to be rewarding. Donors who were amazed and thrilled that a Board member would take the time to call them would often turn the conversation around, offering praise and gratitude to the volunteers for their contributions to the organization.

Board members would finish their calls feeling as good as, if not better than, the donors themselves.

SO EASY . . . AND SO EFFECTIVE

Since publishing the original study in 2000, I have heard from dozens of charitable organizations about the success they have achieved by simply calling donors to thank them for their gifts. Charities have reported improvements in revenue as high as 500% among donors who received a personal thank you call. Here is one example from the YMCA of Dane County, Wisconsin:

> *I am a strong believer in making "thank you" phone calls to donors . . . regardless of the size of the gift. It is a personal touch that impacts all involved!*
>
> *The first time we made thank you calls, I recruited my volunteers who typically make fundraising calls. The reaction from the volunteers and the donors was amazing. The donors were pleasantly surprised that we were calling and NOT asking for money . . . but instead showing our appreciation and letting them know how their dollars made a difference for us that year. The volunteers felt wonderful making phone calls which were always so well received, and they loved being thanked by the donors for being volunteers!*
>
> *The following spring, every one of the volunteers who made thank you calls came back to make fundraising calls on those same donors. Both our donor retention and average gift levels increased.*

> *Call your donors. Start with, 'this is a thank you, not a request.'*
>
> *There is every reason in the world not to call donors—time, awkwardness, inefficiency, fear of rejection—but the relationship that begins as a result of just one phone call is so inspiring. Calling donors is the one thing we do as an organization that usually sets us apart from the others.*

You probably received a donation from someone today. Why don't you pick up the phone and give that person a call. Your donor will be thrilled, and you'll feel great. Fundraising isn't all about mass volume campaigns and struggling to get to goal. Sometimes you can secure a partner for life through a thirty second call.

7
Test Everything

AT THE USED CLOTHING DEPOT

I was turning the radio dial, trying to find some decent music, when a conversation caught my attention. The director of a charity that relies on contributions of used clothing and goods was being interviewed. She was complaining bitterly that vandals were raiding the drop-off box at night before her staff could get there to pick up the goods. The cumulative loss to the organization was about $60,000 in the last year alone. The conversation revolved around the lack of morals in today's society and the interview came to an end. No solutions were offered.

"What a completely 'fixable' problem," I thought. For about $30,000 the organization could station some-one at the depot every night. The presence of a real person would keep the vandals away but the worker could also be on hand to say thank you to the donors who dropped off their goods. Conversations could be initiated about goods in demand, which would likely increase volume and make contributions more targeted to current needs. A mailing list of donors could be developed for a fundraising program that currently has no way of identifying its contributors. The worker could sort goods during the slow periods, reducing those costs at the distribution center. An unemployed person would have a meaningful job. A $30,000 investment would likely erase an immediate $60,000 loss, offset expenses elsewhere, and increase fundraising revenue. Most important, donors would feel good about what they had done and would be more likely to give again.

"What an easy thing to test," I thought. I reached for the dial. "There's just no good music anymore."

Objective research data lights the path for those who are curious enough to explore new ideas. Testing is the splendid companion to research; it imbues the curious with the confidence they need to break away from the status quo.

The research statistics in this book suggest what could happen to charities in general if they were to implement donor-centered fundraising. Because over four hundred subjects participated in this research, you

What I've always appreciated is personal respect, and the personal contact I have with the charities I support. When I get that I continue to give. My advice to any charity would be to make sure you have close and respectful relationships with your donors and, if you do, you will reap the rewards.

Providence Child Center does an excellent job of developing meaningful relationships with their corporate supporters. They recognize our past giving; they are more concerned with us than with our gift amount. All their supporters are treated equally and with very high regard. We feel like we're part of the team.

can be confident that the statistics will point you in the right direction. The test of personal thanks described in the previous chapter, however, was conducted with one charitable organization only. The Paraplegic Association's unique characteristics, fundraising priorities, and historical relationship with its donors affected the results that the thank you test achieved.

You need to conduct your own tests, not only on the impact of personal calls on donor retention, but on other donor-centered concepts. Testing gives you specific information that you need to reliably forecast revenue and expenses, but it also gives you much more than that.

Testing demands objectivity and decision-making based on results actually achieved, even if those results advocate deviating from accepted industry practice. For instance, high donor attrition in direct marketing programs is a current fact, but not a future inevitability. When you look past the program configuration itself and study the statistical and financial implications of donors who stop giving, it makes you want to take action. Then, the testing you do will tell you whether a new approach to fundraising can retain more donors and make more money. Testing will also tell you how long it will take to achieve better results.

Testing considers a question without presupposing the answer and does so in a non-judgmental way. Test results are not an evaluation of the person who commissioned it or posed the original question. In the context of research and testing, being right or wrong is irrelevant. The answer is what the answer is, and that's all there is to it. This is more important than you might think. People become less and less willing to try new things as they get older, and this can only be partly attributed to the accumulation of wisdom. It's also the result of feeling burned or embarrassed at finding oneself on the losing side. Only the most ardently confident people sustain a lifelong willingness to stick their necks out. For everyone else, testing offers the opportunity to be innovative while limiting exposure.

That psychological safety net gives practitioners the freedom to have creative ideas—not just to add a new twist to an existing methodology but to really consider novel concepts.

Testing prevents you from forging ahead based only on others' experiences (i.e. being too trusting). This book is a good example. Though just about every point I make is backed up with data, no single statistic could be applied literally to your organization. The Paraplegic Association's test of personal thanks, for example, produced a 39% increase in giving among test group donors from their direct mail program. If your organization also uses direct mail as a fundraising strategy, this test and the research study that surrounded it are telling you that you will likely achieve better results through more personalized gift acknowledgment; but the actual level of improvement you will achieve depends on many factors that differentiate your organization from the original test subject. These include the nature of your business, your surrounding marketing, your organization's unique advantages at the time the test is run, the effectiveness of those who make the calls, and many other things.

Your own testing will yield the donor retention and revenue numbers you need in order to do longer term, realistic forecasting. I know of charities whose results have been much more dramatic than experienced by the Paraplegic Association, including a few whose test groups performed on average 500% better than their control groups. Though a well planned and executed controlled test limits the variables as much as possible, every charity is different and every test will yield different results.

Testing puts others' fears and doubts to rest. OK . . . not every boss is a living, breathing example of open-mindedness and innovation. And not every employee is good at putting his case before the boss in a way that demands attention and influences change. The most effective way to get what you want in the face of doubt, opposition, fear of the unknown, and belligerent resistance is by conducting a test and letting the test results speak for themselves. This eliminates a "you versus me" situation, allowing decisions to be based on real evidence.

The best advantage of all is the leverage that testing gives you at the Board table. Board members speak the language of results; they understand numbers; they make their decisions based on reliable information. When the information they have at hand is incomplete, suspect, and anecdotal rather than evidence-based, they hesitate. A Board hesitates by saying "No." If you need investment to expand donor-centered fundraising, take your test results to the Board of Directors and just see how fast they take action.

TESTING IS NOT DIFFICULT

There are only a few things you need to know before you conduct a test, and specialized knowledge is not required in order to be successful.

1. How to articulate the objective of your test

Be clear about what you are testing and define your test as a question that does not presuppose the outcome:

I knew a film producer who used to tell people who came to him with lengthy scripts, "If you can't write your idea on the back of this business card, you don't have a good idea." The same thing applies in communicating with donors. If you cannot acknowledge a donor in three sentences or less, you have a lot to learn. Being succinct is the key.

A personal touch is the key to success. Add a handwritten note to a standard, otherwise dry letter; call your donors occasionally. This will make donors feel much closer.

This is an example of a test question phrased appropriately:

Are donors who are thanked personally for their gifts more likely to give again and give more than other donors who do not receive personal thanks?

This phrasing is not appropriate, implying the possibility of failure:

The objective of this test is to personally thank donors for gifts so that they will continue to give and give gifts of higher value.

2. Controlled tests and variables

A controlled test is one in which two groups undergo identical procedures except for a single variable or difference that is particular only to the test group. For a test to be completely reliable, there should be only one variable so that any subsequent difference in performance between the control and test groups can be attributed to the variable. For instance, in the case of the test of personal thanks with the Paraplegic Association, the only variable was that 10% of the whole group of donors received a personal thank you call from a member of the Board of Directors.

If your test sample size is large enough to begin with, it is possible to subdivide the test group and introduce one or more new variables. (You can also run a test with multiple variables right from the start, but I don't advise it if you haven't done this kind of thing before.)

3. Duration and complexity

A controlled test can be a simple, one-time function, or it can carry on over a longer period of time, producing new information as time passes. Without ever doing anything with the test group again after the initial thank you call, we followed the Paraplegic Association test and control groups for two years and found that the test group's average gift value continued to improve against that of the control group. This allowed us to conclude that a single personal interaction with a leadership volunteer can have a beneficial and long-lasting effect on donors.

The following pages describe how to replicate the test of personal thank you calls conducted with the Canadian Paraplegic Association. Because it is a detailed explanation, it may seem intimidating on first read. But, if you assign someone to manage the test and allocate a little time for analysis, you will find that it is not difficult to implement. The test procedure identifies eight things that could be impacted by the single act of thanking donors personally within these five categories: gift value, retention, movement to major gifts program, multiple giving within a single year, promptness of response. You do not have to run reports on all of these things if you think that is too much to handle. You can simply monitor gift value and retention, but the wider range of possibilities is included here for those who want to know more about the effect of improved donor communication.

The sample script, instructions to volunteer callers, phone call log sheet and post-test survey may be copied for your own use.

How to Conduct a Thank You Test in Your Organization

You can conduct a meaningful test in any fundraising program—direct mail (acquisition, renewal or both), telemarketing, canvassing, major gifts, corporate campaign—as long as the program includes or can generate enough donors to make a test worthwhile. I chose a direct mail acquisition program precisely because of the arms-length nature of this type of fundraising and the comparatively poor retention rate of first time donors. I felt that if personal contact could make a measurable impact with these donors, then there was a good chance that longer term donors would also be influenced by better communication.

You can also conduct a successful test whether your chosen program is new or has been in existence for some time. The latter is revealing in different ways because the test is launched with more data on hand, drawn from several components of an existing program. The overriding issue, though, is that you do conduct a test prior to full implementation. Comparative data is vital in order to build a solid case with decision-makers and in order to create a plan for donor-centered fundraising and communication across your development department.

THANK YOU TEST PROCEDURE

1. Select the fundraising program on which your test will be conducted.

2. Select either your acquisition or renewal program. Newly acquired or renewing donors support your organization for different reasons, have different needs, and require different approaches (see Chapter 3–Donors are People). You can conduct more than one test at a time if you are running simultaneous campaigns. However, you should assess the amount of time that you have to manage more multiple, simultaneous tests as well as the number of donors who can reasonably and logistically be called by Board members within that time frame.

You don't have to do a lot; it doesn't take much to keep donors informed of your work and that you appreciate them.

Get your message across effectively about why you need the money, what you will achieve with it. There are thousands of good causes and donors have to figure out why they should support one over the other. Charities need to believe in their mission and express it credibly and passionately.

3. If you choose to test donors in your renewal program, remember that existing donors include those who are being solicited for only the second time (they were acquired in your most recent acquisition campaign) and donors who have been giving to you for longer. These two groups are not the same. You can either select a group of donors with the same "loyalty" characteristics or you might test a representative sample of donors at different stages of loyalty.

4. The following information will be needed at the time test results are analyzed and performance is compared with the control group.

Information Required for the Test	How to Collect the Information
Sample Size *This is the number of donors you need to include in your test to produce reliable results.*	If your database is relatively small, you can include up to 50% of your donors in the test. While it is unlikely you will have sufficient resources to test giving levels with statistical certainty, in order to generate reliable results, avoid allowing any single test donor to represent more than 1% of the entire test group. In other words, your sample should include at least 100 donors. If you do not have enough donors to produce a sample group of at least 100, you can still conduct the test and the information you gather will be anecdotally important.
Rate of Response *This is the percentage who gave of the total number solicited.*	Rate of response is determined by taking the number of donors who gave to a specific campaign and dividing it by the number of prospects who received the mailing. Be sure to include donor numbers that represent the entire campaign, including any follow up mailings that would be considered to be part of the original campaign.
Average Rate of Response	You may wish to test donors from more than one campaign. For example, you might want to test a representative sample who gave at least once in the last two years during which time you conducted, say, six campaigns. If this is the case, it will be sufficient for you to determine the average rate of response for each of the six campaigns and then average those six rates to produce a response rate across the two-year period.

Information Required for the Test	How to Collect the Information
Average Gift— Single Campaign	Calculate donors' average gift value for a single campaign by dividing the gross revenue by the number of donors who gave. If that campaign included both an acquisition and a renewal component, calculate the two average gift levels separately.
Average Gift— Multiple Campaigns	To calculate the average gift value across a series of campaigns from which your test group may be drawn, add together the average gifts for each campaign and divide by the number of campaigns to produce an average over the period.
Rate of Attrition *This is the rate at which donors leave or become inactive. It will be required to determine whether thanking donors once or intermittently influences long term loyalty.*	If you have already established a period of time that defines a donor as "lapsed," then use it for this calculation. Many organizations use the benchmark of non-giving over an 18-month period as a determinant. If you only solicit once a year, however, a donor may not be considered lapsed until after 24 months of non-giving. Regardless, pick a timeframe, then double it. If it's 18 months, go back 36 months from now. Create a file of donors who gave at least once in the earliest 18-month period. Calculate the percentage of these same donors who gave at least once more during the most recent 18-month period. The remainder percentage is your rate of attrition. If you conduct a "thanks test" now, you will not be using this statistic for awhile. However, it will be valuable when the time comes.
Rate of Promptness of Response *This information is valuable in determining whether donors who are personally thanked respond more promptly to subsequent requests. This calculation helps determine whether test donors have become more actively supportive of your organization or, perhaps, have singled you out for prompt attention.*	Determine the number of weeks that your last renewal campaign was in execution. For the purpose of this test, day 1 of week 1 is the day your first gift was received. (If you haven't tracked this information in your donor records, then you cannot determine this statistic at this time, but you should do so in your next campaign.) The last day of the last week is the date that your last gift to the campaign was received before you officially closed that campaign off. Chart the number of gifts received each week. (It would be valuable to plot this data on a line graph.) Do the same for each campaign in the past two years, then create a line graph that represents the average flow of responses weekly during your campaigns.

Information Required for the Test	How to Collect the Information
Annual Average Rate of Response *If you conduct more than one renewal solicitation annually, this calculation determines the average number of gifts per donor per year.* *This information is important in determining whether test donors give more often than other donors. Like the rate of attrition, you won't be using this information immediately, but it is very valuable.*	Let's assume that you do three solicitations per year in this example. Look at two 12-month periods. Capture the names of all donors who gave at least once in the first year, and calculate the percentage of those who gave in one, two, or three campaigns. Do the same for Year 2, then take the average for the two years.
Rate of Transfer to Major Gifts Program *This is a calculation of the number of donors who move up and out of your direct marketing program into major gift status each year, and their average gift values.*	This is the least scientific calculation as donors seldom move into higher giving programs on their own. Success here depends on whether or not you have a regular and proactive process for encouraging donors into higher levels of giving. If you do, you should be able to easily identify how many donors in the last two years have graduated from your direct marketing program into the major gifts category. (Of course, each organization defines the value of a major gift relative to their own overall fundraising portfolio and income level.) Take an average of both the number of donors and gift levels each year for the past two years. If you do not have any major gift donors outside your direct marketing program, then make a note of what the average gift value is of the top 1% of your donors.

Information Required for the Test	How to Collect the Information
Flow of Gift Income *Similar to the line graph created for rate of promptness of response, the income flow graph charts the peaks and valleys of revenue over the course of the active campaign period.*	In telemarketing or canvassing programs, the flow of income is directly related to the number of donors called or contacted per night and the number of callers or canvassers on duty. But, in direct mail, donations flow from a single date solicitation and there is a period when you receive a concentration of gifts. If your organization tends to "batch" input information, then you may not know what your real flow of income is. However, you can probably get a good idea by reviewing bank deposit records. Using the mail drop date as Day 1, create a flow chart of the income received each day over the period of the campaign.

5. Create a critical path for the test. This is especially important since Board members are being asked to participate. Work both forward and backward from the mail date of your campaign, allowing enough time to accomplish the required tasks. An example of a critical path for a direct mail campaign follows:

Timing	Activity
1-2 months prior to drop date	• Gather the comparative data referred to in the above chart. • Determine the sample size. This will involve estimating the number of donors expected to give and deciding how many to call. • Determine the number of Board members required and the calling schedule that ensures calls will be made within 24 or 48 hours of gift receipt, even during peak times. • Determine the information to be captured in calls.
1 month prior to drop date	• Secure the commitment of members of the Board.
1 week prior to drop date	• send Board members the sample script and instructions.
3-4 days into the campaign	• Put Board members on stand-by for first calls to early donors.
first calling day/evening	• Orient Board members to the process.

continued on next page...

Timing	Activity
daily following the previous day's/night's calling	• Input data. • Take action on any extraordinary calls.
weekly during the active campaign	• Ensure that calling quotas are met and that a sufficient number of donors is being called for sample validity.
within twenty-four hours after completion of Board members' calls	• Thank Board members personally for their contribution to the test.
end of campaign	• Report to the Board on results of the test.
end of the following campaign	• Conduct initial analysis of the test, comparing the performance of the test group against the control group in each statistical category referenced in the table on Pages 66 to 69.
long term	• Continue to measure the influence of a single personal call through ongoing analysis.

6. Choose the Test Sample

In the test we conducted, every tenth donor was captured in the test group. This is a perfectly acceptable way to accrue a random sample as long as you start at the very beginning of the campaign with the first donations received, and continue to add donors to the test group until the end of the campaign. This is important because donors who give immediately and donors who wait for some time before giving may display different characteristics. It may be that in your organization the average gift value of donors who give in the first half of the campaign is higher than that of donors who give in the latter half. You want to be sure, then, to sample the entire donor group. Your future analysis may investigate whether late donors give earlier the next time if they receive a personal call.

Use information from past campaigns plus the size of your prospect group to estimate how many gifts you will receive and how large your sample should be. Be practical, too. It is counter-productive to over-burden Board members with too many calls. If each Board member has to make ten calls a night for five weeks, they won't do it.

If this is your first campaign and you have no historical data on which to base your organization's and your donors' performance standards, you can still conduct a test. Results from test donors will be compared with the results of all other donors in the same campaign.

In order to generate statistically significant results, your test should include a minimum of 100 test donors representing no more than 50% of all donors in the campaign. However, if you have only 30 donors, calling 15 of them will still give you good anecdotal information that will help you plan your future donor-centered fundraising program. **Do not call all your donors. If you do that, you are not conducting a test; you are implementing a program and you will relinquish the benefits that testing provides.**

7. Create the calling script and caller orientation materials

There is nothing more straightforward than the script for a thank you call.

Three sentences comprise the full extent of your Board members' responsibilities. Any conversation that takes place after this point should be initiated only by the donor. Many donors are quite satisfied to end the call after the Board member expresses his appreciation; some will comment on the organization's work; some will praise the Board member for his contribution to the organization; and some will talk about why they gave. Whether the call evolves into a conversation or not is not the issue; the fact that someone important in the organization took the time to call is.

Following are sample instructions to Board member callers (which can be adapted to suit your charity's process) along with a sample caller sheet and an evaluation questionnaire for Board members making personal calls.

Dear Members of the Board of (organization),

Thank you for agreeing to make calls of appreciation to donors in our test taking place from (date) to (date). Here is some background information for your calls:

What you should say

The intention of the call is ONLY to thank donors for their gifts just received. To that end, we would like to ensure that each donor receives a personal call within 24 to 48 hours of his gift's arrival at our office. To make this possible, we will be processing gift information immediately and will fax or deliver calling forms such as the attached sample to your home (office) by 4 pm each day. There will be one form per donor; the information that must be recorded is in bold. Additional space is provided for anything else that transpires in your call which you feel is noteworthy.

We have found it to be most effective if you say something like this:

"Hello, Mr./Mrs X. My name is Jane Brown and I'm a member of the volunteer Board of Directors of (name of organization). I am calling to thank you for your support of our organization. We just received your gift today (yesterday) and I wanted to let you know in person how very much we appreciate it."

— we need to add this to our info.

At this point, simply pause and wait for a response. Some donors are quite startled and don't know what to say. Usually, they are very appreciative and gracious.

Most calls are very short, simply ending after you express your thanks. We would appreciate it if you do not make any comment that could be construed as another request, such as "We are grateful for your gift and hope that you will continue to support us in the future." This hints of another solicitation, and we want to avoid leaving that impression. You could end the call by simply wishing the donor a pleasant evening.

Sometimes a caller will ask you about how our organization is doing or they will want some information about our programs and services. If you are comfortable answering their questions, by all means do so. If not, perhaps you could ask them if they would like the Executive Director (or other staff person) to contact them separately. If so, please note that on the form. If a donor expresses an interest in giving more or in volunteering his time, you can definitely engage in that discussion. Other organizations' experience with thank you calls by Board members has shown that a small number of donors want to discuss making an additional gift and sometimes it can be significantly higher than the gift they have just made. The Board member's call is not manipulative, in this case; it is the opportunity for the donor to realize an existing desire.

Additional information to be gathered

If donors offer information about themselves, make comments about our organization, or say anything else that you feel is worth noting (and in fundraising, almost everything is worth noting), please record it on the attached form.

Reaching voicemail or another occupant

If you reach voicemail, try the number again later. If you still do not reach the donor in person, carry this call over for one more day. Try making your call at another time of day. If, by the end of the second evening you still have not reached the donor in person, please leave a brief thank you message on his answering machine.

If you connect to someone else in the household and the donor is not home, you have two choices. If you know you are speaking with the donor's spouse or someone in whom you have confidence that the message will be passed on as intended, you can choose to leave a message of thanks. However, it is probably safer to let the person know that you will call back later and to ask for a convenient time to call.

You could say something like this which lets the person know that this is not a solicitation call:

> *"I'm a member of the Board of Directors of (name of organization) calling to let (name of donor) know that we just received the donation she sent and I simply wanted to thank her for her kindness. I'll call later or tomorrow when she is at home. Is there any best time for me to call? (Wait for the answer.) If I don't connect with her, would you please pass on (name of organization's) thanks for her contribution? Thank you."*

What happens with the results of these calls?

Donors who receive a personal call (including those donors who received messages left on their answering machines) will be specially coded, and any additional information gathered during the calls will also be recorded.

The next time these donors are solicited along with other donors who did not receive a call, we will be comparing their average gift levels, their rate of response, the promptness of response, and other information. We will continue to do this for a period of at least two years, which will also allow us to measure long term loyalty of the two groups. Though we anticipate that donors who receive personal calls are likely to show greater loyalty over time and make increasingly generous gifts, we need reliable information from this test for future planning and forecasting.

We will not be calling these donors again for some time. However, if this test produces meaningful results, we will extend the calling program to include other donors. At the end of this test, we will provide the Board with a report on this program.

The attached form

Please use one call sheet per donor. Information you will need to make your calls appears in the shaded area. We would appreciate it if you returned the forms to us by fax or in person within 24 hours of completing your calls.

A final request

Equally important as receiving information about the donors you called is receiving your own impression of this task. Please take a moment to complete the attached brief survey and return it to us with your completed call sheets.

Thank you so much for your assistance. If you have any suggestions or questions, please do not hesitate to contact (name and title of staff person) at (phone number).

With best regards.

Sincerely,
(preferably signed by the Chair of the Board or CEO)

(Name of organization)

Information for Board Members Making Thank You Calls
Please complete one sheet per donor and fax it back to us at (fax #) or return it in person within 24 hours of completing your calls.

Name of Donor _____   Donor's Phone # _____

Donor File # _____   Date Gift Received _____

❏ First time donor   ❏ Donor for less than 2 years   ❏ Long term donor

Volunteer Caller's Information:

Start Time of Call: _____   Finish Time of Call: _____

❏ Spoke to donor in person   ❏ Left message on voicemail   ❏ Left message with another person

Check any of the following that apply:

❏ Brief call; said thank you; no particular feedback from donor; difficult to assess whether donor was pleased or not

❏ Donor pleased or very pleased to receive the call though there was little or no follow up conversation

❏ Donor actively engaged in conversation. Please check if any of the following apply:

   ❏ donor interested in volunteering on the Board or on a Committee

   ❏ donor interested in volunteering in the office or in direct service

   ❏ donor interested in giving another gift (caller: please indicate who should call donor back if this is the case)

   _____

   ❏ donor interested in visiting the organization

   ❏ donor wants follow up call from staff person to answer question or provide more information on (please explain):

   _____

❏ Other: (please explain):

_____

_____

Additional comments (if warranted):

_____

_____

_____

_____

Information in the shaded box at the top of the caller sheet (previous page) is to be provided to callers in advance. The donor's gift amount is not recorded for two reasons. First, these forms are faxed back and forth and could be seen by several people, compromising the confidentiality of this information; second, this activity focuses on appreciation for the act of giving, not the size of the gift. Only the donor himself can define generosity within his own means. A $25 gift from someone on a modest pension is generous by comparison with a $100 gift from a millionaire.

Board Member Calling Program Survey

When you have completed all your calls, please fill out this brief questionnaire and return it to us with your call sheets to (fax #). _____

Board Member's Name: _____

1. Please indicate whether you agree or disagree with the following statements:

	Agree	Disagree
• On the whole, the experience of calling donors to thank them for their gifts was pleasurable.	☐	☐
• On the whole, donors appreciated receiving the thank you calls.	☐	☐
• I was able to find the time to make my assigned calls within 48 hours.	☐	☐
• I would do this again if asked.	☐	☐

2. Do you have any advice concerning how the process of calling donors personally could be improved in the future?

_____

_____

3. Do you have any other comments?

_____

_____

_____

_____

As part of a new commitment to donor relations at our university, one of our Deans sent a stewardship report on an endowment fund to the daughter of a late professor who had established the fund some thirty years earlier. The report included personalized thank-you letters from the award recipients. Soon, we received a letter in return which read:

"This is the first time I have personally heard from any recipient, and I must tell you in all truth, that I was unclear if the award was still being given...It just warms my heart to know that Daddy's memory lives on in the department he so loved and where he devoted so many of his years!...In the hope that this tradition will continue, I am enclosing a check for $1,000, which I hope will bring a little joy to a few more students this year and enhance their studies in some small way."

There are ways to make thank you calls to donors less time-consuming for volunteers. If you spread the calls out among many people, each individual has only a few calls to make. We do ours monthly and it works well. Each Board member spends only about an hour a month on phone calls. A small price to pay for donor loyalty.

If a member of the Board of Directors phoned you within one or two days of the receipt of your gift, just to say thank you, what would you think?

Wow!! Totally on the ball.

I would be dumfounded.

I would fall off my chair.

I would be amazed.

I'd drop my pants!

I'd be astonished.

Fabulous!

I'd be impressed.

I would think that they really cared about my gift.

I'd think they have a great board!

It would be very cool.

It would make me feel good.

It would be nice.

That would be great.

I'd be surprised.

I'd pass out!

I'd think it was incredibly generous of this person's time.

Very nice. I'd be impressed because they were obviously well organized.

It would be great . . . but it never happens.

I'd be shocked.

I'd be more impressed if they said, "Do you have anything you want to say about our work or how we're doing it?"

I just had a call recently. I wouldn't have given again without it.

Why it is important for Board members to make these calls

A donor seems to have to earn the right to be noticed by the Board of Directors. When Board members' time and attention is concentrated solely on the group of donors giving at the highest level, it sends a message that only the amount of the gift is important and not the act of giving itself. Many corporate and individual donors in the study said that they tend to increase the value of gifts to certain charities over time and that a key factor in retaining some partnerships and walking away from others is the quality of the relationship which has developed.

When a Board member acknowledges a donor's gift and does so immediately, the donor knows that the organization has really made an effort. First, there must be communication and coordination from the front desk all the way to the board room. Two or more departments may have had to cooperate and move quickly to process the gift and pass the appropriate information on to the Board member who makes the call. Though the donor may not know exactly what has transpired behind the scenes, she knows that a sincere effort has been made and she is impressed.

As the top authority in the organization and as the group of people who embody the highest ideals of voluntarism, there is no substitute for the Board of Directors. The single greatest honor that can be bestowed on a donor is recognition from the Board. We tend to mete out recognition by Board members as if their capacity to say thank you were somehow in limited supply. Or we hesitate to ask for Board members' time because they have more important things to do. What could possibly be more important than communicating with donors? Chapter 13 includes more information on the role of leadership volunteers in donor-centered fundraising.

Finally, no statistic in the study was more compelling than this one. Corporate and individual respondents alike were asked this question:

If a member of the Board of Directors of a charity to whom you had just made a contribution called you personally within a day or two of the receipt of your gift just to say thank you, what would you think?

95% of respondents would be appreciative and impressed. As well, this simple gesture would influence 72% to give more the next time they were asked, and 74% would continue to give indefinitely or longer than they might otherwise have considered.

The act of showing appreciation will create change. It will influence how everyone thinks about and interacts with donors. It will bring Board members closer to the people who give, people whose opinions are less subjective yet still supportive. It will lessen the need (and accompanying pressure) to ask for money. In an environment where everyone is as interested in the donors as they are in the money, things change—for the better.

Time is of the essence in making thank you calls to donors

It is the combination of a call from a leadership volunteer and the promptness of the call that is so influential with donors. Calling two weeks or a month after the gift may be misconstrued as another solicitation and callers may have to do some fast talking to reassure donors about the call's purpose. Though this is not a calamity, why put Board members in a situation that forces them to explain themselves and which risks upsetting donors, even if only momentarily?

The importance of restricting the number of variables

A controlled test identifies a group of donors whose performance will be compared with another group of donors. In a straightforward test, there is only one variable (difference) between the control group and the test group. In this case, the test group receives a personal call; the control group does not.

It is important that all other things remain the same in future solicitations; otherwise, you may not be able to prove that your data is a result of the personal calls. For example, if you conduct this test in your direct mail program, it will be important that all donors—both control and test group donors—are sent the same letter, on the same day. If you are also testing a secondary letter, that is fine as long as a similar percentage of test donors as control group donors receive this alternate letter. Make sure this is flagged in your donor files so that your analysis is based on like data.

It is possible to test for more than one thing at a time. However, doing so can limit your sample size too much and it can introduce a level of doubt about the impact of each independent concept being tested. As you are attempting to demonstrate to Board members that their personal calls make a tangible difference, you may wish to avoid including any secondary testing so that results are unquestionably conclusive.

Data Input and Analysis

Here is an overview of new information to record in donor files and the basic data analysis functions required to provide meaningful test results:

Don't spend so much time preparing for the call that you never make it. Just get out there!

A one-minute phone call can represent the equivalent of one year's worth of solicitations. You never know why or what someone might give.

Timing	Data Input Activity
from Day 1 of the campaign from which the test donor group is drawn.	• Identify donors as test donors. • Record gift received date (actual date that gift arrived, not processing date if later). • Identify name or initials of Board member assigned to the call. • Accommodate information from volunteer call sheets. • Allow room for extraordinary information.

Timing	Analysis of the Test
post campaign	• Report on the reaction that donors had to being called, the number of donors who offered or inquired about making another gift, the number of donors who offered to volunteer. • Report on the reaction that volunteers had to making the calls. • Create line graphs showing the flow of donations and the flow of revenue across the campaign.
prior to execution of the next campaign	• Compare the percentage of donors in the test group who gave another (unprompted) gift between the end of the first campaign and the beginning of the next one against the percentage of donors in the control group who did so. • Compare the percentage and average gift value of test donors who became major gift donors against the percentage of control group donors who did so.
after the next campaign	• Compare the average gift size of test group donors with control group donors. • Compare the percentages of test and control group donors who gave. • Compare the promptness of test group donors' giving with their own performance in the previous campaign. Compare the line graphs which showed gift and revenue flow for both campaigns. • Compare the performance of test group donors who were reached in person with donors who received a message on their answering machines or a message passed on by someone else in the household.

Timing	Analysis of the Test
at the end of a full year of campaigns, if applicable	• Compare the annual average rates of response, average gift levels, etc.
at the end of three years (or the period of time you use to calculate lapsed donors)	• Compare the attrition rates of test donors and control group donors.
ongoing	• Continue to monitor the test group against the control group for all relevant information. • Note the point at which the beneficial effect of a single phone call begins to wane, if it does.

How Long Do I Have to Keep This Up?

Isolating a number of donors in a control or test group indefinitely is impractical. Three years from now you may want to introduce new innovations in donor communication across your entire donor base without concerning yourself about whether or not you are compromising your testing. You will still have a legitimate test sample as long as you introduce other changes or enhancements across both the control and test groups simultaneously.

Observing your test group over the long term gives you just as valuable, though different, information from what you gathered in the first year. If you plot average gift and frequency of response over several years without ever calling test group donors again, you will learn how long that single phone call continued to influence test donors' giving. As donors who renew tend also to give more over time, your long term study of this group will reveal how influential personal thanks is in setting a new standard of giving.

You may choose to split your test group (assuming you are working with a sufficient number in the first place) and test new theories, using half the group as a new control group. For example, you could call half your test donors again after two years, then monitor the two groups' performance at the end of the third and fourth years of the program. By doing so, you could answer questions such as:

- Do donors who are called twice in four years give more and/or give more often?
- Does a higher percentage of those donors who are called more often move into the major gifts program?
- Is it meaningful if the same member of the Board of Directors calls a donor the second time?

Data analysis and controlled testing are two of the three keys to success in fundraising. The third is donor-centered fundraising. Objective analysis takes nothing away from innovation or creativity; it makes them possible.

Forecasting Revenue Using Test Results

Though results from a single test are meaningful, decision-makers will be increasingly supportive of donor-centered fundraising as they see the results it achieves over a series of campaigns or years. A donor communication strategy which demands time from Board members as well as an investment in staff will only be supported if decision-makers can see the long term as well as the immediate benefits. If the results of your test are positive, your immediate (next campaign) improvement will pale by comparison with the cumulative impact of donor-centered fundraising over several years (see Chapter 11).

Cost Implications of a Personal Thanks Calling Program

You can run a limited test without impacting your budget if you are prepared to reallocate some staff and volunteer time for a short period. Advance planning is the key to success here. Though a sudden shift in work priorities can have an adverse effect, most organizations can plan ahead to incorporate a short-term activity without having it drain resources from other areas. The test results you generate will then tell you whether you can raise more money, how much more money you can raise, and how quickly you can raise it if you make donor-centered fundraising your new priority.

Saying thank you to donors promptly and personally makes more money; but even if it didn't, thanking donors well would still be the right thing to do. Making these calls may also be the best application of your Board members' time in the fundraising process. If they do nothing more than communicate their gratitude to donors, they will provide the ultimate gift to their charity—the gift of time, meaningfully applied.

FROM TESTING TO IMPLEMENTATION

After conducting your test and demonstrating the value of incorporating personal thanks into your donor communication program, your attention will naturally turn to your entire donor base. Now you need a systematic approach to thanking every donor on a set schedule within a formula that is the least disruptive of your time or that of your volunteers, right? Wrong. The moment you are tempted to take a mass marketing approach to acknowledging your donors' support is the time to put the heart back into your work. If you are determined to thank all donors as quickly as possible, your personal thanks will soon become impersonal and just another obligation.

When you move beyond written thank you letters into the much more personal realm of voice or in-person contact, the slightest inflection, the merest hint of mood is perceived and processed faster than the speed of light. Donors may not be able to articulate those feelings but they certainly know that they have been transmitted. The atmosphere that surrounds the call, therefore, says much more than can ever be captured in a script. If the call is a duty and not a privilege, it will be noticed by the donor and the effort will be counter-productive. Every call involves a volunteer as well as the fundraiser's time in supporting that volunteer. The number of calls that can be made in a set period will be limited by time.

Here are some guidelines to help you handle the implementation of more personalized communication with contributors over your entire donor base:

1. If you presently run such a large direct marketing campaign that it would be difficult to thank each donor in person within 48 hours, return to the testing you conducted and the questionnaire completed by your volunteer callers. Ask yourself these questions:

- How many calls can a Board member handle in a single evening and still easily fulfill this commitment?
- How many nights a week is it reasonable to ask volunteers to call?
- Over how many weeks can volunteers sustain their interest in making calls?
- Is a good portion of the donor base reachable during the daytime?
- If so, are there Board members available for daytime calling?
- How many Board members of the total group were willing to make calls in the test? Can that number be increased now that the test has proven successful and Board members have had a good experience? (If that is so.)

It's good for Board members to be involved in recognition and have personal relationships with donors. Board members can speak effectively about why they give their time to the organization. This gives a human face to the charity at the very top.

General "fear of asking" prevents our leadership volunteers from experiencing the rewards that come with developing closer relationships with donors. Getting our Board members to simply communicate with donors, even without an ask, can be a real challenge.

With the number of willing Board members, their estimated available time, the length of time it takes to make a call, and your knowledge of the flow of donations (see page 69), you can determine how many donors can be called in each campaign.

2. Do not worry about equitable treatment. If you feel that you must call every donor to avoid treating anyone unfairly, it will become a reason to call no one at all. Even a limited calling program can be dramatically productive.

3. Donors do not need to be thanked in person every time they make a gift— nor should they be. As you continue to monitor your initial test group, you will know when or if that first call ceases to influence donors' future gift levels and frequency of response. Calling donors to thank them for gifts is not the only thing that influences their future giving. (See Chapters 9 and 10.)

4. Incorporate personal calls to donors into your own schedule. I know I have been saying that immediate in-person thanks should be done by Board members and that is so. However, that does not mean that hard-working professional fundraisers should be barred from the privilege. If fundraising staff started and ended every work day with one phone call to a donor and one personal note, that would be four a day or 672 a year per staff member—allowing for holidays, sick days, and days away from the office for other reasons. Apart from the increase in revenue that could be expected in the following year, imagine how good staff would feel knowing that every work day started and ended with the best job perk imaginable. No matter how good a donor feels after getting a call or reading a heartfelt letter, the one who places the call or composes the letter feels even better.

If you focus on what has been achieved, not on the number of donors not yet reached, you will continue to make progress and feel good about it at the same time.

Changing How You Think and Act in the Face of New Information

Testing is not yet a part of fundraising culture. It's not that the industry has rejected the notion; it's simply that testing has not surfaced in fundraising as a smart business strategy.[14] When taking on new work as well as a new way of working, you run the risk of going to the trouble of getting the job done but not

---

[14] with the single exception of testing alternate letter copy in direct mail

using the results. This happens so often in strategic planning, for instance, where the detailed road map to success gathers dust in a binder on the CEO's bookshelf. In testing, an organization may go to the trouble of conducting a test, the test produces positive results, the test results are presented and studied . . . and nothing changes. Even in the face of statistical evidence that is astonishing, change does not take place automatically. Chapter 15 offers some insight into the barriers to change and how they can be overcome.

You'll be surprised how much information about your donor you can acquire with a simple phone call.

If we wait for donors to make a major gift before we make a special effort to acknowledge their support, most of them will never get there. It is direct contact with donors and the evident gesture of respect that reinforces their giving and influences supporters to give again. In essence, the thank you is the ask. It's as simple as that.

8

All That Donors Want

THE GUEST SPEAKER

Our organization is a treatment center providing habilitation and rehabilitation services for children and young adults with physical disabilities. Our largest fundraising event is the annual Dinner Dance Gala. Over the years, we have tried a number of different things to ensure that attendees are not just filling out a table at yet another charity event, but are informed about our charity and the work their contributions are supporting.

We have tried giant video presentations inside the hall, smaller video presentations in the front lobby, speeches by local politicians, board members, volunteers—but none of these seemed to accomplish our goal. Then, one year, we decided that the best proponents for what we do are the clients themselves. This immediately caused a concerned reaction from several members of the Board and staff who felt that using clients to extract cash from donors was both exploitive and unethical.

We searched for and found the middle ground. We invited a few older clients from our Youth Advisory Committee to attend the Gala. This is a group of 12–22 year olds who make recommendations from a user's perspective. We even found a corporate sponsor to cover the cost of their table at the Gala. One member was selected to speak on behalf of all our clients and to tell the guests what the center has done to make a difference in her life.

When she rose to speak on the night, she introduced herself by saying: "Hi, I'm Rose and I'm what you are paying for." The crowd was riveted. By the end of her speech, everyone in the room knew why they were there. As for the clients, the experience was just as positive, if not more so. They were real participants, they met influential members of the corporate world, and they got to express their feelings and ideas.

This was a turning point for us. The annual Dinner Dance Gala continues to this day. It is a much happier and more meaningful event for participants now because the people they help are enjoying it with them.

One of the biggest challenges that will be faced by practitioners in trying to implement donor-centered fundraising is convincing decision-makers to invest time and money in communicating more effectively with donors. (That is why testing is so important and why I give it so much attention. Test results are the argument in support of investment in new strategies to raise more money more effectively.) Another challenge is helping decision-makers and program personnel understand why *designated giving* is an essential tool for building donor loyalty.

Designated gift fundraising is simply the commitment of a charity to use donors' gifts for one or more specific purposes which comprise only a portion of the programs or services in which the charity is engaged.

Designated giving: reward for major donors or antidote to early attrition?

Charities need to turn their thinking upside down about designated giving. Designated giving is offered as a privilege or benefit for major donors when it should actually be a tool to attract new donors and breed early loyalty.

The relationship between organization and donor is most tenuous at the time the first gift is made. This is evidenced by the attrition pattern in direct marketing programs in which more donors lapse between the first gift and the second ask than at any other time. (See Chapter 3.) With this in mind, practitioners need to ask, "What is loyalty?" and "What does it take to turn a first-time or occasional donor into a committed philanthropist?"

Loyalty is the by-product of trust and trust has to be earned. So, when someone gives for the first time, she is more hopeful than trusting. Something influences her to contribute to your organization—it could be your superior marketing that surrounded the campaign, your charity's prior reputation, a personal affiliation for the cause—whatever it is, she gives you the benefit of the doubt that you will act responsibly, but she has no real way of knowing in advance whether or not you will. Your job now is to turn that first tenuous gesture into continuing, confident giving.

Prompt and personal gift acknowledgment goes a long way toward making your organization stand out in the mind of a donor who may give to several causes simultaneously or who is living with sour memories of past communication disappointments. But, more than anything else, information in the form of measurable results is what influences donors to give again. In order to provide measurable results, a donor's contribution must be designated to a specific end purpose. Since gift designation is used as a reward for higher level contributors, donors who give small gifts don't learn what their effort achieved, and so they stop giving.

While our immediate preoccupation in fundraising is always to make money, we are also responsible for helping prospective donors and tenuous donors learn about the joy of giving. Gift designation is one of the tools at our disposal for creating resilient philanthropists.

At the other end of the giving spectrum, relationship-building reduces the need for gift designation. Ask anyone working in planned giving. When planned gift prospects begin to discuss the possibility of a bequest or other deferred gift, it is quite common for them to want to designate to a specific end use. As there is no guarantee that a fifty-year old donor's current interest will be a focus of the charity by the time the donor dies and the bequest is realized, undesignated bequests are certainly preferred. How does a planned gifts officer move a donor from a desire to designate to a willingness to provide an undesignated gift? The relationship is the key. Donor cultivation is a sharing of information and exchange of ideas which progresses until the donor feels comfortable with the solicitor and well informed about the organization she represents. At some point, they both know that a state of trust has been reached and it is now possible for the donor to make a commitment.

WHY CHARITIES RESIST DESIGNATED GIVING

Charities discourage the idea of assigning donors' contributions to specific programs and services because they assume that designated giving:

- restricts charities' ability to capitalize on new opportunities. Organizations feel that if too much money is designated by donors to one program or only to certain programs, it will be impossible to finance other areas of service without the freedom to move revenue from one program to another.
- places too much power in the hands of donors. Charities feel that donors will tend to designate their gifts to the most popular, well known or least controversial programs and that lesser known but equally important programs will not be adequately resourced.

Both these fears are unfounded. But, there are real, underlying issues that foster a resistance to designated giving and they are worth exploring:

23% of study donors always or most of the time receive measurable results on their gifts at work; **29%** receive this information sometimes; **55%** never or rarely get this information. A number of other questions in the study confirmed that measurable results influence donors' future support more than anything else.

93% of individual donors would definitely or probably give again the next time they were asked to a charity that thanked them promptly and in a personal way for their gift, and followed up later with a meaningful report on the program they had funded. Under these circumstances, **64%** would give a larger gift and **74%** would continue to give indefinitely.

The World Society for the Protection of Animals goes places and gets involved in things that other organizations don't do. Their solicitations are project specific and they report on their progress by project, too, which is very satisfying.

I only ever get information about gift allocation from smaller organizations; the big ones never do this.

93% of corporate donors said that they would definitely or probably continue supporting a charity that provided them with measurable results without being prompted to do so. **91%** of them would definitely or probably increase the size of their contribution.

When giving for the first time, **67%** of donors always or sometimes give a smaller gift or grant than they could. When asked what they are looking for that would cause them to give a larger gift the next time, **68%** said measurable results; **9%** said personal contact, and another **9%** said prompt gift acknowledgment.

The newsletter will sometimes make reference to the programs a charity is executing, but you never know if your money actually went there.

1. Gifts must be undesignated to allow for maximum flexibility in programs and services.

If this opinion is prevalent, the charity is likely working without a strategic plan. In that case, there is a much bigger problem in the organization than a disagreement over designated giving. The most important attribute of a strategic plan is its ability to bring purpose and productivity to an organization. A strategic plan focuses everyone's attention on a limited number of programs and services, each one with a measurable set of objectives to be reached this year and a few years ahead. For fundraisers, a strategic plan forms the basis of their communication to donors about why money is required, where it will be applied, and what it is expected to achieve. This makes for very compelling solicitations. More important, a strategic plan puts controls on the entire organization to do what it has promised to do and to produce measurable results. This is precisely the information that donors say they need in order to keep giving. Maximum results is the objective, not maximum flexibility.

If gifts cannot be designated, then fundraisers are relegated to talking to donors in general terms. They may reference specific programs and services, but only as examples of the work that the organization does as a whole. Without specifics to guide their decision-making, donors are hard pressed to find something on which they can focus their imagination and their philanthropy. The result is watered-down solicitations that elicit lackluster response, opening the door for higher attrition and lower gift values.

2. Some programs or services are unsaleable.

It is always easier to write or talk about the core service or the more popular programs. New or less understood initiatives are more difficult to position to donors in a compelling fashion. Just as professional marketers are a boon to donor acquisition (see Chapter 3), they are also most skilled at positioning new or difficult-to-sell programs and services. Sometimes organizations shy away from designated giving because they feel that some or most of the programs for which they need money will not be attractive to donors. If they weren't vital, though, they wouldn't be part of the programs and services mix. It may simply be a matter of not knowing how to describe them in ways that are appealing to the public. Programs staff and the CEO can be very helpful in explaining the rationale for chosen programs and approaches to fundraisers, and inviting the types of questions that donors would be likely to ask.

3. We will lose donors if they designate their gifts to a program that does not produce the desired results.

You will lose some donors, but at a rate no higher than donor attrition without designated giving. When asked whether they would give again to a charity whose last program had been unsuccessful, 62% of respondents said definitely or probably and 32% more said they might. It seems that charities can count on the majority of their donors remaining loyal contributors as long as they learn from their experience and put controls in place to minimize the possibility of repeat failure.

4. Designated giving grants too much power to donors.

Designated giving means that prospective donors are offered information about how their gifts will be used *before* they commit to give. Designated giving does not mean that donors are offered free rein to choose from among all possible program options at the time they make their gifts. It is always within the charity's unilateral control to select the programs or services that will be offered to donors as funding choices. If a charity needs more money for program B than for program A, then B is the one that should be showcased in solicitations.

In most charitable organizations, donations from private sector donors are not the sole source of income. Government grants, revenue from admissions, product sales, and memberships, for example, constitute income that can often be allocated anywhere the charity sees fit. These funds are best assigned to programs that are less attractive to donors, making the job of creating compelling solicitations much easier. Of course, the more you get to know your donors individually, the more you will discover how diverse their interests are and how willing they are to fund risky or less popular services—as long as they are kept informed of your progress.

Donors do not want to run the charitable organizations that they support; they are much too busy running their own lives, families, and businesses. But when they don't know whether their money has been put to good use, they lose confidence, and when that happens, donors do one of two things: they either stop giving or they start making more demands. If the latter, it may seem like donors are trying to dictate how an organization should be run. In reality, they are just trying to hold staff and volunteers accountable for the expenditure of their money.

Occasionally an organization may encounter a donor who offers a substantial gift on condition that the charity adopt a program or service other than the ones currently available for funding. This is another instance when having a

62% of corporate donors require a progress report on the effect of their previous contribution before considering another gift to a charity. They estimate that fewer than half of the charities they support provide this without being prompted.

59% of individual donors and **81%** of corporate donors say that an economic slowdown affects their giving.

The bigger and more established charities feel they don't have to report on their results. "Why should we have to explain ourselves?" is an unfortunate but common attitude.

I am proud to be a supporter of the 200 Club which provides scholarships to deserving students. Sometimes I hear from their parents who cry openly on the phone when we tell them we can award a scholarship to their child. Many are first generation Americans. It's very gratifying.

When corporate donors have to reduce their charitable giving, the charities that continue to receive their priority support are those for which their employees volunteer (**36%**); those with whom a long term giving relationship exists (**18%**); and those who provide the best exposure or recognition (**18%**).

When individual donors have to reduce or modify their charitable giving, the charities that continue to receive their priority support are those for which they volunteer (**31%**); those in which they are confident that results are being achieved (**19%**); and those which affect them personally (**14%**).

Dillon International is an international adoption agency that is very effective in communicating. I get periodic pictures and information from their orphanage in Vietnam and when its Director comes back to Tulsa, I meet with her and get a first hand report.

strategic plan is incredibly valuable. If the donor's interest is within the plan's objectives, then a terrific opportunity is on the table. If not, then the donor is appealing to the wrong organization and should be redirected to one of the other 865,000 charities that might be able to provide a better fit. Any organization that takes the time to make a considered referral will gain both the donor's and the other charity's respect. And, of course, what goes around comes around.

5. Designated giving grants too much power to fundraising personnel.

Fundraisers are always asking, "What's the money for?" If there is no clear strategy or if management cannot provide information that is specific enough to satisfy donors, fundraisers will push for this vital information or even write the operational strategy themselves. This is definitely not the preferred course of action but it is not unusual for fundraising to be the catalyst for strategic planning.

This can be unsettling to some executive directors who may feel that development staff are attempting to dictate programs and services priorities. Sometimes this seeming reversal of authority is exacerbated when fundraising personnel have direct access to and close relationships with members of the Board, the critical fundraising leadership group.

Without information in a planned context, development staff (and all staff, for that matter) can only take orders. While this kind of management style definitely reminds everyone who the boss is, it comes at a price. A fully informed staff who feel just as responsible as the CEO for the plan's success, delivers results, usually well beyond expectation. However, they also tend to challenge the status quo, offering creative ideas that the boss hasn't thought of. A confident leader knows that her success is directly related to the inventiveness and success of her staff, encouraging their creativity within the confines of the plan's goals. A less confident CEO leaves staff in the dark.

When fundraising staff aren't enjoined to the vision and to the plan, they lose the ability to be compelling—their copy writing becomes predictable and dull; their faces don't light up when they're talking with donors. They gradually lose the urge to "get out there," spending more time in arms-length fundraising activities. Their confidence wanes; the work becomes harder; they look elsewhere.

6. Gifts must be undesignated in case a new opportunity comes along that requires immediate funding.

An extension of point 1 above, this speaks to the unfortunate fact that too many charities are willing to quickly abandon a current priority or add to a defined roster of services. This, in turn, implies a lack of faith in existing programs and a less than required appreciation for the time and attention that should be afforded a new concept before it is adopted. New programs need to be vetted against the organization's mandate, researched, budgeted, tested, evaluated, assigned to staff, and blended into the entire programming strategy. That simply takes time.

By all means, the executive director and programs staff should think big—but that thinking should be followed by planning, controlled testing and, only then, by full execution. A new program requiring private sector support cannot be shaped, tested, adopted, and marketed adequately within a single year. An effective strategic plan will include a provision for accommodating new ideas and opportunities, one that allows exploration, research, etc. in the current year, but does not disturb the integrity of existing programs. Things go wrong when staff and volunteer time are suddenly diverted to the new concept, leaving current programs inadequately supported.

You may think that a discussion about strategic planning is somewhat off topic for a book on donor communication, but it is not. If your organization is one which tends to switch horses easily, then it is very difficult for fundraising personnel to create compelling literature and donor solicitation pieces. It also suggests that your charity thinks it doesn't matter what donors are told in order to get their money. It does. Donors do read and are influenced by the content of direct mail and other solicitation pieces. They become suspicious when they cannot find references to the programs or services they thought they were funding. They look for reports in correspondence, newsletters, on charities' websites. When they don't get them, they feel duped and become concerned about how their contributions are being used.

Charities that don't or can't articulate their long term strategy miss out on big gifts. Donors' decision-making processes when considering gifts of significant value can be lengthy. If you start your fiscal year with a particular course of action, then see it change mid-year, the efforts of your most senior (and usually most expensive) development staff are compromised.

Staying the course becomes doubly important when you are negotiating with a donor who came to you with a specific, off-strategy designation request. Skilled fundraisers can help prospective donors understand that funding an existing priority will produce better results than charting a new course in the middle of the race. So, don't send a mixed message by being inconsistent.

Charities rely on staff and volunteer fundraisers to be the essential information link to donors. It is impossible for them to do their job if the very programs that donors thought they were supporting are now gone or relegated to a lesser status. When fundraisers are constantly selling new programs rather than reporting on progress, they are forced back into a cycle of acquisition and re-acquisition. This means that all the time, money, and skill that went into capturing donors in the first place have been wasted.

7. Planning places onerous controls on staff.

Many Executive Directors and program staff resist planning because a strategic plan puts performance expectations in very tangible terms. Just as fundraisers should be expected to work to specific financial objectives, administrative and program personnel should also have tangible and measurable expectations for service and institutional growth. Instead of measuring gross and net dollars, though, their measurements are in terms of numbers of clients served, program growth, audience enjoyment, research progress, etc.

When programs and services are specifically defined and targets are time-limited and measurable, it becomes possible for the Board of Directors to do its job. Sometimes staff feel that if Board members are kept in the dark as much as possible, they will not interfere with day-to-day operations. The opposite is actually true. A Board with no roadmap and no realistic benchmarks for achievement has no option but to step in and have a look for themselves. But, armed with a pragmatic plan that measures growth and staff performance, the Board retreats to its position as policy-makers and governors, knowing it will be easy to determine whether or not the organization is on track.

8. We cannot offer designated giving to donors until we know how much money has been raised.

Fundraisers are sometimes told that designated giving cannot be offered to donors before the money is raised because, until then, the charity will not know how much there is to spend and where those funds would be most appropriately allocated. This is not a valid argument. Every organization has a budget, and the budget is set and approved by the Board before the start of any fiscal year. In order to establish a budget in the first place, the Board and CEO (and others) would have to know what they are planning to do with the money.

Of course, it is possible that the fundraising goal does not get achieved, but that makes contingency planning for different levels of funding both pragmatic and strategic. As you introduce a more donor-centered way of fundraising, however, your annual and multi-year forecasting will become increasingly accurate. This is because you will lose fewer donors, the donors you retain will be more satisfied and dependable, and you will be able to control acquisition costs better.

Once the budget has been established, it should not be changed. Some charities treat their budgets as works in progress, altering revenue and expenses as the year unfolds. This is inappropriate as it relieves managers of their responsibility to plan and forecast accurately, and to deliver the services that donors believed they would be funding when they made their contributions. It also has the regressive effect of denying staff and Board a vital sense of accomplishment. If employees and leadership volunteers don't know what the goal is, how do they recognize success?

Fluid budgeting is a disaster for fundraisers. Many charities think nothing of adjusting the current year's fundraising goal upwards when the year is already in progress, or choosing a goal for an untried fundraising event that, miraculously, matches the amount required to balance the budget. Actions like these leave professional and volunteer fundraisers feeling like Rumpelstiltskin: "Just go into the next room, dearie, and spin that pile of straw into gold, too." If they are successful, it's due to luck, not skill, and luck has a way of running out at the moment that expectations rise.

For donors, the effect of fluid budgeting is equally harmful. One of the most common frustrations expressed by donors in the study is that they often do not hear about success. They respond to compelling appeals but don't get to enjoy the good news after the money has been raised. If fundraisers are doing their work without the benefit of a strategic plan or to expectations that are always changing, they never know if they and their donors have succeeded. They are denied the opportunity of reporting successful results, which also means that, for all intents and purposes, they are denied the tools they need to engage in donor-centered fundraising.

IS FUNDRAISING PROACTIVE OR REACTIVE?

$20 x 8 = $77,000

From the title, you may be convinced that I flunked simple arithmetic, but I assure you that the above equation is absolutely correct!

In the 1980s, for eight consecutive years, a donor faithfully responded to our annual giving appeal with $20 each year. We always sent her a cordial personalized thank you letter and all other communications that our donors received regularly. Because she lived in a very modest part of town, we never

Great story!

A youth orchestra that I support sends me information on the musical programs that the children have performed and a schedule of where they have played in a handwritten note.

Does donor-centered fundraising work? The short answer is yes. We (University of Saskatchewan) started last year by changing our fundraising event format to put more emphasis on stewardship. The response was immediate. Donors kept thanking us for our efforts and for giving them what they really needed: quantifiable, qualitative information about the impact of their giving on the lives of our students and on our university as a whole.

aggressively tried to upgrade her giving. Our reasoning was that her zip code area didn't warrant more costly efforts.

Some time after that, we were stunned to receive a check in the amount of $77,000 as a bequest from the donor's estate. We subsequently learned that she was single, had worked all her life as a secretary at a local company, lived thriftily, and left an estate of over a million dollars. Our organization was one of about a dozen who benefitted from her amazing philanthropy.

We never really know what a donor is capable of giving. Stories like this one prove that every day. But typical fundraising methodology assumes that donors will only edge up their gift amounts over time. The statistics which support this theory, though, are actually a product of how fundraising programs work and not a reflection of donors' tightfistedness.

In addition, essential information is provided to donors only after they have reached a level of generosity that covers the cost of dispensing that information. For 90% of donors who stop giving before they learn that they have made a difference, this is simply too late.

In typical fundraising, gift value triggers communication, forcing programs and practitioners to wait for the donor to make a significant move. Typical fundraising can only react. Donor-centered fundraising sees the donor himself as the prize from the moment he is acquired. The value of his first gift is assumed to be tied to the fundraising program that generated his support, and not an indicator of his true potential. Essential information is offered to every donor and a direct line of communication is established as early as possible. Donor-centered fundraising is proactive.

In a donor-centered context, the weight of fundraised revenue shifts from low average gifts through direct marketing programs to gifts of significance raised through meaningful relationships. Consequently, donor-centered fundraising raises much more money.

If you offer gift designation early, you will find that you need it less and less as you draw your donors closer to your organization through meaningful communication. In the end you, your CEO, and your Board will get what you want—the majority of monies raised undesignated—but you'll have to earn your donors' trust first.

9

How to Communicate With Your Donors

THE RETIREMENT PARTY

When I was Executive Director of a local branch of the Big Brothers organization, we enjoyed tremendous fundraising success through events, particularly 'Bowl for Big Brothers,' which raised almost half the agency's budget each year. It was a typical pledge-per-point fundraiser where teams of bowlers from companies competed for industry trophies and prizes while raising a lot of money for our organization.

Over the years competition had become quite fierce, especially among the banks who vied for the coveted "Financial Industry Trophy." But every year the same bank won, thanks in large part to the spirit and dedication of one man—Jim Strong. Now, it didn't hurt a bit that Jim was a senior executive in corporate lending and started every meeting by pushing his pledge form across the desk and suggesting a generous commitment. We were never surprised that out of some 3,000 competitors, Jim won the "Most Money Raised by an Individual Bowler" trophy every year.

When Jim announced his retirement, we were honored with an invitation to his retirement party. It was a great event with lots of funny tributes. We were scheduled to speak last, right before Jim himself. My President of the Board and I shared the honors.

My President summarized Jim's long and successful history with Bowl for Big Brothers, ending with . . ." In almost a decade of support for our organization, Jim single-handedly raised over $60,000, which represents the cost of finding big brothers for twenty-seven boys on our waiting lists and supporting those big/little brother relationships. In short, Jim's superb efforts on our behalf have made life a lot better for twenty-seven children who really needed a big brother."

The jovial crowd fell silent during our President's speech. I could see tears in Jim's wife's eyes and Jim couldn't look at anyone directly. We had planned to present Jim with his "Most Money Raised by an Individual" trophy for the last time at his retirement party and it was my happy job to announce that he had won yet again.

The trophy was a beautiful west coast native design with Jim's name on ten brass plaques around the base. I held it up to the crowd as I said, "Jim, there is no more room on the trophy's base for the new winner next year. So, once again, we would like to present you with the trophy for 'Most Money Raised by an Individual Bowler' but ask you to keep it permanently as a memento of the years of support you have given our organization." (Ooh's and applause from the crowd.) "But, as we will be needing another trophy for our new winner next year, we have commissioned an identical award which we have brought with us tonight to show you." I pulled the new trophy out from behind the podium and held it up. "You can't see it from here, so I wanted to read the inscription, which is:

Bowl for Big Brothers
The James H. Strong Award
presented annually to the individual who raises the most money."

At the mention of Big Brothers' most prestigious award being named after Jim, his colleagues and friends burst into applause, his wife started to cry openly, and Jim looked down at the floor. Eventually, he got up to speak.

Jim thanked everyone who had spoken during the evening and then turned to acknowledge my President and me. "Having this award named after me is quite an honor, for which I thank you most sincerely. But nothing could be more important to me tonight than learning that the money I have been able to raise has matched twenty-seven children with big brothers. You see, my own father died when I was seven and I could have used a big brother myself. You cannot imagine how much it means to me to know that I have helped these children."

Successful fundraising is not the process of accruing an ever-increasing volume of donors; it is recognizing the ones with potential for contributing progressively generous gifts, then making it as easy as possible for them to do just that.

Retained donors are increasingly cost-effective over time because they tend to give more while requiring less investment based on cost-per-dollar raised. Maximizing return on investment from a manageable number of donors within a portfolio of fundraising programs is the key to success. How, then, do you bring a donor to that coveted state of loyalty and progressive generosity?

All the heartfelt appreciation in the world will not be enough to retain a donor indefinitely unless he can fulfill the quiet commitment he has made to himself to do good. He needs you to be on the alert, monitoring the program that he has supported and communicating with him when you have something important to say. Most definitely that includes providing measurable results and doing so before you ask him for another gift.

Measurable results are tangible and can be quantified. How the measurable results of a charity's work are expressed depends on the nature of its programs and services and the time frame for the program that donors are funding. Measurable progress in medical research, for example, takes longer to realize than does premiering a new play. However, there is always meaningful and measurable information that can be reported to donors in between solicitations, regardless of the duration or complexity of the program or project. Measurable results that are meaningful for donors include both a qualitative and a quantitative component. Donors seldom receive either. Most often, anecdotal information, reported quite subjectively, fills charities' newsletters and annual reports. This includes claims of being "the best" or "the biggest" or "the first," usually without the evidence that supports such statements, and often without considering whether these claims matter to donors. Fundraisers' passion for the cause is admirable; but donors should not be expected to make their repeat giving decisions void of demonstrable evidence that the program in question is superior to alternatives and is serving more people. Charities that provide reliable and tangible results will be richly rewarded.

That said, it is a challenge to gather qualitative and quantitative information. The former requires objective program analysis; the latter requires evidence of real growth. Measuring net growth in service, or reduced suffering, or improved quality of life is demanding. However, it can be done. The greatest ally of a charity in this work is its objectives-based strategic plan, without which it is impossible to prove to itself, let alone to donors, that the organization is moving progressively forward.

When donors give to a charity for the first time, they are responding to its established reputation and/or reacting to a persuasive solicitation. Donors' attention and support have been won for now, but the relationship is by no means secure, as evidenced by the high attrition rate after the first gift. If the charity has adopted the first two tenets of donor-centered fundraising—prompt, personalized gift acknowledgment and confirmation that gifts have been set to work as intended—then donors are reassured that they did the right thing when they gave their support. But what will really establish a life-long relationship between a charity and its donors are measurable results, something that can only be provided after donors give the money to make those achievements possible. Communicating results is the most important thing a fundraiser can do to ensure ongoing donor loyalty.

An ideal partner is a charity that values personal communication, consistently finds ways to recognize our grant throughout the year, makes contact with us when not asking for money, and asks our company what they can do for us. Especially during an economic downturn, we prize this kind of proactive partnership.

I'm not confident in fundraising that goes on with no business or strategic plan and where there's a lack of communication regarding the effective end use of funds.

When I first established my Trust, I wrote to a well known international agency asking them to tell me how they would use the money if I made a gift. I never got a response. About a year later I got a phone solicitation and I mentioned my prior correspondence. They said they would have someone get back to me but no one ever called. I gave them one or two small gifts but I could have given them a very generous grant if they had responded.

Court appointed special advocates (CASA) has 900 chapters around the country and our company supports many of them. They really have their act together in spite of the incredibly difficult job of getting committed volunteers who come with special skills. The organization is very hands-on; they were one of the first charities to use on-line training effectively. They are so good that our boss joined their national board. Their ongoing communication with us is superior and it has had a direct impact on the amount we give and the length of our relationship.

It takes very little effort to influence my decision to give more. Once, for instance, I was acknowledged at a YMCA meeting and the next time I they solicited me, I gave them a larger gift.

What persuades me to give a larger gift is learning about specific accomplishments with the original gift. I'm on a Foundation Board; in processing grant requests, this is precisely what we're looking for in reports after the first installment. One charity I support deals with teenage suicide. The Director, who is outstanding in communicating with teens, invited me to attend one of her classes to see their work first hand. This was very effective.

MEANINGFUL DONOR COMMUNICATION

Communication is one of those catch-all words; it can mean just about anything. In fundraising, the words *acknowledgment*, *communication* and *recognition* are sometimes used interchangeably, but they mean quite different things to donors.

Acknowledgment: *private* affirmation that the donor is appreciated. Activities that acknowledge a donor's support include writing thank you letters for gifts, making thank you calls, expressing appreciation one-on-one in other ways that do not involve public recognition. Acknowledgment is highly valued by donors. It is very rare for someone to not want to be privately acknowledged.

Communication: the provision of meaningful information about the charity, its work and its progress, the most important information being measurable results achieved through donors' contributions. Communication vehicles take many forms such as newsletters, forums, charities' websites, and annual reports. Communicating can also be done one-on-one through phone calls and visits, or by letter or email. I have never encountered a donor in over thirty years in the business who does not want to know what is being achieved by the charities he supports.

Recognition: the public acknowledgment of donors for their contributions. Donor recognition events, awards, media stories on donors, published lists of donors' names in newsletters or annual reports are examples of public recognition. The majority of individual donors do not want to be recognized. However, more time, money and effort goes into charities' efforts to recognize donors than into providing them with meaningful information. Corporate donors and sponsors usually do want to be publicly recognized. Chapter 10 deals with donor recognition in more detail.

Meaningful information is, in itself, a form of acknowledgment. As a matter of fact, it is the ultimate acknowledgment for donors. There is a great deal of research in the industry on why donors give. Sharing with those who have less, giving back to community, being personally asked to give, and to fulfill religious obligations are the top reasons cited in the most recent edition of *Giving and Volunteering in the United States.*[15] But not all reasons are

---

[15] *Giving and Volunteering in the United States*, 2001, Independent Sector, Washington, DC, 2002

outwardly focused. Donors also give to fulfill a private commitment they make to themselves to do good. Philanthropy is not only an act that benefits others; it is a measure of the character of donors themselves and an element of their personal journey through life. Donors depend entirely on the charities they support to provide them with relevant information. When they get it, their commitment to themselves has been fulfilled.

RETHINKING DONOR COMMUNICATION FROM A DONOR-CENTERED PERSPECTIVE

Newsletters

Length

It's not just what donors need to know but how it should be communicated to them that matters. The most riveting information will be irrelevant if it is buried inside a quarterly newsletter that lies unopened on the donor's coffee table, only to be thrown out along with the other magazines and periodicals two months later. Newsletters are charities' most common communication vehicle. 88% of study respondents publish a newsletter and 59% of them produce newsletters that are between eight and sixteen pages long. But, 66% of study donors said they don't have time to read charities' newsletters thoroughly and 58% said outright that charities' newsletters are simply too long.

If information on what charities do is the essential ingredient of good newsletters, then maybe it should also be the only ingredient. Most charities create newsletters to a fixed length rather than letting the information itself determine the length of the publication. 65% of individual donors and 87% of corporate donors suggested that instead of a multi-page newsletter, they would rather receive a one-page bulletin that concerned itself with the program or service to which their gift had been targeted. Bulletins have the built-in advantage of being more likely to be read because they appear to be more urgent or vital. Their "late-breaking news" appearance and timely content get noticed.

Some donors said they would like to get a one-page news bulletin most of the time, rounded out perhaps once a year with a more descriptive communication piece that puts the program they are funding within the bigger picture. This is an excellent suggestion, as once donors are confident that their gifts are achieving a specific benefit, they will be motivated to do more. This includes giving more generous and/or more frequent gifts to support their widening interests. Other practical suggestions included focusing on a single theme in

---

 # issues of newsletter published per year by study charities

more than 4 **13%**
4 **35%**
3 **23%**
2 **15%**
1 **2%**
no newsletter **12%**

newsletter size

more than 16 pages **15%**
9-16 pages **17%**
8 pages **27%**
6 pages **12%**
4 pages **22%**
2 pages **5%**
1 page **2%**

newsletter content

space devoted to programs/ services **52%**
space devoted to fundraising **24%**

The newsletters I enjoy the most have an interactive feel about them. They don't focus so much on "what's going on" articles; their content is more like that of magazines with a decidedly educational slant.

each issue of the newsletter to cut down on content and to help focus readers on an important issue, and flagging articles of particular interest.

When charities produce lengthy newsletters with high production values, donors are more influenced by the physical product than by its content. Donors have two reactions to such newsletters:

They become concerned about cost of the product.
Perceived cost leaves a negative impression that can overshadow good content. Having your newsletter sponsored does not alleviate this concern because it means that the sponsor's money has been devoted to communicating with donors instead of being directed to programs and services. If you pay for your newsletter yourself, it is still a problem. Your own promotions or communication budget is the evidence. What percentage of this chronically under-resourced cost center is devoted to just the newsletter? It is probably too much.

They feel they should not throw them away.
Even if donors are reluctant to throw away your high quality newsletter, it does not mean that they are reading it. Lengthy newsletters created with the production values of a small magazine are set aside for leisure reading. But things that are put aside tend to remain unopened, especially when they were not purchased specifically by the donor. The longer the newsletter sits there, the less likely it is to be read at all. Its fate is either to be thrown out unread or, at best, scanned as "old news" before it is tossed. In the end, the only person who won't throw out your newsletter is you, so strike a balance between production and content.

Learning that donors are looking for shorter newsletters will be a relief to most writers and editors who have to plead with and threaten colleagues for articles and reports. I know; I used to be responsible for the newsletter in several organizations. The day after putting one issue to bed, I'd be panicking over the next one. I still shudder when I think of it.

Look at this issue from the donor's point of view and be merciful! On average, individual donors represented in this study support over twenty-five charities a year; corporate donors give to hundreds. With newsletters averaging ten pages and the majority distributed four times a year, that means that individual donors are expected to read one thousand pages of information from charities they support; corporate donors must attempt to digest over eight thousand. For donors, newsletters are the not for profit equivalent of Tolstoy's *War and Peace.*

There is an exception in the issue of newsletter length and that is newsletters written for supporters as a benefit of membership. Many are fabulous, particularly those produced by health issue charities, which are loaded with research information, articles on managing disease, and much more. Though written specifically for those living with the disease and their caregivers, much of their content would be of interest to donors as well in a shortened format.

Format

In a one-page bulletin, you will have only two thirds of the space available for news because the following elements will be part of every issue:

Masthead: eye-catching, reflecting the charity's brand image, including your website address.

Photo with cutline: depicting your work in action (no "smile for the camera" shots of someone handing someone else a plaque or a check, unless this is a bulletin you are creating only for the donor who is the subject of the photo).

List of your Board of Directors, Campaign Cabinet or Fundraising Committee: donors are positively influenced when they see the names of leadership volunteers, even if they do not know anyone on the list personally.

Contact information: including specific staff person's name, title, address, phone number, fax number, and email address.

You might try sketching that out on a piece of paper just so you can see for yourself the amount of space you have to work with. See how this forces you to cut to the chase in the copy you write. With less space to work with and bottom line results as your theme, your news bulletins will be focused, visually appealing, and newsworthy.

Content

Study donors reserved their strongest criticism for content. 63% of donors rated charities' newsletters low for compelling or exciting content. Charities will have much less trouble in this area if they get news out when it is still exciting to read and have only a few paragraphs to work with instead of several pages.

Testimonials, success stories, and articles which "humanize" programs and services are meaningful and welcomed by both corporate and individual donors because they allow donors to picture the results of their philanthropy in a very tangible way.

Some donors expressed concern over newsletters which are thinly veiled promotion pieces for upcoming fundraising events or campaigns. You may wish to review your newsletter content and count the number of articles and overall space that is devoted to your planned golf tournament, a wrap up of your last

---

68% of donors would prefer to receive a short, one-page bulletin that concerned itself specifically with the program or service to which their donation had been targeted. **12%** would prefer the one-page bulletin most of the time, rounded out with an annual newsletter that was more comprehensive; **19%** are satisfied with the current length of charities' newsletters.

Donors want to hear from you and to know what is going on through statistics that verify results but they want to get this information in an easy to follow and well laid out format. Show donors that their contributions are making a difference, especially in emotional work—a success story accompanied by some statistics that relate to the story—that would work well for me.

Improve the quality of writing in newsletters. Most are just verbiage and cliches. I'm not moved by anecdotal exhortations. I need evidence.

Provide readers with examples of things that donors can do to plug into an organization—not just more ways in which they can give money but more things that they can do. It's easier to give money but it feels much better to give one's time as well.

% of study donors who agree with these statements

Newsletters provide useful information on charities we support **91%**

Newsletters provide useful information on specific program/service to which contribution was directed **71%**

Newsletters are too long **64%**

I don't have time to read newsletters thoroughly **69%**

Newsletter content is exciting/compelling **33%**

There is too much fundraising content in newsletters **31%**

I am concerned about the cost of newsletters **53%**

I don't need a fancy newsletter; a simple letter including a thank you and some information on their programs is sufficient.

Don't assume that donors are not interested in atypical topics. For instance, Yale produces a report on investment activities for endowment funds which communicate with donors and alumni as if they were partners. Many less sophisticated charities don't provide this important information. Either they keep it hidden or they don't feel donors are interested in reading it. Charities want your money but they don't want to share the information about what they're doing with it.

event, profiles on your volunteer fundraisers, and your enclosed "gift opportunity" advertisement or pledge card. Remember that the purpose of a newsletter is to provide the third essential element of a donor-centered fundraising program: information on donors' gifts at work.

Newsletters, like all communication pieces produced by not for profit organizations, need to look sharp and professional but not expensive. In-house publishing software makes this entirely achievable today. The savings you can accrue through shorter production time, lower printing costs, cheaper postage, etc. can be turned back into programs and services or devoted to other communication enhancements. My choice would be to put that saving into contract writers. Local, national, and especially international organizations' newsletters would be much better if local correspondents were hired to write the stories, much as newspapers do. For instance, if a non-government organization providing third world relief finds it difficult to obtain timely and compelling stories from their service people on the front lines, they might try using stringers who are filing stories for American dailies. They could be paid a stipend to write "from the front" articles on the organization's overseas work. Not only would the stories be well composed but the reporters' influence with their own papers might get these stories more broadly published. Creative alternatives become possible when some of the newsletter production budget is available for the most important aspect of the newsletter, which is content.

Frequency

Just as there is no set rule about newsletter size, there is also no rule about the number of issues of a newsletter that a charity should have. Producing a semi-annual or quarterly newsletter is more about keeping you on a disciplined production schedule than it is about communicating with your donors. After all, it's called a newsletter because it's supposed to contain news . . . right? The problem with newsletters produced on a pre-determined schedule is that the content is old by the time the donor reads it. Things happen in charities that are exciting, vital, that create a buzz. The moment something significant happens, it grabs attention; later on, it's just something that donors will get around to reading at some point—maybe.

Content should drive your production schedule as well as your format. So, when something happens, you need to be able to get the information out right away. Otherwise, if you have nothing to say, don't say it. As the sole means of communicating, newsletters are costly, time-consuming to produce, and they are received at the other end with mixed reviews. In donor-centered communication, your newsletter is only one tool (albeit an important one) in a larger and more varied mix of communication options. In this context, the pressure is off the newsletter to be the be-all-and-end-all communication piece for donors, an expectation that it seldom can live up to.

73% of charities publish their newsletters on a schedule of two, three, or four times a year. The problem with that is news doesn't happen on an organized quarterly or semi-annual schedule, making most charities' publications old news before they arrive in donors' mailboxes.

Most newsletters are neither filled with news nor are they the length of a letter. Charities need to remember why they communicate information to donors, and change their ideas and actions concerning newsletters. Publishing news when it really is news might mean communicating with donors three times in one month and then not again for several months. If you limit what you say to one page and take advantage of modern-day technology to help you get this vital information to your donors quickly, your communication will be much more effective. Your donors will actually read it because it really is news and they'll retain the information because you're not asking them to absorb a short novel. Keep in mind what you are trying to achieve. You want your vital information transferred from the page to the donor's brain. The only one who will want to keep your multi-page newsletter forever is you.

Fundraising through the Newsletter

When I open newsletters that come in the mail from charities I support, the return envelope falls to the floor or the coffee table reminding me that no matter how many pages of information I am holding in my hands, the purpose of this mailing is really to ask me for money. If I'm not inclined to give at that time, I feel kind of guilty about reading the newsletter because I know I am resisting what the organization really wants me to do. The newsletter kind of loses its appeal for me at that point.

I am hard pressed to think of a charity that doesn't include a solicitation piece in every issue of their newsletter. As a matter of fact, most categorize newsletter revenue as a fundraising program. However, providing information and asking for money at the same time is contrary to the principles of donor-centered fundraising. If newsletter donors are so responsive that they will give through this type of indirect appeal, perhaps you should be talking to them in person and turning them into major gift donors. If charities move to simpler,

---

How study donors feel charities' newsletters could be improved

provide more targeted information on how donations are being used **54%**

include more human interest stories **12%**

reduce newsletter size **9%**

Of the charities who choose to publish lists of donors' names in their newsletters, **33%** do so in every issue and **33%** limit publishing donors' names to one issue per year.

81% of individual donors and **71%** of corporate donors say having their names published in a charity's annual report, newsletter, or program has no influence on whether or not they will give again.

Make sure the content isn't dated. I often get charities' newsletters after the event is over, for instance.

47% of individual donors and **59%** of corporate donors would like to receive information on their gifts at work via email.

Charities' reasons for communicating with donors via email
informing donors about meetings and non-fundraising events **75%**
informing donors about fundraising events **57%**
informing donors about gifts at work **49%**
thanking donors for gifts **41%**
soliciting **18%**

47% of charities do not communicate with their donors via email. Their main reasons are: not having donors' email addresses, feeling that email is too impersonal, lack of staff/budget.

Newsletters are designed for stakeholders but they're not money well spent. I'd rather charities we support didn't issue a newsletter as we actually need the information when a funding request is under consideration, not after the fact.

If it's a charity that I've been wanting to become involved with, I can go to their website or read their materials to make myself more informed. However, when I give and I'm promised a newsletter and then it takes six months to get it, I'm concerned because it shows they're not organized.

bulletin-type communiques, newsletters will no longer have the space and structure for stitched or enclosed gift cards and return envelopes; but then, the lower production values will not necessitate a fundraising drive to underwrite the cost.

ADDRESSING INDIVIDUAL AND CORPORATE DONORS' DIFFERENT NEEDS

Corporations and individuals read charities' newsletters with different objectives in mind. Most corporate donors scan newsletters for references to their own company's name. They photocopy articles that feature their company's philanthropy and distribute them internally. Corporate donors are far less receptive to lengthy communication; they need specific information and they need to be able to find it quickly.

Individual donors look first for evidence of gifts at work and they are less focused on seeing their own name acknowledged in newsletters. However, if you choose to list donors' names, it then becomes very important that no one be left out and that everyone's name be spelled correctly. (See Chapter 10 for more information about publishing donors' names and giving levels.)

When producing newsletters for your corporate donors, write with a view to making it as easy as possible for them to find pertinent information, lift it from your newsletter or bulletin, and re-distribute it. Your writing style should be concise, and content should be results-based with specific references to corporate supporters' involvement and contributions. Photos and cutlines are very effective because they tell the story without you having to "write the thousand words." (Of course, this means you should always have a camera on-hand wherever you go on behalf of your organization.)

Email

One day I received an overseas call from a young man who had found our California-based agency on the internet. He was very interested in what we do and asked us to send him a package of information. We fell to talking and I learned that he used to be in a situation similar to the clients we serve. He was only nineteen years old, but he sincerely wanted to help.

For two years now he has been sending us a regular contribution of $10 which arrives promptly and predictably at the start of each month. Last year he was able to spend the summer in California and volunteered for our agency.

Though his giving is modest by major gift standards, I am confident that this young man will continue to support our Center long term. We treat him with the utmost respect and send him update notes on our programs. You just never know.

Email offers wonderful opportunities for the dissemination of information to donors. 59% of corporate donors surveyed said they would prefer to receive targeted communication via email, especially when their companies are specifically referenced in the copy. Emailed newsletters can be redistributed quickly and efficiently to employees, a boon to harried Corporate Contributions Officers who are as concerned as fundraisers about communicating results. Though in the minority, some companies in the study were not supportive of receiving information via email and were very vocal about it, saying they are inundated with unwanted email already. I suggest you ask your corporate donors individually whether or not they would like to receive email news from you before you risk sending it to someone who would find it irritating or invasive.

Over 90% of individual donors in the study use email as a form of communication and 47% said they would appreciate receiving charities' newsletters and other information electronically.[16] For the 51% who said they do not want charities to send them information via email, the issue is not the medium but the feeling of being bombarded by junk email and other unwanted solicitations. In all cases, then, it will be important to ask donors' permission before putting them on your email list.

Charities that convert a substantial portion of their newsletter to electronic format will realize yet another cost saving. As well, they will be able to transmit late-breaking news to donors and give them an easy way to respond quickly with their comments if they so desire. Like regular newsletters, however, it is important not to depend on electronic communication as your only information link to donors. It should be part of your overall communications strategy.

Websites

Some corporate and individual donors do not want you to send information directly to their email address, but may be willing to receive a short notice about information that has been posted on your website. It could read something like this:

> *We have just posted a report on the XX program on our website. Please go to (link) if you would like to see the progress we have been able to make so far, thanks to your generous support.*

I can't imagine a donor who could resist clicking that link. This is, after all, what donors said they want. Once they go there, make sure your information is

Put your newsletter online so I can download it when it's convenient. Include headlines that I can click on so I can scan it easily. Once a year, it should say that our company supports your program. Tell us who's running the organization. The Board of Directors list should be easily accessible, for instance.

I used email to communicate with many donors during our campaign. It was an easy way to verify phrasing on recognition plaques. I also used email to keep donors informed of the campaign's progress and also just to casually say, "hi" and let them know we appreciated their commitment.

I get everything I need and want but from some charities I get too much. That is where my dissatisfaction lies. I sometimes have to search through a lot of mailings, emails, etc. to get down to the information I really want.

Keep your communications brief and concise. Get to the point quickly; we don't want to read a novel. Brief emails are terrific. Copy us occasionally on releases and other information that demonstrate that you are doing your work well. Give us top line information in headline form, written in a way that makes it sound compelling, makes it worthwhile reading.

---

[16] This is a significant increase since the first research study we did on this subject two years ago.

At times we have supported a crisis unit which goes into homes where children are threatening suicide or violence. When I read about their achievements in their newsletter, I feel good knowing that I was a part of that.

Some charities put us on their mailing list even when I ask them not to. I get hundreds of annual reports from universities every year that I just trash.

STAR (Society to Advance the Retarded) is very good at communicating with our company. Their newsletters are very upbeat and the charity is highly visible in the community. They did an interesting fundraising promotion last year where they commissioned a group of artists to create six-foot tall sculptured stars which were displayed at critical points in the community. They generated a lot of positive publicity.

results-oriented and concise and does NOT include a solicitation or a link to the donations page in the body of your copy. No doubt you have permanent click-throughs in your header or sidebar, so donors who are impressed and want to give you another gift immediately will be able to do so easily by clicking on your existing donate button.

You will need to be very careful about the message line in this kind of email. Spam pleading for financial assistance or offering highly suspect business deals (always with appalling grammar—a dead giveaway) litter everyone's inbox daily. Make sure your message header does not make it appear that your email is one of these. You might want to inform donors that your message heading will always start with or include a particular phrase so that they know it is from you.

If you build a good relationship with your organization's web master or information technology director, you will realize some additional benefits of driving donors to your site:

- You will be able to track the hits and know for sure how many of your supporters are responding to your email and reading your information.
- You will know which other pages donors peruse once they are on your site.
- Donors will be able to communicate back to you immediately. (Be sure to include a link back in your communication copy, preferably to a specific name and title, not just to "contact us.")

For donors who prefer to receive printed information by mail, make sure you always include your website address on your newsletter with an accompanying explanation of how you alert your email supporters to late-breaking news. Gradually, more and more people will migrate to electronic communication as it becomes more commonplace and as long as you don't overdo it.

Of course, hundreds or thousands of donors and potential donors will go to your website without being guided there by you, so consider the following:

Include an edited, up-beat mission statement on your home page. You would be surprised at the number of charities who do not provide a statement explaining what they are in business to achieve, or who bury it somewhere deep in their site.

Offer something before asking. Most charities feature fundraising so prominently on their websites that they leave the impression that they're asking for contributions before giving readers a reason for wanting to give.

Include concise financial information for donors and prospects who wish to anonymously review your credentials before contributing.

Provide your most recent annual report in portable document format (PDF).

Make it easy for donors and prospects to find out who runs the development office and provide links and phone numbers to specific contacts.

Include the names and business affiliations of the members of your Board of Directors.

```
This acknowledges receipt of $25.00 to American Society
for Whatever. Do not reply to this notice. This is an
automatic response to your online transaction and not
an official receipt. Thank you.
```

If I gave online and got this kind of reply, I would never give again. If you use an external supplier for fulfillment of online contributions that does not specialize in fundraising, or if the internal staff who handle website matters are not in the development office, it is important that you retain responsibility for the content of anything that donors will read on your website or receive in response to making a gift or inquiry.

On-Site Visits

Inviting donors to your site to see your programs and services first hand is a gesture that is viewed very favorably by donors. 93% of corporate donors and 74% of individual donors said that they have been asked to visit one or more charities that they support. Though corporate donors are particularly strapped for time, 30% of those interviewed who offered comments about site visits and open houses said that they insist on them as a prerequisite for giving or for continuing partnerships over time. Fully 94% of corporate respondents offering comments said that site visits are worthwhile and important. Many mentioned that they appreciate the invitation whether or not they are able to attend. Only 6% of corporate respondents said they would never make an on-site visit and reasons always related to lack of time. 84% of individual donors said that visiting an organization that they fund to see its work first hand is very appealing.

Be careful of trying to achieve too much at once by asking many donors to visit you at the same time. This is more of an open house and will be interpreted by donors as an event. This puts a whole different spin on things and donors may perceive an ulterior motive.

72% of study donors have been invited on site to one or more charities they support to see their work first hand. **77%** said that this is appealing and that the invitation is appreciated even when they are unable to go.

Our company seeks to develop "integrated relationships" with the charities we support. We want to be involved; we want to work with them to promote their objectives and help them reach their goals.

With regard to on-site visits, I often can't take them up on the offer but the invitation itself is meaningful.

47% of individual donors and **87%** of corporate donors in the study have been asked to speak at conferences or events hosted by charities they support.

Do communicate with your donors. Build stronger, more deeply integrated relationships with them. Use the resources available to you by your funders. For instance, if you need staff to clean up your camp for children, come and ask us. If you need promotional expertise but don't know how to work with the media, ask us, we can help you.

Don't make a nuisance of yourself. Charities need to be more understanding of the amount of pressure that companies and their donations officers are under. We worry about hundreds of requests at a time while the applicant thinks only about their own submission. Be more efficient in making proposals. Make them easier to read; don't overwhelm us with paper. It doesn't make the impression you think it does.

COMMUNICATING WITH CORPORATE DONORS AND SPONSORS

Ultimately, the needs of individual and corporate donors are the same. All donors want to know what the charities they support are achieving with their money. But corporate and individual donors process information differently and work under different constraints, and this should be taken into account when planning your communication program.

If you think fundraisers are overworked and that development departments are understaffed, try working in the corporate contributions office of a large company. Like a fundraiser, a donations officer is pulled in several directions. Company executives count on the donations officer to justify to shareholders and to the Board of Directors that their commitment of philanthropic funds is a worthwhile investment. Employees and their representatives want to know that wise decisions are being made with their payroll deductions. Everyone wants to know whether sponsoring an event had a measurable impact on the charity's programs and services and furthered brand awareness. Donations officers work under an avalanche of solicitations and within budget restrictions that are as bad as, if not worse than, those within development departments.

Whatever charities can do to save their corporate supporters work and time will be appreciated and it will be fruitful. Donations officers expressed dismay at how hard it is to get the information they need to justify both their contributions to specific organizations and continuation of their companies' philanthropic programs in general. 72% of corporate respondents said that charities do not communicate with them about their gifts at work before asking for another gift. Only 18% of corporations in the study said that they usually receive meaningful information in the form of measurable results even though 40% of study respondents indicated that reporting is a requirement. Some respondents noted that many charities fail to capitalize on the availability of renewed gifts or subsequent installments because they do not report on achievements made with the original contributions.

TIMING DONOR COMMUNICATION IN LIGHT OF THE SOLICITATION SCHEDULE

Though the first two requirements of donor-centered fundraising can be satisfied immediately following receipt of the gift, that is not so for the provision of measurable results. Obviously, a period of time must elapse during which donors' gifts are producing the meaningful and measurable results that will be communicated later. But other issues come into play in the timing of communication, and they concern both the sensibilities of donors themselves and the schedule of charities' fundraising solicitations.

Organizations often provide information on donors' most recent gifts at work within the body of the next direct mail letter or in a rushed information blitz just before making the next call. This does not work for donors. Donors need time to consider what you have to say and to weigh your measurable results against others' claims (or to notice that yours was the only organization that bothered to communicate results at all). When you use the renewal letter or telemarketing script to account for how you spent their last contributions, donors see this move for what it is: a poorly executed attempt to make up for a failure to communicate while you drive home the real intention of the call. This is equally frustrating for telemarketers. On their clients' behalf, professional call centers present passionate arguments to donors about giving to achieve something important. At the time donors are acquired, callers provide assurance that they did the right thing and that their contributions will be put to good use. Six months later, these same callers are on the phone again, trying to overcome donors' reluctance to give for the second time because they have heard nothing from the charity concerning their gifts at work in the interim. Instead of these calls being progressive as they should be with renewing donors, callers are struggling once again to get to first base. This forces call centers into a perpetual acquisition mode, limiting both the number of successful asks and the growth in gift size.

To better understand how donors feel about and react to communication, or lack thereof, think of the process of providing information as if it were the kind of retail transaction you make every day. You go to the hardware store to buy a drill; as you pass your money across the counter you are striking a deal—your money for the store's product. The receipt you get is merely the confirmation of your purchase; the agreement is only fulfilled once you get the drill home and find out that it works. So, too, with your transactions with donors. Look at the thank you letter as if it were the donor's receipt. It is their important record of the gift having been made but it is not the agreement fulfilled. The difference in a giving transaction, however, is that donors rely entirely on you to plug the drill in and show them that it works and that you made something with it. You must tell them that they made a good investment. Then, with that knowledge, they are much more likely to "buy" from you again when you have a new line of drill bits to sell them.

68% of charities with EFT (electronic funds transfer) programs communicate with these donors in the same way and with the same frequency as they do with all other donors. **18%** communicate less frequently or not at all.

Charities feel that the most common reason for attrition among EFT donors is that they receive less information about their gifts at work because their monthly giving is automatic.

Take the time to become aware of your potential funder's priorities. Seek out an opportunity to discuss your proposal in advance to make sure you are both on the same page; and provide follow up after getting the gift. It's important for community organizations to use their funds wisely and keep their overheads under control.

In general, charities make considerably more effort to communicate with planned gift donors than other donors. For instance **54%** make personal calls and **61%** make personal visits to keep planned gifts donors informed about their work versus **26%** making calls and **19%** making personal visits to other donors on a regular basis.

Most common communication tools for planned gifts prospects:

educational literature on making a planned gift **92%**
stories on planned gifts donors in newsletters, brochures **80%**
educational sessions on wills, financial planning **55%**
promotion of planned giving through allied professionals **55%**
direct contact and visits with prospects **11%**

33% of study charities create a discrete newsletter for planned gifts donors.

67% of planned gifts newsletters are issued two or three times a year; **24%** are issued four times a year.

A separation of time between providing information and asking for another gift dispels any hesitancy on the part of a donor who would otherwise be bracing himself for a premature ask. If your solicitation follows prompt and personal gift acknowledgment and meaningful reporting on the effect of his last contribution, you significantly improve the chances of getting a next gift, one which is even more generous than the last.

WHICH DONORS DESERVE DONOR-CENTERED COMMUNICATION?

When I first came to work in the development office of a public institution of higher education, I insisted that we recognize couples who give by linking their names together in formal recognition, no matter what their sexual orientation. This was a challenge to achieve since we are located in a very traditional part of the country and views were old fashioned. I stuck to my guns, though, and a same sex couple's names appeared together in our donor recognition.

I began cultivating this couple, inviting them to dinner, sending notes to them under one cover, as I would with any couple. It wasn't long before they let me know that, although they genuinely appreciated the contact, they had commitments to other charities and we would not be receiving major consideration when they made their allocations at year end.

Our stewardship continued unabated. It wasn't long before we began to see this couple's contributions increase in size and frequency. We began to offer them a more public connection—inviting them back to campus to speak, and bestowing honors on them as we would for any other significant donor. I think they were pleased to be treated so respectfully by an institution they loved but that hardly knew they existed in the past. I encouraged the President of our institution to visit them which he did on several occasions, often with his wife.

When our capital campaign began, we knew this couple could be major donors. They owned a large company which had recently been sold for a healthy profit. In the midst of the campaign, the couple came to the campus and announced that they would like to make a gift of $100,000! This was the largest gift to our institution by living alumni. We were thrilled, and to this day we continue to steward these donors, making them full partners in our growth and progress.

There is a strong tendency to equate the value of information with gift size—the larger the gift, the more personalized and more frequent the communication. This is why many charities have a policy of not receipting gifts below a certain amount, or not providing newsletters to donors whose gifts are below a certain value. **On a gift-by-gift basis, budgeting communication and recognition relative to gift size seems to make sense, but it is actually the *opposite* of what we need to do if we want to retain more donors and increase the average value of contributions.** We make the mistake of designing and budgeting communication as a post-gift activity instead of what it really is—the investment cost of securing the next gift.

Which donors need the most diligent investment from you? The answer is the ones whose loyalty is not yet secure, the ones whose current affiliation with your charity may still be tenuous. And who are they? They are your first time donors, those new contributors who demonstrate the highest rate of attrition between the first gift and the next ask. They are also the donors who contribute gifts of lower average value, as average gift value tends to increase with giving frequency. On a cost/benefit basis, these are the donors with whom we make the most meager investment even though they need the most attention. Many fundraisers take the position that since such a large percentage of first time donors is not going to renew, investment should be minimized for this uncommitted group. In fact, fewer first time donors renew precisely because they do not receive the information needed to warrant a second gift. From the moment their first gift is committed until the moment they are asked for the next one, the power is in the hands of fundraisers to keep those donors or to lose them.

I have had many calls from charitable organizations over the past two years who were preparing to implement a personal thank you calling program. In every case, they had segmented their donors into categories by gift size and were planning to call those who had given above a certain benchmark amount. Though making personal calls to high end donors is a good thing, the more productive thing is to expend your precious staff and volunteer time at the other end. Improving your retention rate will have a positive impact on numbers of continuing, active donors and gift size and the speed at which donors move into your major and planned gifts programs.

Improved communication will act as reinforcement to new donors, assuring them that they did the right thing by making this first step and boosting their comfort level about giving again. For renewing donors whose gifts have hit a plateau, enhanced communication provides the reason for giving at a new, more ambitious level. For loyal high end donors, personal communication is an expected part of your growing partnership and an opportunity for charities to help donors fulfill their, and your, long term goals and dreams.

Donors shouldn't have to ask to get the annual report. They are the equivalent of a company's investors and investors expect to see an annual accounting of the state of the business.

When considering whether we will support a charity again and increase our gift, we try to determine how responsible the charity is in managing administrative costs and we look at where they focus their time and energy. We assess how prepared they are for meetings with us—does the office look "together" or do they look like they're falling apart. We get a lot of information from the things that charities do and how they behave, rather than from what they say or put in a proposal.

The things that influence me to give more vary with the charity. In the case of my college, it's the closeness of the relationship. I go to college events with like-minded people and that enhances the bond I feel for my institution. When I give to other organizations like the United Way, however, I don't have any personal relationship so only the pleasure of giving to a good cause influences me to give.

61% of donors would definitely or probably support a charity again whose program had been unsuccessful, as long as they knew what had gone wrong.

It would boost my confidence to know that a charity I supported was actually measuring their effectiveness, even if they found that a particular program was unsuccessful.

Charities are reluctant to report failure because they're afraid we'll think they screwed up. Yet, as a foundation, we would appreciate getting information from a self-evaluation and we would use the example to help other charities that we fund.

Honest communication is what I want. Tell us when your project isn't working, tell us when you haven't raised the required amount or if there has been a controversial internal change. Don't embarrass us with awkward surprises.

So what is the answer to the question, "Which donors deserve donor-centered communication?" All of them do, of course.

WHO SHOULD COMMUNICATE WITH DONORS?

A donor seems to have to *earn* the right to be noticed by the CEO or a member of the Board of Directors. Gift size and frequency are things that trigger their attention. This, too, is contrary to what should happen if charities want to solidify relationships with new donors and help them increase their giving over time. Our test of personal thanks (Chapter 6) is an example of the influence that a charity's top people can have on new donors. Whether a donor has given $25 for the first time or $100,000 after ten years of loyal support, the gesture of support is heartfelt and important, and should be acknowledged by the people in the recipient organization who represent its highest level of authority.

COMMUNICATING POOR RESULTS TO DONORS

Our study asked donors: "If you received a report from a charity you supported which revealed that the program funded had not been successful and why, and that as a result of this experience the charity now had another program they wanted you to consider, would you give to this organization again?" 61% of donors replied "definitely" or "probably." Only 16% said "no" or "probably not." Happily, donors are very generous as long as you give them accurate information and a reason to believe that you have the situation under control. Even if a program has not been successful, donors are likely to continue to support you if they feel that there is less chance of failure the next time. The new program for which you are now seeking funds should certainly be designed to learn from past mistakes, though, as donors are less likely to be as forgiving with repeated under-performance.

COST

More personalized and consistent communication with donors will probably mean more time, and this is likely to place demands on your development office. Additional personnel or re-allocation of current staff priorities may be required to ensure that donor communication is repositioned as equally important to making the ask. You will, however, be able to realize cost savings by streamlining other parts of your fundraising operation and by spending less on commodities. You will also increase revenue substantially through a combination of personalized thanks and meaningful communication. The money will be there over time to implement donor-centered fundraising and communication and to fund more and better programs and services.

EVERYTHING COMMUNICATES SOMETHING

Everything you do that is read, heard, seen, or attended by even one of your donors is a part of your donor communication inventory, whether you intend it to be or not. With that in mind, you may want to rethink your annual general meeting, golf tournament, public service announcement, the script of your CEO's next speech—whatever reaches beyond the boundaries of your administrative offices.

Providing too little or too much information to donors will be on your mind, but your own intuition and experience will be the most valuable guide when deciding what, when, and how to communicate. For instance, if you find yourself staring at your blank computer screen wondering what to write, your donors probably don't need to suffer along with you.

Convey news when it is news and it will be noticed. Pass along what you think is important and your donors will think the same. Trust your judgment and be ready to act quickly.

I strongly believe that charities who evaluate the effectiveness of their programs, whether they have been successful or not, should be rewarded. I would double my gift to a charity that could tell me, in measurable terms, why their program had failed.

Make it clear to your donors that you invite questions about your work and that you will address any concerns that arise. Donors should be able to call the charity and feel welcome when they do so.

Stay true to your mission; deliver your product with integrity, and in those instances where you have problems, do your best to address them.

10
Donor-Centered Recognition

THE DONOR WALL

I was privileged to have been a member of the Board of Directors at a regional theater company when they were raising money for a beautiful new steel and glass building in the downtown core. The most special part of my association with this wonderful company was getting to know their Artistic Director who had founded the group some twenty years before.

During a full week of celebrations that surrounded the opening of the new building, the theater unveiled its Donor Wall in tribute to the many supporters who had contributed gifts to the Campaign. The wall's designer had captured the spirit of the theater and its audiences beautifully. Donors' names seemed to rise out of a row of applauding hands. I commented to Peter, the Artistic Director, that the hands were so lifelike you could almost hear them clapping. Delighted, Peter pointed to a pair of particularly enthusiastic hands and said, "See those—they were made from a mould of my own hands."

Just a year later, the theater and all of its supporters were shocked when, at the age of 51, Peter died suddenly from a heart attack. The Donor Wall's unique design, already so beautiful and appropriate, took on a new meaning for me. Now, whenever I attend a production in that theater, I spend a minute looking at the Donor Wall and its applauding hands . . . and I think of Peter.

To Recognize or Not to Recognize . . .

A donor gives to achieve results through a cause that is personally important. To give again to that cause, the donor needs to be confident that the original gift satisfied the obligation he made to himself and to society. You are an essential part of the donor's quest for satisfaction through philanthropy because satisfaction comes from information and information comes from you.

If donors are given the information they need, then, is there still a place for recognition? Yes, there is.

How charities recognize their donors:

include donors' names in annual reports, programs, brochures **74%**

offer donors gifts in recognition of their contributions **58%**

recognize donors in giving levels, honor rolls **55%**

hold donor recognition events **54%**

have a donor wall **45%**

publish stories on donors in newsletters **42%**

create special awards **38%**

submit donors' names for prestigious community awards **34%**

issue certificates or plaques **18%**

Most effective recognition activities, according to charities

thank you letters **78%**

publishing donors' names in newsletters **32%**

publishing donors' names in annual reports **31%**

donor recognition events **30%**

donor clubs/honor rolls **25%**

We support a local botanical organization. We were unable to attend their annual event for members this year, so the organization asked us over to their office for a special tour, took us out to lunch, and later sent us a plant that we had admired during the tour. It was a lovely experience.

Every year, a charity sends me a pin with their logo. I don't want it and I definitely don't need it. I want the money going into the charity's work. I have ten pins now from one charity—good grief!

Though donors stress that public recognition is not necessary and, in fact, for some donors it is completely undesirable, recognition can be effective if it is a carefully designed adjunct to, and not a substitute for, your donor communication program.

53% of individual donors said they do not want to be recognized and another 18% were ambivalent, meaning that being recognized is not something that they think about when they give, but they would not be opposed to being recognized. 29% do appreciate being recognized for the giving they do. The picture is quite different for corporate donors, however. 69% want to be recognized, largely to encourage staff in their philanthropic and volunteer efforts, and also to demonstrate to customers that they are investing in the communities that make them profitable.

90% of donors said that they would want to be asked first if a charity were planning to recognize them.

Only thirty donors in the study could recall a specific situation wherein a charity they supported did something unusual or out of the ordinary to recognize their philanthropy. Nine mentioned a special dinner or event and four talked about receiving a special award. But over half considered memorable recognition to be things like these:

- Being remembered when in the hospital.
- Being asked to speak about philanthropy at a non-recognition event.
- Developing a good relationship with the CEO or development director.

On the other hand, charities' activities in donor recognition are very tangible and costly. 30% of study charities' fundraising budgets is devoted to recognizing donors, far surpassing the 19% of budget spent communicating with them. It seems that there is room to bring charities' activities more in line with donor sensibilities and that there are funds already in charities' budgets that can be re-allocated in ways that work better for donors.

You mean I'm actually supposed to wear this . . . ?

When you establish a partnership with a donor and provide her with the information she needs to stay loyal, many of today's common recognition devices or commodities are no longer necessary for thanking donors. But, these same things may be useful for other purposes. Consider this example: You are the fundraiser for a social service agency. A donor who believes in your cause gives you a gift, is promptly and warmly acknowledged by you for that gesture, and is then kept informed of the good work her gift is achieving. Why, then, would she need a pin? You already know she will give again and you risk having her attention diverted to wondering about the cost of the pin, how many might have been produced, and whether you really needed her contribution. Now, consider the same pin in the context of another example. Let's say you are a new member of a service club and at your first meeting you are presented with a Club pin by the President of the Chapter. Is the pin appropriate in this context? Yes. You have joined a team of volunteers dedicated to raising money for charitable causes. One of the roles you take on as a member is encouraging other people to join, too. Wearing a pin identifies you as part of that group and helps you in both your fundraising and recruitment efforts.

When I'm writing a book or an article, my housework improves. I'd like to think it's because I'm a talented multi-tasker, but it's really because I'm trying to avoid the inevitable. I only mention this because in one of my desperate cleaning forays I found nineteen pins in various sock and incidental drawers. I dare say that if I ever get around to moving the furniture, I'll find a few more. I cannot identify the origin of most of them now, but I guess I've kept them because they were given to me and because they cost somebody time and money. I'm pleased to report that I have now freed myself from this obsequious feeling by throwing them out. The onus is back on the charities that issued them in the first place to provide me with a more satisfying memento of my giving—information on my gifts at work.

While I was counting pins, I also took a tally of sweatshirts and T-shirts—twenty-one. Included in the bundle is a sweatshirt with the name of a disease emblazoned across the front; not "I'm working toward a cure for ABC disease" or "I support the ABC disease Foundation"—just the name of the disease. Needless to say, I have never been seen wearing that one in public, nor the others. Why do I have so many? I get lots of T-shirts and sweatshirts as gifts for speaking at conferences or attending events. Come to think of it, I used to hate it when, as a teenager, my mother picked out my clothes.

Apparel and other products for participants related to fundraising events can be a good marketing tool for sponsors and a smart move for charities. T-shirts for the annual 5-K race, for instance, promote the cause to onlookers, engender a spirit of camaraderie among the participants, and carry sponsors' logos. They play an important role in the event's ability to make money.

The study asked individual and corporate donors for their opinions on

When asked to comment on gifts given to donors for the contributions they make, **28%** of individual donors said they are inappropriate under any circumstances; **21%** felt they were appropriate in cases of exceptional giving; **17%** said that gifts are acceptable if they are obviously inexpensive.

Corporate donors were decidedly more adamant about gifts for donors. **79%** felt they were always inappropriate; **14%** felt they influence future giving in a positive way.

86% of individual donors expressed negative views about token gifts such as address labels or fridge magnets. These included comments that token gifts were worthless, not an incentive to give, a waste of money, and that they sent the wrong message to donors. **100%** of corporate donors agreed.

A charity that we support once sent me a monogrammed briefcase. I called them immediately to chastise them for spending their money this way. They told me that the briefcases had been donated and that only twelve were sent to special donors. I felt a bit better after they explained things.

Keep it simple; keep it cheap. We get too many expensive (and irrational) gifts. For instance, once I got a real brick with our name etched into it. What am I supposed to do with that?!

76% of individual donors receive plaques or certificates that acknowledge their philanthropy. Only **5%** display them; **73%** either throw them out immediately or store them in a cupboard and throw them out later; **12%** keep a few and throw the rest away.

Corporate donors appreciate receiving plaques and certificates. **72%** display them; **71%** are displayed in high traffic areas, especially where employees will see them; **29%** are displayed in the Executive offices.

71% of individual donors and **94%** of corporate donors have received photographs or personal letters from people who have benefitted from the charity's work. **76%** of individual donors and **94%** of corporate donors say that this is very appealing and meaningful and plays a role in maintaining their support.

We display the plaques we get for two weeks only, then they are put away. In fact, our company tries to keep them out of sight because we don't want other charities to feel that they should give us plaques as well. We are inundated with them and we certainly don't want any more.

The Executive Director of a charity I supported used to send donors his picture about once a year. Why would I want that?!

several common donor recognition commodities, and their responses were significantly different. In general terms, corporate donors are more likely to use physical recognition commodities to communicate a message to employees and executive decision-makers. Tangible recognition for corporations serves an important internal marketing purpose. However, individual donors who have no need to convince anyone else that their philanthropy is worthwhile would rather see you spend the money and the time on charitable pursuits.

Plaques and Certificates

100% of corporate donors and 76% of individual donors said they receive plaques or certificates acknowledging their philanthropy. 72% of corporate donors display them, most often in an area where they will be seen by the largest number of employees. Certificates that come already framed are more likely to be displayed. If you are wondering how they should be framed, I suggest you call the donations officer for advice. The company may already have a style and size that they like and you won't go wrong on cost if you heed their advice. If the certificate or plaque is being directed to the executive office, the president's assistant could give you an idea of the office style and color scheme. Even better, where your gift negotiations include meetings at the corporate donor's offices, take note of the surroundings and color scheme for future reference. Then you will not have to ask and your gift acknowledgment will be a happy and fitting surprise.

Corporate donors in the study who said they did not display certificates or plaques most often cited lack of space, but some said they objected to the cost.

Though 76% of individual donors said they receive plaques or certificates, only 5% said they display them. Most (73%) throw them out immediately or put them away for awhile, then throw them out later.

Plaques and certificates are another reminder that individual and corporate donors cannot be satisfied with a one-size-fits-all approach to recognition.

Photos and Testimonials

By far the most popular recognition commodities are those which are unique to your organization. 86% of corporations in the study and 65% of individual donors report having received photographs from organizations they have funded, often depicting their gift at work. 84% of corporate donors and 68% of individual donors said they were very appreciative of this kind of recognition and saw the photos as important. Similar to plaques and certificates, if the photos arrive already framed (tastefully but not expensively), they are likely to be displayed, especially by companies. Most common display locations of framed photos are the executive offices, the main lobby, staff cafeteria, or staff meeting room. Of course, photos need cutlines, identifying your organization and the event or situation that is depicted.

You should be sure to take a camera with you wherever you go on behalf of your organization. Unposed, unplanned photographs are so much more vibrant; they really tell your story and they become a conversation piece for your donors.

With prior permission from corporate donors, photos can also be sent electronically, facilitating their direct distribution to staff via internal broadcast email. Let's say that a local branch of a financial services company contributes twenty staff for a Saturday spring clean up and renovation blitz in preparation for the opening of your summer camp. You are on site with your camera and the following Monday morning, a selection of photos is waiting to be downloaded when the company's donations officer arrives at work. What fun for both of you to give and receive such a personal thank you.

Photos really are worth a thousand words—photos with cutlines and a simple "thanks" on the back sent immediately after a fundraising event are great for expressing appreciation to event volunteers as well as donors.

Donors expressed particular delight about receiving letters of appreciation from people who have been helped because of their contributions. Study respondents most often cited letters from students who received scholarships, but said that any genuine personal testimonial is enthusiastically received.

Donor Recognition Events—The Good, the Bad, and the Ugly

The Black Tie Fundraising Dinner

The Chairman of one of the country's largest financial institutions was also the Chairman of our University's campaign. He had agreed to lead our efforts to establish an Endowment Fund for the creation of a Chair of Environmental Studies. His tireless efforts on our behalf for over a year had been tremendously successful. Now the campaign was culminating in a black tie fundraising dinner which the Chairman generously offered to host in the beautiful dining room at the Bank's head office.

We were so indebted to this wonderful man and wanted to thank him appropriately for his contributions as both Campaign Chair and major donor.

71% of charities hold donor recognition events. **74%** of those events are designed exclusively to recognize donors and are not combined with any other event.

68% of donor recognition events are held annually; **12%** biannually; **19%** sporadically.

83% of donor recognition events include donors who are not being recognized.

We are huge supporters of XX charity. They hold big events for donors at which there is a lot of time spent introducing the "important" people. I'm not keen on that.

Bowdoin College holds alumni weekends with donors where we can get a first hand impression of what goes on inside this institution. This is very appealing.

A donor recognition event is successful when the donors actually attend!

34% of charities include a fundraising element in donor recognition events.

I don't like recognition events when we are charged an admission fee to attend.

Ideally, the event should leave donors with a greater understanding of what we've done with their donations, a true sense that we appreciate their efforts, and the motivation to give more at some point down the road.

Simple elegance, an opportunity to meet with the president, an opportunity to meet fellow donors, and in the case of the college, fellow alumnae, visiting with faculty, eating, and a concise well delivered presentation on how their gifts are used. That, for us, is the ideal donor recognition event.

Inviting students to a donor recognition event is really effective. Our donors love to see the tangible effects of their philanthropy and meeting with students gives them immediate gratification.

The typical tokens of appreciation just didn't seem to do justice to his philanthropy and leadership. So, we set out to learn more about him. To make a long story short, we presented our Chairman with his family genealogy at the Dinner, which was assembled by the Chief Herald of his country of birth. The parchment was a spectacular document and our Chairman was thrilled. But, the best was yet to come. Near the end of the evening, several musicians entered the room and took up position on the dais. There followed a musical/memorial tribute to the Chairman's late father, the music's composer.

The Chairman was overwhelmed and broke into tears. The guests rose as one with a standing ovation.

To this day, the Bank Chairman supports our cause and has a special place in his heart for our University.

Among the many things that charities in the study believe play a role in retaining donors or moving them to higher levels of giving, donor recognition events were rated number three behind thank you letters and publishing donors' names in newsletters or other publications. But, even though charities are confident that recognition events play a substantial role in ongoing donor cultivation, they still had many questions about cost, perceived cost, content, and about whether donors really appreciate or just endure donor recognition events.

It seems that charities' hesitancy is justified. 87% of corporate donors and 81% of individual donors in the study have attended one or more donor recognition events. The study asked them to provide their opinions on what they like and dislike about them, and their comments were revealing. Individual and corporate donors are often looking for different things and most definitely have different sensibilities. For instance, corporate donors place a high premium on being singled out for recognition while individual donors think recognition events are enjoyable if they are not singled out. A company represents the collective efforts of a group of people, so when a corporation is singled out and praised for its philanthropic efforts, it is a rewarding experience that is shared by everyone and not focused on a single individual. Although all donors respect the trouble you go to and the genuine appreciation you show through your events, it is the manner in which that appreciation is offered that elicits a reaction. Both individual and corporate donors agreed that excessive recognition is uncomfortable and something definitely to be avoided.

The study included several corporate respondents who attend donor recognition events on behalf of their companies. They are particularly appreciative when the event can accommodate many employees and not just the donations officer or president, so that the message about the company's philanthropy spreads beyond the donations office and into the entire firm. 24% of corporate donors said that they do not have time to attend donor recognition events. However, several said they wished more charities would recognize their company at the company's own offices so that internal recognition and donor/charity relations could be maximized.

Events that are too long are an endurance test, not recognition, and they make donors think twice about attending the next time. Recognition events should be designed to deliver these three things:

- The charity's expression of genuine appreciation to those in attendance.
- Communication of the charity's message about gifts at work.
- An opportunity for guests to network or socialize.

When these three things guide your planning, other time-consuming agenda items can be eliminated. Gone is the urge to thank a long list of donors unable to attend; gone is the mind-numbing speech from the local politician; gone is the lengthy report from the Chairman of the Board.

Scheduling donor recognition events at a different time of day can help you keep them from dragging and can boost attendance. A healthy attendance communicates the vibrancy of the charity and avoids the embarrassment caused by organizers outnumbering guests. Holding your recognition event at breakfast or over lunch solves the problem. I attended a breakfast book launch recently. The room was packed; I networked at a table with eight people I had never met before; I listened to a ten-minute precis of a fascinating book; I met the author; and I was in by 8 a.m. and out by 9 a.m. What a great way to start the day.

Individual and corporate donors agreed that learning more about their gifts at work is one of the three most important benefits of well designed donor recognition events. Several donors cited testimonials from scholarship recipients, researchers, and other beneficiaries as highlights of events they have attended. Of course, showcasing disabled children or people suffering from a disease may be outside the bounds of policy or good taste. How charities communicate the tangible results of their donors' gifts at work is the issue, not whether they should do so. Event organizers can be in full control of how service recipients are positioned in public events. For example, produce a short video, have the program director or social worker relate a story

According to donors, the most attractive things about donor recognition events are learning more about the charity's work (**28%**), seeing others who support the same cause (**20%**), and socializing or networking with other guests (**19%**).

Least attractive aspects of donor recognition events include being too long (**18%**), singling donors out for recognition (**14%**), and being a waste of money or a perceived waste of money (**13%**).

Only **12%** of charities feel their donor recognition events are too long even though this is the number one complaint from donors who attend them.

The mark of an effective donor recognition event is that guests walk away having had a great time and feeling immensely proud of our organization.

The best events are those in which all donors feel equally welcome and appreciated, regardless of the amount of their gift.

Staff are more than twice as likely as volunteers to shoulder the responsibility of organizing donor recognition events.

We hold a nice cocktail reception in the President's Suite around convocation. It has developed the reputation of being exclusive but fun. We make sure that the corporate donors who attend only send their most senior people, and all our Board members attend as well. Recently we added some of our prominent individual donors and they were very flattered to be invited. We don't know if this event is particularly unique but our donors seem to feel it is special.

I recently attended a donor recognition event. The key official from the charity was unable to attend and the message from the podium was, "he had an important engagement elsewhere!"

Board members should be at events talking to donors, not with each other.

without identifying anyone by name, or best of all, include service recipients in the event, treating them with the same dignity and courtesy afforded any other guest. Donors and beneficiaries will find each other and they will do just fine.

What donors can learn about your organization and about their gifts at work can be limited or enhanced by event location. It is hard, for instance, to gain an appreciation of an environmental organization's groundbreaking work in wetlands conservation while you're sitting in a downtown hotel ballroom. Recognition events that draw donors to the site of charities' achievements can be thrilling while eliminating other concerns related to venue, food, entertainment, etc. No one expects you to serve a five-course dinner while standing knee-deep in a bog!

Some recognition events can take hold as permanent fixtures for their sheer innovation and entertainment value. A small rural university took a handful of donors on an archaeological dig a few years ago. They had such fun that now a convoy of three rowdy busloads of donors heads into the country for one day each summer to hack away at the dirt and enjoy a picnic lunch. It's the event of the season. All the fancy hotel room galas can't hold a candle to it.

Events and Leadership Volunteers

> *I was invited to attend a Donor Recognition event last year for a charity that our company had supported with one of our largest ever contributions. When I arrived, everyone seemed to be engrossed in conversation, so I hung on the edge of the crowd, trying to be unobtrusive as I scouted for someone I knew. After ten minutes or so, someone from the charity noticed me and, much to my relief, came over to introduce himself. "Hi, I'm John Doe, from the Board," he said, as he observed my name tag. "I see you're from ABC Inc." "Yes," I replied with a smile. "So," the board member said, "what brings you here?"*

Leadership volunteers can make or break a donor recognition event. They need to arrive at the event well ahead of the first guest and fully informed of the giving history of invited donors. Their job is to meet and greet the guests and to introduce them to others in the room. To make this a handleable task, volunteers should be assigned to specific donors. At all times, the charity's volunteer leaders are "on the job" at donor recognition events; they are not invited guests themselves. They should be continuously scanning the room for donors who are unengaged, making sure they are connected with compatible people. Those introductions become easy if volunteers have done their homework in advance (which means that the professional fundraiser has to lead this initiative). If a group of volunteers is clustered together conversing with each other, they are falling down on the job. Your volunteers are the party's hosts and the success of the event is entirely dependent on them. Great volunteer hosts can overcome lousy chicken, a video machine that won't work, and air conditioning that is growing icicles on the tips of the guests' noses; but no amount of A-class catering, lively entertainment, and nifty venues can compensate for lack of hospitality.

Recognition Event Bloopers and How to Avoid Them

When considering venue, catering, etc., you should review your donor list to make sure you are not inadvertently creating awkward situations. For instance, if the president of a hotel chain is among the corporate guests you are honoring, it is advisable not to hold the event at a competitor's hotel. Completely unintentional as they are, oversights like these make a stinging impact.

The number one complaint about donor recognition events is their real or perceived cost. You can reduce cost by holding events on your own site, at a donor's offices, or in an intriguing location that is not commonly considered to be a party venue. Use the local college's chef school for the catering, perhaps, to cut down on the cost of food and to bring awareness to another deserving group.

It is very difficult to be objective about your own organization. You might consider hiring an event planner or a public relations professional who could give you creative ideas from a third party perspective. Consider hiring just for the imaginative insight, then executing the event yourselves. Or, as a starting point, you might draw together a few people (not the donors you are going to honor) in a focus group and find out what they would want to know about your organization and about the kind of event that would make them feel welcome, entertained, informed, and appreciated. If you keep your thinking and planning inside the organization, you are likely to merely adjust what you do already rather than break out into a whole new way of thinking.

If the story about your gifts at work becomes the central focus of your donor recognition events, you will find it easier to solve another problem that disturbs donors. When you hold an event, you are putting on a show which means that entertainment, drama, and building to a climax are important. If

66% of charities feel volunteers contribute meaningfully to the success of donor recognition events.

What leadership volunteers do at donor recognition events (according to staff)
greet and entertain guests **74%**
make speeches **63%**
nothing in particular **15%**

It is important not to go overboard and make the event too lavish. It must be exclusive enough that people want to come and are impressed by the event, but not so lavish that they feel the organization is wasting their money. It is a fine line.

Sometimes we connect our donor recognition event to a previously scheduled event with a noteworthy guest speaker, for instance. This makes it more appealing and boosts attendance.

We try to have a family member come to the recognition event with his or her child and present a warm and gentle story about how the Child Center has helped the family. This helps us show donors what a special place we have and why their support is so needed and cherished in many different ways. We also hold the function in our facility to allow us an opportunity to show off the place and demonstrate to donors exactly what their money has achieved.

recognizing your donors is the show-stopping item on the agenda, it stands to reason that the recognition event is going to be structured to showcase the top contributors. Some respondents in the study said that they feel intimidated at donor recognition events if they are not in that group. They feel that either they are there to "get the message" that their giving could be higher or they are somewhat embarrassed if they are perceived to be in the "also ran" category. They are definitely being told that their giving is not as important as the ones at the top. 11% of respondents made unprompted comments about feeling uncomfortable or like a stranger at donor recognition events.

Using recognition activities as fundraising strategies is a poor substitute for the more sophisticated methodologies and tactics available in today's diverse fundraising marketplace. If you are asking for money, do so; if you are saying thank you, do that. Simplicity and straightforwardness will win the day.

So much goes into the decision to give. Only the donor is fully aware of the opportunities and constraints that come into play in deciding how much to give and only the donor can define generosity within his own means. I have spoken with donors in the past who felt that their significant six-figure gifts were no longer meaningful because they had been usurped by donors giving $10 million or more. If the focus were less on the amount of money and more on what that money has achieved or is in the process of achieving, all donors would feel that their contributions are worthwhile. Even a single gift of $20 million to build a new facility will not be enough to get the job done completely. It takes hundreds or thousands of donors pulling together to achieve the goal.

In the context of a donor recognition event, if you focus on what you are trying to achieve or have achieved, and if you follow a philosophy that all donors did their very best to get you to where you are today, the tone of your event will make everyone feel part of your success. And, isn't that what you want? It's out of a feeling of confidence and satisfaction that donors will go on to give you more in time. If they are made to feel embarrassed or of less importance, they will give to someone else or, worse, stop giving altogether.

Finally, donors expressed considerable dissatisfaction with charities who use their donor recognition events to ask for money or design them in such a way that guests feel that they should be giving. This is counter-productive. The impromptu auction may be fun for you but it sends an entirely different message to your donors. If you cannot afford to hold a donor recognition event without including a fundraising element that covers its cost, then you should not hold the event. An entirely acceptable alternative is for your Board members to personally call each donor who would have been invited to thank them for their ongoing support.

Publishing Donors' Names

Gift Clubs and Honor Rolls

I was newly hired as the university's donor relations officer, and one of my first assignments was to create the list of donors who had given over $10,000 to the capital campaign. The list was to be included in the final campaign report, an important and prestigious publication.

    *While going over the list I noticed two people with the same unusual surname. I placed an asterix next to the names as a reminder to myself to check later to see whether they were married and should, perhaps, be listed together. Unfortunately, my small notations made it all the way to the printed publication where these two donors, who are very much alive, are footnoted as *deceased.*

    One of those donors won't take my calls to this day. I still tremble whenever my colleagues suggest we should publish a regular honor roll.

93% of study charities recognize their donors by publishing their names in newsletters, annual reports, house programs, or other publications. 67% publish donors' names by gift size (graded donor recognition) and 22% do so alphabetically. Less than half feel that publishing donors' names influences them to continue giving; only 17% feel that it encourages donors to give more.

Connecting donors more closely with the organization, giving donors a sense of belonging, and tangible recognition were cited by charities as attractive or appealing things about their honor rolls or gift clubs. Most common weaknesses of graded recognition programs were poor benefits or lack of distinction in benefits from one gift level to the next. Charities also agreed that gift categories tend to lock donors into gift levels rather than play a role in moving them up. An additional concern expressed by many charities was that graded recognition programs need to be promoted to be worthwhile, and that takes both time and money. Most charities in the study said they under-budget or do not budget at all for the promotion of their gift categories, then fail to reap the hoped-for benefits.

Honor rolls or gift clubs with defined gift value categories like the "Gold Level" or the "President's Club" are examples of dual-purpose recognition. From direct mail to major gifts, gift value is tied to fundraising strategy. But, in some circumstances, gift clubs also play a role in donor recognition. Gift levels often determine the size and location of a donor's name when published in the annual report or house program. They also sometimes carry with them certain benefits such as receiving the newsletter for free or getting an invitation to an

---

93% of charities recognize their donors in some fashion in their newsletters, annual reports, or programs. **65%** do so by gift level or category; **22%** alphabetically.

62% of charities have gift clubs, honor rolls, or other gift recognition categories. **72%** believe they contribute to maintaining donor loyalty; **56%** believe they are effective in moving donors to higher levels of giving.

59% of charities' gift clubs reward donors with tangible benefits or gifts such as discounts on merchandise, pins, etc. **54%** offer a distinct array of benefits for each giving level so that donors can easily discern the advantages of one level over another. Charities say that **27%** of donors take advantage of the majority of benefits offered but that **19%** do not use any gift club benefits.

According to charities, the benefits of publishing donors' names are:
attracts other donors **49%**
encourages ongoing loyalty of existing donors **47%**
showcases philanthropy as newsworthy **19%**
encourages gifts of higher value **17%**

My husband and I have tried to deal with several charities that keep pressuring us to have our names included in their publications. Their rationale is that these lists influence others to give, but it makes us very uncomfortable.

annual lecture. I don't object to graded donor levels or clubs per se, only to how dual-purpose recognition influences the way charities interact with their donors.

If gift clubs' primary purpose is to influence gift value, do they work? According to individual donors in the study, 91% have had their names published in giving levels like the Gold Club or the President's Circle but 71% said that it does not influence them to give at a higher level than they would have otherwise considered. As well, 58% said that giving levels do not influence them to maintain subsequent gifts at their current level when they might have been considering lowering the amount for some reason.

Neither charities nor donors feel that giving levels are demonstrably effective but neither are the statistics a condemnation of the practice of publishing donors' names. There may be some positive influence on non-donors who happen to see friends' and colleagues' names on a list of supporters, but only if they get the newsletter (which is unlikely if they're not donors themselves) or read the names in a house program while waiting for Act II to begin—which is a little more likely, I suppose.

The more important issue is allocating time and cost to an activity whose benefits are uncertain when there are proven successful alternatives for improving donor retention and increasing gift values.

Publishing donors' names is one of those "systematized" things that charities do because it is part of accepted donor recognition practice and because it deals with a lot of donors all at once. But when charities opt for handling the volume instead of reaching out to the individual supporter, they cover the obligation but miss the opportunity. Though publishing donors' names by gift level might keep some donors in a holding pattern for awhile, it won't be effective long term in helping charities with their progressive fundraising efforts. In fact, gift levels may actually lull charities into a false sense of security. If a donor maintains his giving in the Silver category year after year, has he actually been locked into a giving ceiling when he could have given much more? Only by communicating with him directly will a fundraiser ever know.

As long as practitioners think in categories, donors will respond in kind. They cannot break free into "giving generously within their own means" until fundraisers break out of these categories themselves.

Donor Walls

Nearing the end of our last capital campaign, a permanent donor wall was created to recognize campaign contributors.

Now, however, we have more donors who contributed late in the campaign and their names are not on the wall. Some of our early donors whose names are on the wall never fulfilled their pledges. As well, some donors who were among the first group of contributors have now given us more and qualify to be listed in a different category on the wall. Though it may seem that we created the donor wall prematurely, if we had waited it would have been years after the campaign had ended before donors got the public recognition we had promised them. We are now in the expensive process of trying to fix this problem. It's a waste of time and money.

Charities had a lot to say about donor walls and most of it concerned the logistical headache and cost connected with keeping them current. They also questioned whether donor walls were relevant to donors.

32% of individual donors and 50% of corporate donors felt that donor walls had some influence on whether or not they contribute to a capital campaign. This means that donor walls could be a worthwhile component of a multi-faceted solicitation strategy, though not a prime motivator for giving. Charities should keep in mind other statistics in this study such as the high percentage of donors who do not want to be recognized under any circumstances; during asks, position recognition on donor walls with discretion.

When a donor wall is already installed, 36% of individual donors and 55% of corporate donors felt that seeing other donors' names on a donor wall plays a role in inspiring them to give.

Charities themselves are uncertain about the impact that this form of recognition has on donors. 58% felt that donor walls were of questionable value. Even when questioned on the effectiveness of donor walls as a tool for negotiating lead and major gifts for capital campaigns, 50% of charities said they were not particularly effective.

My key frustration right now is keeping the list accurate and setting up proper guidelines for who we list and who we don't list. Our database does not sort the listing alphabetically like we would like to have it on the wall, so we have to go through the list and rearrange it, causing more room for errors. We also encounter frequent problems with donors who give on an individual basis both personally and through their personally-

47% of charities had some kind of donor wall at the time this study was conducted. **43%** were established to recognize capital campaign donors; **28%** recognize annual fund donors; **16%** recognize planned gifts donors.

47% of donor walls organize donors' names by gift size; **25%** alphabetically; **28%** by date of gift or randomly.

42% of charities with donor walls feel that their donors feel these installations are important; **19%** do not; **39%** do not know.

Charities' top five frustrations concerning donor walls:
staff time required to make changes/additions
cost of walls and name plates
poor/low traffic location of donor wall
dated appearance
inconsistent criteria for qualifying donors

How people wish their names to be listed when our criteria are complex is a real issue in our organization. For instance, many times one donor may want to "split" his/her gift among many memorial or honorarium names. I have received a gift as small as $100 which the donor wanted to divide among five people, meaning there would be five separate lines of recognition for that one modest gift.

For **63%** of individual donor respondents, the prospect of having their names on a donor wall does not influence them to give; however this does play a role in the giving decisions of **32%** of those surveyed. Donor walls have a somewhat greater impact on corporate donors, with **50%** being positively influenced to give.

Donor walls may play a minor role in promoting the concept of philanthropy. **55%** of corporate donors and **36%** of individual donors feel that seeing other donors' names on a donor wall can be inspiring.

I like the idea of donor walls because I think they do influence some people to give and they offer naming possibilities to donors, making fundraising easier. On the other hand, I've been in buildings where every last doorknob and entranceway is named and that turns me off.

There are two donor walls in our building. The donor wall in the lobby was for the capital campaign which is still used for larger donations to the organization IF the donor requests to have his name added to the wall. The other wall was constructed for anyone who establishes a Memorial and each listing on this wall includes the memorial itself and the names of all the donors who gave in memory of that individual. They are both a nightmare to keep organized, accurate, and updated.

owned businesses. If the amount for each doesn't make it to the required level for recognition, we still try and list them as a combined entity. Tracking this can become complicated.

72% of charities organize their donor wall either alphabetically or by gift size. This contributes to the problems they experience in maintaining their accuracy and avoiding embarrassing errors. The most common complaint about donor walls was the staff time required to make name changes or additions or to move names around to accommodate new contributors.

The frustration among charities responding to this part of the questionnaire was evident and donors' views on the subject are not definitive. As the data does not point to a clear solution to the problems charities are experiencing, I would recommend the following:

- Since the majority of individual and corporate donors in this study have the capacity to make major gifts to campaigns, and since a number of respondents reacted positively to these questions, donor wall recognition may be a worthwhile negotiation advantage as long as solicitors predetermine prospects' individual sensibilities concerning public recognition.
- Donor walls should be designed during the planning phase of a campaign so that public recognition can be used as a negotiation tool. Discussions with donors will be more fruitful if solicitors can show prospects the donor wall design, its planned location, and how donors' names will appear.
- Do not pressure donors to have their names included on a donor wall for the purpose of influencing others to give. Donors who prefer to give quietly or anonymously do so for reasons that are private and significant. Suggestions that they should serve as an example to other donors are very uncomfortable for some donors. Make sure you know your donor well before making this kind of request.
- An exciting opportunity exists for companies that create and market donor walls to design systems that work better for charities. Designs which fix names permanently to an installation are problematic. There is a need for alternate design formats using electronic name recognition, for instance, or transportable donor walls which can be easily moved to better locations as building structures grow. It is time for

unconventional concepts. Donors are not that focused on donor walls and they are certainly not tied to any pre-existing design format. Suppliers who solve the problems that charities are currently facing will get the future business. Being beautiful isn't enough; charities' donor walls must also work for the people who are left to deal with them after the campaign is over.

- Finally, if you have been getting along just fine without a donor wall, don't feel you have to incorporate this form of recognition into your fundraising program. In the end, it's still one-on-one communication and relationship-building that matters most, not public recognition.

Membership: The Double-Edged Sword

If you run a membership program in your organization which you feel is really successful, by all means continue to do so; but if you are concerned about its cost effectiveness and whether it generates long term loyalty any better than your fundraising programs, the following perspective may be helpful.

Like donor clubs, membership is used to serve fundraising, donor retention, and recognition purposes simultaneously. It can work—in special cases. However, in many membership programs, the advantages are questionable and liabilities clear. The most practical benefit of a membership program is the inherent commitment that charities make to communicate on a regular basis. Apart from that, membership programs are usually high cost relative to return, and they are often indistinguishable from programs for non-member donors.

73% of individual donors in the study were members of at least one charitable organization but 79% felt that being a member and a donor were the same thing. Membership was broadly interpreted as just a softer term for a program with exactly the same objective—to raise money.

Membership programs seldom play a measurable role in moving donors to higher levels of philanthropic support. As a matter of fact, they often work against fundraising interests by locking donors into a meager contribution level (the annual membership fee) while compelling charities to provide them with tangible and costly benefits. There are very few membership programs that work well as high return, high growth fundraising programs, and most are overly complicated as communication vehicles. Additionally, by focusing members on what they will get for their membership fee instead of how they can help further the goals of the charity, membership programs often work

---

Why charities have membership programs

revenue generation **76%**
membership improves retention **73%**
major gift cultivation **62%**
advocacy **62%**

Most common membership benefits

newsletter
advance notice of/early registration for events
exclusive receptions/parties
membership card
free/discounted admissions or tickets
discounted merchandise
voting privileges
gifts
special access to facilities (campus/ pool/library, etc.)
cross-promotion benefits with partner organizations

Benefits that charities feel influence members to renew

newsletter **46%**
exclusive receptions/parties **29%**
advance notice of/early registration for events **20%**
none **17%**
discounted merchandise **16%**

66% of charities with membership programs offer donors four or more different membership levels from which to choose.

against the more important objective of furthering the philanthropic spirit.

83% of charities with membership programs offer members a regular newsletter, by far the most typical membership benefit. But should charities not want all their supporters to receive the newsletter? If newsletters are the most commonly used tool for informing donors about their gifts at work or for increasing their knowledge of the charities they support, what is the fundraising advantage of offering this important communication tool to some supporters while withholding it from others? Because newsletters are promoted as a key benefit of membership, charities are forced into a style and quality (i.e. expense) of production and a length that is not necessary for the purpose of keeping donors informed.

Membership programs are more effective for charities whose donors or supporters are the beneficiaries of the products or services they produce. For instance, arts organizations draw the bulk of their membership from subscribers; universities' alumni associations are actually membership programs under another name. Still, vested interest membership programs are more effective as communication vehicles than they are as fundraising programs. All charities would be well advised to periodically assess their membership programs on a cost-centered basis to determine whether they are worth the investment. (This means calculating professional staff time required to design and execute the program as well as hard costs.)

The array of membership benefits offered to donors should be carefully scrutinized. You will probably find that only a few of the benefits offered are actually being used by a small percentage of your members; yet the cost in time and money of developing the program, producing a discrete membership brochure, promoting the program, etc. must be borne by you and your communication budget. 31% of study respondents who are members of one or more charities are attracted by membership benefits. Interestingly, though, 68% never or hardly ever take advantage of the membership benefits they are offered.

Most benefits currently offered through membership could actually be tangible and valuable gift acknowledgments for loyal donors. Consider this example: a loyal subscriber and donor to a local dance company receives a call from the development director who is offering two free tickets to the next performance in addition to the subscriber's own seats. As well, it has been arranged for all four seats to be together in the hope that the subscriber will introduce two friends to the dance company. Both the arts organization and the subscriber win in this situation. The subscriber is singled out and acknowledged for his ongoing support, which makes him feel special, and the dance company stands to gain two new subscribers by being clever enough to strategically allocate two of their unsold tickets. The subscriber is very likely to go out of his way to be an ambassador for the dance company, knowing that the company had honored him with this "responsibility." On top of that, he and his guests will probably go out for dinner before the show, doubling their usual investment in the local economy.

It is hard to find a downside in this scenario. However, if the occasional free tickets were part of a membership package that the subscriber had purchased months or years ago, he might not remember that the benefit existed; or, if he did, he might not feel bold enough to ask for them. But with the dance company making the offer, the subscriber is at ease; and with the development director making the call, personal contact is made with a loyal supporter in the most comfortable way possible. This more creative application of recognition can lead directly into a discussion about another gift.

51% of study respondents said they become members to add their presence to a group of supporters for advocacy purposes. However, just by being donors they do that; it is unlikely that someone would give to a charity if he were opposed to its work. Bylaws which differentiate between members and donors for advocacy and/or voting purposes are unnecessarily complicated, and organizations are not uniform in their definition of a member. Several individual donors surveyed in our study said that they are sometimes informed after making a gift that they have become a member of the charity, even if that had not been their intention.

Recognizing Corporate Donors and Corporate Sponsors

> *"Sponsorships have changed and donations are now much like sponsorships; it's hard to tell them apart. Sponsorships are sales driven and donations are goodwill contributions. Charities and donors sometimes don't know the difference between sponsorship and giving. Today it's more like "donorship" and everyone who contributes should be recognized."*
> —Study Respondent

66% of charities in the study have corporate sponsors as well as corporate donors. Charities were generally confident that they offer a well balanced recognition program for corporate donors and sponsors so that neither group feels that the other is favored. One exception, though, concerned recognition and contribution value. Where recognition programs are built around gift size, charities agreed that sometimes a short-term sponsor may receive more prominent recognition than a corporate donor who has contributed every year for sev-

---

Most attractive membership benefits, according to members
free or discounted tickets/ admissions **31%**
discounts on merchandise **13%**
preferred seating/seat exchange **9%**
lectures/tours/"meet the author" **9%**
none **9%**

Only **10%** of members take advantage of most of the membership benefits offered; **22%** do so occasionally; **68%** never or hardly ever take advantage of membership benefits.

52% of charities with sponsors incorporate sponsor recognition in their overall donor recognition program; **32%** have a discrete recognition program for sponsors.

I usually opt for membership over charitable giving because the membership fee is less than what I would be expected to contribute philanthropically.

eral years. If a donor-centered approach to recognition is adopted that show-cases charities' achievements while recognizing all donors and sponsors more equitably, this concern will be alleviated.

93% of charities were very confident that including sponsors in their recognition program contributes to maintaining their loyalty and facilitates contract re-negotiation. 32% of charities actually design entirely unique recognition programs for their corporate supporters.

> *I am working to change our internal mindset about how best to develop agreements with corporate sponsors. I recognize that their primary concern is gaining name recognition while being associated with worthwhile community efforts. Here I believe a stronger, long-term relationship can be developed in much the same way individual relationships are. We must communicate what we are doing with the money and build commitment to our mission within the corporate sponsor's employee base. That way they are less inclined to donate just for a project, and may become dedicated corporate donors over time.*

Recognizing Planned Gift Donors

70% of the charities in this study have a planned giving program. Not surprising, communication is superior with these donors who are being stewarded by the relationship specialists in the fundraising department. For instance, 62% make personal visits to planned gift donors to keep them informed about their charities' work. This compares with only 18% who visit other donors as a regular part of their donor relations program.

Planned gift donors seem to be better informed in other ways, too. 85% of study charities provide planned gift donors with their regular newsletter, and 31% supplement that with a special newsletter designed just for them. 52% invite planned gift donors on site to see their work first hand; 43% publish articles on these special donors; and 33% hold special events just for planned gift donors.

33% of respondent charities also keep in close contact with allied professionals who have been instrumental in facilitating planned gifts. One very creative organization offers free seminars for financial planners which qualify as a credit towards certification. "This has proven to be effective and it has helped us secure some gifts we might not have otherwise obtained."

Some charities were concerned about providing donors with recognition before their bequests or other deferred gifts had been realized. They also wondered whether recognition should be different for donors who have made a commitment to a future gift than for donors whose gifts have been realized. If recognition is part of a charity's honest appreciation for a donor's generosity, then withholding that recognition until the donor is dead is . . . well . . . strange. It also means denying both him and you the joy of giving and receiving appreciation. If you are worried about the already small percentage of donors who revoke their gift commitments, then donor-centered communication will reduce that even further.

Similarly, charities that concern themselves with listing donors with gift commitments separately from those whose gifts have been realized, or publishing their names in smaller type or putting them on a different donor wall, are seeing donor appreciation only in the context of cash in the bank. This two-tiered valuation of donors' intentions versus monies received sends a message which I am sure charities are not intending to communicate.

In all your dealings with deferred gift donors, don't wait. Tell them how much you appreciate them now.

Prioritizing Communication and Recognition

While charities need to put more effort into communicating with their donors, donor recognition is an area where time and money can be saved. The fact is, not one donor in this study said they wanted more donor recognition events, more honor rolls, or more plaques. On every question concerning public recognition for their philanthropy, a significant majority of study donors said it wasn't necessary and it doesn't influence their future giving.

When offered as a complement to meaningful communication, donor recognition is seen by donors as an act of kindness and respect. In the absence of meaningful communication, however, donor recognition raises donors' ire and focuses them on the money—their money—that they feel you are wasting on things they never asked for.

Real recognition is not something you do at certain intervals in your relationship with donors, nor is it a momentary thing. It is pervasive. Recognition is between the lines in the newsletters you write, it is in the tone of your voice, it is in the welcoming handshakes of the members of your Board of Directors. Recognition is inseparable from the people who give it.

53% of individual donors do not want to be recognized; another **18%** are ambivalent. **29%** say they appreciate being recognized for their philanthropy.

69% of corporate donors want to be recognized and **72%** of them want to be involved in the decision-making about how their company will be recognized.

I don't care or not if my name gets published in the annual report. But leaving my name off the list when everyone else is on it does have an influence. One charity I supported lost a fifteen thousand dollar gift because of that.

I am sometimes put under tremendous pressure to have my name published "in order to influence other donors to give." Occasionally I will comply with this request but I am never comfortable with it.

If charities never printed our names in donor lists, it wouldn't change our lives in any way. It's nice when they do but it's not a motivation for giving.

I'm very conscious of the cost of several pages in an annual report being devoted to lists of donors' names. I also don't like seeing donors listed by their gift amounts. It's offensive.

PART II
Making Donor-Centered Fundraising Work

11
Trapped!

THE FAMINE

A well known international charity was respected in fundraising circles for its extremely large direct mail campaign. Although they were struggling with donor retention, the program's longevity and high volume acquisition meant that it was still a significant source of revenue.

During the height of a prolonged famine in a region of Africa, the charity raised more than six times its average in a donor acquisition campaign. The intense media focus on the tragedy combined with a brilliant marketing campaign by the charity were responsible for this success. But, within eighteen months, acquisition had fallen back to its pre-campaign average and donor retention was at a five-year low.

The "famine" donors were labeled skittish and unreliable because they seemed to respond impulsively to a tragedy that was receiving intense media focus, then disappear as soon as the spotlight was removed. Thereafter, the impressive figures from that year's direct mail acquisition program were reported with a footnote that said "skewed due to unusual response to the famine campaign." Subsequent performance reports were careful to eliminate this year so that year-to-year comparisons would more accurately reflect the lower industry standards within which the direct mail program was once again performing.

With the best of intentions and in the true belief that we were doing the right thing at the time, the not for profit sector has gradually limited its own ability to make money. We have caught ourselves in our own trap.

Fundraisers and donors are victims of the very programs which are supposed to make the job of raising money easier for practitioners and the act of giving easier for our donors. The moment that a new donor is "caught" in the direct mail program is also the moment that she needs to be freed from its constraints. But when will that moment come? There is no time to give her the attention that influences her to give a larger gift because we are too busy trying to make more money.

I will consider a larger gift once I have taken the time to check out the charity more thoroughly. Rather than not give at all when the need is great, I tend to give a smaller gift initially, then do my research which often includes a visit to the organization to meet their people.

Be straightforward. Don't exaggerate claims or charm your way into donors' pockets.

I want to receive a single annual solicitation and I tell charities that. Sometimes they comply and sometimes they don't. Duplicate solicitations are completely avoidable given today's computer technology and getting more solicitations right after I've made a contribution is particularly annoying. It's also a waste of money—my money!

No one is at fault. The fundraising business itself has trapped everyone—staff, volunteers, and donors together—and the more sophisticated that fundraising programs become, the harder it is to escape from the control they exert over practitioners. A relentless schedule of campaigns leaves fundraisers exhausted, unable to capitalize on opportunity, and labeling donors fickle when they decide not to renew their gifts. Taught from the start that this is the way money is raised, no one stops to wonder whether the formulaic approach to fundraising is related to high donor attrition. No one, of course, except donors themselves.

These are the traps in which the fundraising business and its practitioners are caught:

Statistics

Though there is far too little statistical analysis in fundraising, much of the information that is gathered on a regular basis and on which practitioners rely is doing the industry a disservice. Beware the phrase, "industry standards." Who makes up the industry in which a 50% attrition rate after the first gift in direct marketing programs is considered acceptable? Unfortunately, *we* do. We have created our own statistics based on our own unregulated performance and then called them benchmarks. The problem with benchmarks is that we take comfort in them; benchmarks allow fundraisers to continue to operate below par, oblivious to what their level of performance could really be.

This study tells a story that challenges industry standards. If 93% of both individual and corporate donors said they would definitely or probably give again *the next time they were asked* by a charity that provided them with prompt, personal gift acknowledgment and information on their gifts at work, and if donors say that they give to truly make a difference, and if giving makes donors feel good—then why would *anyone* stop? It's not simply a matter of donors not getting around to it; the process of fundraising itself must be making it easy for them to stop giving.

Industry performance standards are not our friend. Statistics become standards when they reflect a level of performance that is achieved on a consistent basis. Fundraising performance shapes the standards and then the standards shape fundraising performance. How will the industry react, then, if donor-centered fundraising performance challenges those industry standards? Will fundraisers be ready to capitalize on opportunity, or will they retreat to the familiar?

Categorizing Donors by Gift Size

Give a gift at the top of the suggested gift range in the annual fund campaign and a donor might receive a letter signed by a volunteer; give in the middle range and he gets a less informative letter signed by the director of development; give at the bottom end and he can look forward to receiving a pre-printed card. Fundraisers have adopted a reward and punishment approach to gift acknowledgment by meting out recognition and information according to gift size. This is both insulting to donors and self-defeating for charities. If your policy is to send the newsletter only to donors giving $50 or more, how will your $25 donor get the essential information about his gift at work that influences him to give again and give more? If he gets nothing, how will he even know what he's missing? What is the incentive to give again?

We are so preoccupied with the revenue that we overlook the donor, passing judgment on the people themselves through the actions we take or fail to take. By withholding information and personal appreciation, we are really saying, "That just isn't good enough." If we equate the amount of information or consideration due a donor with the size of his gift, we will only hurt ourselves by limiting philanthropic growth among new donors and those who are contributing more modest gifts.

Urgent Appeals

When charities are faced with an immediate financial need, it is hard to remember that *their* emergency is not the donor's emergency—it's not even the donor's problem. Though donors will respond when the cause is serious and well promoted, their loyalty cannot be sustained by continuous urgent appeals. After awhile, donors want to know that they are working with you to resolve problems long term, not simply responding to unpredictable crises. Fundraising strategies for getting and keeping donors are not the same; fundraising methodologies need to take this into account.

Failure to Plan

Charities fail to maximize the value of donors' contributions by not clearly articulating the specific end use of funds. The majority of not for profit organizations operate without a strategic plan, with no long term blueprint for growth

Don't equate communication and recognition with gift levels. I need information no matter what level of gift that I give.

It is difficult to assess whether or not giving levels are effective and it has been a subject of ongoing debate. As a religious higher education institution we have those who believe all gifts are of equal value in the eyes of God and we should not be ranking people by the size of their gift. Others argue that "to whom much is given, much is required" and gift clubs serve as good motivators for increased giving. So, some years donors' names are published and some years they are not and this inconsistency makes it impossible to evaluate the effects of the program.

We do not use our giving society/ levels as a marketing tool. We communicate with donors after the fact, telling them that they are now in such-and-such giving level because of the gift they have already given.

It's just a list. I don't think people give to our organization to be on a list of donors, but I may be wrong.

Giving levels may actually be compromising our fundraising potential. Our highest gift level is $1,000. Everyone in that level gives exactly $1,000; no one gives more.

On my desk right now sits a pile of year-end appeals. I'm saturated and I've become immune to all requests because there are so many. They're all 'urgent,' they are all introduced in the same way. It's past my threshold of pain!

Two years ago my wife and I made the decision that we would give a significant gift to a limited number of charities and stop giving to everything else. We wanted to be more deliberate and give more significantly. It's also because fundraising is annoying.

I don't like it when fundraising letters suggest how much I should give.

We recently received two $100,000 gifts from alumnae, our largest gifts ever. Both of these gifts resulted from simple cultivation strategies started over seven years ago.

Donors all come in at the lowest giving level in our gift club...and no one moves up!

of service and innovation of product, and with no short term goals to guarantee results. Charities expect donors to fund on faith.

Failure to Test

For a sector that is otherwise very conservative, charities are often risk-takers in the extreme when it comes to fundraising. It is not unusual for an idea for a new fundraising event to emerge as a concept, be adopted, and set into motion in a single board meeting. Buoyed with enthusiasm for an inventive concept, decision-makers can quickly attach an expectation for net revenue to the event that, coincidentally, equals the projected operating loss for the year. An event date is set three months hence, and the meeting is adjourned with assurances that there will be no impact on staff time.

Under stressed conditions and with the right-minded intentions of demonstrating leadership and productivity, fundraisers and decision-makers guess, hope, and assume. Sometimes they get lucky and sometimes they don't. But the option is always available to limit exposure by testing a concept prior to full implementation, by researching others' experiences, by finding a partner to limit risk, or by simply spending more time thinking before acting.

Being Unrealistic About Time

There is no such thing as short term fundraising. The reasons for fundraising success or failure today can be traced back to what was done, not done, or done poorly two or three years ago. Pressure is placed on professional and volunteer fundraisers to close deals for major gifts and sponsorships within time frames that are simply unrealistic or which fail to take donors' decision-making processes into account. Charities lose donations and sponsorship opportunities because they need the money now, rather than negotiating to the company's next unencumbered fiscal year. They lose opportunities to engage prominent fundraising volunteers because they recruit at the last minute to fill current vacancies instead of securing commitment now for future postings. Being realistic about time and being willing to wait one's turn can reap so many rewards.

Solicitation/Attrition

The direct marketing programs that house the bulk of a charity's donors become increasingly demanding as these programs get larger. No sooner has one direct mail campaign been put to bed than the solicitation letter for the next must be drafted. If revenue levels off, solicitations increase. This causes donor burnout which, in turn, causes higher attrition; so prospecting increases. There is no time for follow up, so attrition climbs . . . so prospecting increases again. Fundraisers cannot get off the treadmill long enough to think, to analyze fundraising programs in depth, to test a new theory, or just to distance themselves momentarily from the work in order to regain their objectivity. Direct marketing programs are designed to be methodologies for finding donors; they are not meant to house donors indefinitely. Fundraisers spend more and more time immersed in the programs and, in so doing, distance themselves from the very people they are trying to reach.

Relying on Fundraising to Be Marketing

42% of the charities in our study had no marketing budget at all, and of those who did, the average expenditure on marketing was a mere 6%. If yours is one of the many not for profits with no discrete marketing plan or budget, now is the time to look seriously at your performance to date in donor acquisition and ask yourself whether your message is penetrating the giving community. So many charities are vying for donors' attention and many are your direct competitors for private sector funds. Your message needs to get out and it needs to reach the donor/consumer in non-traditional ways.

Fundraising programs do play a role in the overall marketing mix but their purpose is income-generation, not awareness-building. Direct mail, telemarketing, and canvassing are great at getting right to the donor, but they are selling and doing it very assertively. Fundraising events can vary widely in theme and content but they do not cast a wide net and they are not cost-effective as marketing programs. In an unprompted question about charities to which study donors would not contribute financial support, 12% said they would not support an organization with which they were unfamiliar. Potential donors need an opportunity to learn about your organization. They cannot be expected to go from no awareness to writing you a check in a single step.

The full range of promotional vehicles in today's highly sophisticated communications marketplace is available to the not for profit sector as it is to the corporate sector. You cannot hang back just because you are a charity and hope that donors and volunteers find you. You have to get in the game.

Our long term donors are as high on our donor relations priority list as are donors who have given us a single, large gift. Planned giving has taught us that loyal donors are our future endowment pool. Long term loyalty needs to be recognized equally.

When we run events, I compile the marketing materials in a display folder and send it to my main contact at the sponsoring company. When next year's event is being planned I take a duplicate folder with me to negotiation meetings. This is helpful in providing evidence that their sponsorship was worthwhile and it comes in handy if there has been a staff change at the company.

If I see write-ups in the paper or other external endorsements of a charity I have supported, then I have the confidence I need to consider a larger gift the next time.

I confine my giving to locally-based rather than national charities. Greenpeace is an exception because they put their lives on the line. I get more dependable information from local charities and their activities tend to get published in the local newspaper.

Marketing . . . communicating . . . educating toward the "need to give" as opposed to "giving to a need" is a tight wire indeed. Donor monies must obviously be stewarded and accounted for with the utmost care. However, we as a community must do a better job in articulating the real and acceptable costs of doing so.

Most of our Patron Services Director's time is spent exchanging tickets for our patrons rather than working with the Director of Development to cultivate donors. This situation bleeds time, energy, and resources from our staff.

It's often hard to distinguish between being a donor and a member. I am often made a member automatically when I contribute over a certain amount so the benefits of membership are irrelevant to me.

I don't like getting membership cards when I give; it's so frivolous and meaningless.

Fundraising Expense

In some not for profit organizations, saving money is more valued than making money. Volunteer boards, including members who built their own businesses by investing now in the calculated expectation of future return, think nothing of denying even the most modest investment in fundraising. This is such an important issue. Attempting to run progressive fundraising programs with insufficient investment holds all fundraising back, and it will certainly scuttle donor-centered fundraising before it has a chance to prove itself in your organization.

"Donors should be neither seen nor heard"

Some charities (not their fundraisers, just the charities) have a love/hate relationship with donors. It could be because of the time and resources that are diverted from programs and services to deal with fundraising matters; or maneuvering among the most privileged members of society may not sit well with those who are trying to help the least privileged; or some organizations see donors as people who should feel privileged to be able to give and expect nothing in return.

Actually, donors *do* feel privileged to give and they *don't* want anything in return for themselves. But it is important not to confuse having no vested interest with having no interest. Two reasons make it vital for charities to keep donors informed as best they possibly can and to remind them from time to time that they are appreciated. First is the sheer volume of competition. Though donors are very generous, they cannot support everyone. Your meaningful communication is what sets you apart from all other charitable organizations. Second, donors have had some bad experiences in recent years. The high profile ones stick in everyone's mind and make donors more cautious about giving. If you want their money, you'll need to prove that you deserve it and that you will be reliable stewards of their contributions.

The Fundraising System

All businesses must develop systems in order to run efficiently and predictably. Without defined practices and common standards of performance, it would be impossible to achieve results. But systems can become ingrained to the point where practitioners have difficulty seeing any other way of doing business, even when the benefits of doing things differently are significant. Resistance to change in any business is a common thing, so common in fact that an entire industry of change management specialists has emerged to help companies move from less to more effective ways of operating. It is not at all unusual to find owners, managers, and workers all wanting to achieve an exciting new goal but unable to adopt the new methodologies and new ways of thinking that will get them there.

It's no different in fundraising. Though fundraising in its current configuration can claim many big successes, it has not done a good job of controlling donor attrition. Tinkering with the system will not solve this problem; new priorities are required. In follow up research to the first edition of this book, we surveyed a group of charities concerning implementation issues in donor-centered fundraising. Those who had wanted to improve their communication practices but had not done so said that it was because there was no time to take on anything else due to the heavy schedule of solicitations. Though they knew that a donor-centered approach would retain more donors and reduce the required number of campaigns, they couldn't break out of the system they were in long enough to test an alternative.

Feeling that Charities are Beyond Reproach

Fundraising is a largely unregulated business and it is a diligent guardian of its methodologies, even in the face of strenuous complaints from donors. When in the rare instances donors make their concerns known publicly, the third sector responds with bewilderment. It's as if charities feel they should be exempt from controls or limitations on their practices just because they are charities.

83% of adult Americans gave to charity in 2000. That's an incredible rate of participation in philanthropy. So, when the people decide to challenge fundraising methodology, whether directly with charities, through the media, or even in court, it's not just some angry citizens who don't know how fundraising works; it's our donors trying to send us a message. We need to listen more carefully and be better prepared to change the way we do business to meet the needs of the people who keep us in business.

Focusing on "What" rather than "Why" in Fundraising Research

The ebb and flow of national giving averages year to year tells practitioners what is happening in the fundraising marketplace. This is interesting and important information, especially when the numbers are going down, as it helps

I have to keep a binder of who I have given to and when during the year because I get so many multiple requests in a single year. I spend a lot of time monitoring how many solicitations I get and whether or not I've already given. I used to ask charities to send me only one solicitation a year, but they would tell me that it's too hard to do that because everything is computerized. Eventually, I just stopped asking.

Get rid of that feeling of entitlement that so many charities have. Many groups feel we should be obligated to fund them either because they are prominent charities or because they reside in our city. They are sometimes cocky and too confident; they get used to being successful and this attitude is not helpful.

I throw out about seven requests for money each day. Last year I gave for the first time to a fledgling charity. Now I'm on the list of dozens of similar organizations from all over the country. It's very irritating.

I don't like being put down for a pledge before I've agreed to give one.

practitioners realize that they are not alone and why they are working so hard just to stay even. But these statistics don't delve into the underlying problems. Rarely does research go beyond reflecting what is happening to ask, "*Why* is this happening?" Although we should know how much money was raised this year compared with last, which kinds of charities got the lion's share of it, what is the age/marital status and income range of a typical donor, etc., the industry needs more comprehensive research to guide fundraising strategy and programs modification, and to shape donor relations.

BREAKING OUT OF THE TRAPS

The things that prevent charities from instituting donor-centered fundraising are real and serious but they are also of their own making. Because charities have set the trap and caught themselves in it, they can also break out of it if they so choose.

As you read Part I of this book, you may have been concerned about trying to implement donor-centered fundraising in a development office that is already running flat out and under-financed. It can be done—not all at once, of course; but, by applying donor-centered fundraising principles to your work as you are able, you will generate measurable results more quickly than you think. Here are some tools and information that will help you break out of the traps:

Statistics

As long as you are not tied to the standards and statistics that reflect the fundraising industry as it currently exists, you will succeed. If you experience a dramatic increase in giving because of donor-centered fundraising, it will not be an aberration. The 39% increase in giving among donors in the Paraplegic Association test is impressive; but many charities have reported even better results through improved communication with donors. As you become more engaged in donor-centered fundraising, anticipate that your statistics will change and be ready to capitalize on opportunity.

Categorizing Gifts and Donors

Cost-centered budgeting attributes the real costs, including salaries, to individual fundraising programs so you know whether a program is really making money or not. As salaries and fees make up the largest expenditure in fundraising, this is an important way of looking at return on investment.

Return on investment cannot be measured on the head of a single donor, however. If we slot donors into categories and then limit the cost of recognition and communication to a percentage of the value of their gifts, most donors will never experience the things they need in order to keep on giving. The cost of donor-centered communication needs to be shared across the entire donor pool and across all your fundraising programs.

Categorizing donors by gift size is dangerous because no matter how well you think you know a donor, you never *really* know his potential. You know what she last gave and you may even know a fair bit about her personal holdings, but the philanthropic spirit that is behind the act of giving is not restricted to a set percentage of net worth. If you use giving levels to define your donors, it becomes much harder to see them as the unique individuals they really are . . .

> *One fall, our conservation organization decided to take some donors on a tour of conserved properties. Among the group was an older woman who had given us about $250 a year for the last decade. After the tour, she sent us a $1,000 gift and that was followed by several other similar-sized gifts. We kept in touch with her, which I think she appreciated, though whenever we tried to schedule a visit, she always said she was too busy to see us. We thought this was her polite way of avoiding us; after all, she was 85 years old. Surely, she couldn't be that busy.*
>
> *Then, last July we received another letter in the mail which read:*
>
> *"I was going to give this to you in my will, but I figured, why wait. I would like to remain anonymous."*
>
> *Enclosed with the letter was a check for $100,000.*
>
> *A week later, the Executive Director and I took her out for lunch. She told us that her financial advisor had suggested she invest her money differently as it wasn't making much at the bank. Her idea of a good investment was to give some of it to us. We were very honored.*
>
> *We spent the rest of our lunch talking about wilderness sports. It turns out that she'd just bought a kayak!*

Publishing donors' names is a nightmare. Some of our prominent donors don't always "fit" the criteria (they gave nineteen months ago and our published list only goes back eighteen months) and we make exceptions so as not to offend them but then you struggle with "is that fair?" "are there others who should get special dispensation?" etc.

I feel that publishing donors' names is an important way of recognizing donors that does make a difference. We ask them how they want to be listed and are very careful to adhere to their wishes. If you are going to commit to publishing donors' names then you have to equally commit to the time and effort required to list them correctly.

I'm afraid that in this era of privacy, publishing donors' names is a dinosaur that may not be serving any useful purpose for most donors.

Having a clean and accurate database is the key to success. There is nothing worse than forgetting a donor or mispelling (sic) a name!

The only way to become donor-centered is to *assume* that at any moment in time, all your donors are doing the best they can *within the limitations that restrict their philanthropy*. Some of these limitations are out of everyone's control, like the economy; some are within your donors' control like the number of other charities they made commitments to before you came along; and some limitations are under your control.

You can gradually overcome a donor's hesitancy about investing in your organization by improving your public marketing program. You can overcome his tendency to be cautious when giving to a new charity by reinforcing the importance of that first gift. If you do your part to remove the limitations over which you have control, and combine that with effective, carefully timed solicitations, you will hold on to that donor, and you will get contributions that are increasingly generous within his means.

Urgent Appeals

If your donor attrition is high, you may be focusing on broadcasting your need at the expense of communicating your results. You will not keep donors indefinitely with emergency appeals because even if *you* can sustain that sense of urgency, *they* cannot. Donors need to see your progress; they need to hear from you. Donor-centered communication will provide the balance your donors need between asking for money and demonstrating that their giving is worthwhile.

Failure to Plan

Your Board of Directors holds the key here. The only way a Board can monitor performance and assess productivity is through a strategic plan. The plan articulates the charity's measurable objectives; fulfilling the plan means achieving measurable results. Your donors need these measurable results in order to assess the effectiveness of their giving and decide whether or not to continue their support.

Without a strategic plan, a Board of Directors cannot lead; it can only hope. Yet it remains legally and morally responsible for the achievements of the organization as well as the welfare of its service recipients or the satisfaction of its audience.

It is not a crime if your organization does not currently operate to a well defined strategic plan; but if Board and/or staff refuse to develop and follow a plan, it is. Your donor-centered program will be only as good as your strategic plan. Use all the resources available to you to encourage your Executive Director and Board of Directors to take this essential step.

Failure to Test

You can conduct a test with a very small number of donors at little or no cost. Some time to design the test is required but a good test can be executed without disturbing the entire fundraising operation. Producing results you can rely on through testing will lead to an increasing respect for the science of testing itself. Conducted properly, test results are reliable; you can build on this information and plan accordingly. If you don't test, you are guessing and that is no way to run a fundraising department.

"Test everything" is a winning philosophy. Testing produces numbers that compare one way of doing something with another. This is the language your Board of Directors speaks. They need numbers, facts, weight of opinion; they need a way of assessing future potential; they need information to gauge risk—testing gives both you and them this important security.

Test everything speaks to more than fundraising. When applied to programs and services, hard data also gives you a marketing edge with your donors. You can stand behind a new program initiative with confidence knowing that it has proven itself through advance testing. Your likelihood of success is heightened, your donors' investment risk is minimized, and you stand to raise more money because of the valuable information you bring to the table.

Testing instills a strategic approach to work, it breeds an analytical way of thinking, and it produces decisions based on fact. Testing is fundamental to superior performance.

Time

Time as the enemy in fundraising will gradually be replaced by time as your ally if you engage in donor-centered fundraising. Within a real relationship where you and your donor are communicating, information about what you are achieving now because of his past giving begins to blend with discussions about your future goals and dreams. As your partner, your donor is receiving information and processing it all year round. Because you are always there and available, your donor feels increasingly comfortable about offering his opinion, about asking questions, and about inquiring about your future.

The thing that bothers me about fundraising is its "slickness." I'm looking for organizations that are making a difference; I don't want to be aggressively sold. I want to know the people who are involved and I want them to be able to explain to me why their charity should interest me.

I want my giving to be purposeful. I seldom get information at the time I'm making my giving decisions that helps me be strategic about my philanthropy.

Recent problems with reporting on how donors' gifts are used which got wide national attention have had an impact on my attitude toward giving. The damage has been done. I am now very cautious about charities and their reporting and make more specific demands up front before I give and even more demands before I give for a second time.

We have had at least one for-profit business solicit donors listed in our newsletter by sending a letter saying, "Since we share the same values, you may be interested in learning about our business."

The volume of requests in a single year from a charity is out of control. I get a request again immediately after I've given. Also the huge amount of mail from all charities in direct mail is troublesome. I resent the amount of money all these mailings represent.

I once worked for someone who was heir to a large corporate fortune. I was responsible for going through his mail and was astounded by the volume of solicitations and the crude nature of most of them, as well as how off-the-wall some of their requests were.

Find out whether or not your donor wants to give more than once a year and solicit accordingly.

In traditional fundraising, we ask, we thank, then there's a gap, then we ask again. The gap estranges your donors from your organization, forcing you to start the fundraising process all over again every year. Working like this, it is very hard to get to a level of familiarity where you and your donor are talking with each other; current fundraising methodologies relegate you to talking *at* your donors, and all they can do is react with a decision to give or decline the request.

A donor-centered approach to fundraising and communication will realize much more money but you have to invest the time before earning the return. Professional and volunteer fundraisers have no spare time, so it's a vicious circle. The key is to start small. Begin with one donor-centered activity and limit that activity to a manageable number of donors. Narrow the job at hand so you can deliver an early success. Then the increased revenue will be the proof you and others need to adopt donor-centered fundraising as your official philosophy.

Fundraising Programs and Donor Attrition

You will always be executing fundraising programs, of course; donor-centered fundraising just makes it possible to do a better job. With improved retention and increased gift renewal levels, you will be able to maintain donor acquisition programs at a level that offsets a much lower rate of attrition. You will save both time and money which can then be invested in even more donor-centered communication which, in turn, will produce even more donors and higher gift averages. Success breeds success. The following tables illustrate:

Table 5 shows an initial acquisition campaign that secured 1,000 donors through a direct marketing (DM) program. Industry standards are used to calculate attrition over five subsequent renewal campaigns, bringing the number of retained donors to 170 at the end of the final campaign. This calculation factors in a conversion of 1% of donors from each solicitation to major gift donors, 50% of whom give again in subsequent campaigns. The total of all direct marketing and major gift donors retained at the end of the fifth campaign is 175.

Table 5 – Retention/Attrition of Donors Over Five Campaigns

Campaign	Attrition Rate for Direct Marketing Program	Total DM Donors Retained	Retained DM Donors with 1% Major Gift Donors Removed	New Major Gift Donors @ 1%	Retained Major Gift Donors after 50% Attrition	Total Major Gift Donors
Initial Acquisition	n/a	1,000	n/a	n/a	n/a	n/a
Campaign 1	50%	500	495	5	n/a	5
Campaign 2	30%	347	343	3	3	6
Campaign 3	20%	274	272	3	3	6
Campaign 4	20%	217	215	2	3	5
Campaign 5	20%	172	170	2	3	5

Table 6 – Retention/Attrition of Donors Over Five Campaigns Using Donor-Centered Fundraising

Campaign	Donor-Centered Attrition Rate for DM Donors	Total DM Donors Retained Through Donor-Centered Fundraising	Retained DM Donors with 4% Major Gift Donors Removed	New Major Gift Donors @ 4%	Retained Major Gift Donors after 20% Attrition	Total Major Gift Donors
Initial Acquisition	na/	1,000	n/a	n/a	n/a	0
Campaign 1	25%	750	720	30	0	30
Campaign 2	15%	612	588	24	24	48
Campaign 3	10%	529	508	21	39	60
Campaign 4	10%	457	439	18	48	66
Campaign 5	10%	395	379	16	53	69

Table 6 starts with acquisition of the same 1,000 donors and follows them through five successive campaigns in an organization using a donor-centered fundraising approach. In this calculation, attrition is half the rate of that in Table 5; 4% of donors in each campaign become major gift donors and there is an 80% retention rate of major gift donors campaign to campaign. The number of retained donors by the end of the fifth renewal campaign is 448, a 256% increase. These figures are supported by a combination of our own research and testing, and anecdotal reporting from charities that have instituted donor-centered fundraising techniques. Rapid movement of donors to major giving is due to early, personal intervention by a leadership volunteer. Overall

I gave once to XX in memory of someone and now I'll never get off their list!

We do not have a comprehensive database to track donor relationships, resulting in poor documentation and gaps of information about donors with lengthy giving histories. This limits the number of donor relationships we can move forward.

Fundraisers assume that donors want something for their money. They want to give you address labels, a party or something else. That assumption is not right. I just want to know that my money is going where it's supposed to be going and that it's having an effect.

Gifts are a waste of money and when I receive them I stop giving.

Token gifts like address labels don't replace a good pitch. When I get them I wonder what they cost. Sometimes I give and sometimes I don't when I get incentives in the mail like cards or labels. However, I never want this stuff.

As soon as charities get our gift, they solicit us again—even in the thank you letter.

Table 7 – Revenue Implications Over Five Campaigns Using a Typical Fundraising Approach

Campaign	Attrition Rate	# Retained Donors	Average Gift	Revenue by Gift Type	Total Revenue per Campaign	Accumulated Revenue
Initial Acquisition	n/a	1,000	$25	$25,000	$25,000	$25,000
1 – Direct Marketing		495	$28.75	$14,231		
— Major Gifts	50% (500)	5	$1,000.00	$5,000	$19,231	$44,231
2 – Direct Marketing		343	$33.06	$11,340		
— Major Gifts	30% (347)	6	$1,100.00	$6,600	$17,940	$62,171
3 – Direct Marketing		272	$38.02	$10,341		
— Major Gifts	20% (274)	6	$1,210.00	$7,260	$17,601	$79,772
4 – Direct Marketing		215	$43.72	$9,400		
— Major Gifts	20% (217)	5	$1,331.00	$6,655	$16,055	$95,827
5 – Direct Marketing		170	$50.28	$8,548		
— Major Gifts	20% (172)	5	$1,464.10	$7,321	$15,869	$111,696

Table 8 – Revenue Implications Over Five Campaigns Using a Donor-Centered Fundraising Approach

Campaign	Attrition Rate	# Retained Donors	Average Gift	Revenue by Gift Type	Total Revenue per Campaign	Accumulated Revenue
Initial Acquisition	n/a	1,000	$25	$25,000	$25,000	$25,000
1 – Direct Marketing		720	$31.25	$22,500		
— Major Gifts	25% (750)	30	$1,000.00	$30,000	$52,500	$77,500
2 – Direct Marketing		588	$39.06	$22,967		
— Major Gifts	15% (612)	48	$1,250.00	$60,000	$82,967	$160,467
3 – Direct Marketing		508	$46.87	$23,810		
— Major Gifts	10% (529)	60	$1,562.00	$93,720	$117,530	$277,997
4 – Direct Marketing		439	$56.25	$24,694		
— Major Gifts	10% (457)	66	$1,953.00	$128,898	$153,592	$431,589
5 – Direct Marketing		379	$67.50	$25,583		
— Major Gifts	10% (395)	69	$2,441.00	$168,429	$194,012	$625,601

improvement in retention, whether in direct marketing or major gifts programs, is attributed to improved communication about donors' gifts at work, including measurable results.

The difference in retained donors between Tables 5 and 6 is dramatic, but even more compelling when both the number of donors *and* income from their gifts are taken into account. Tables 7 and 8 start with the same number of donors and average gift value used in Tables 5 and 6. Table 7 shows an average gift increase of 15% for retained donors in each subsequent campaign. Major gift donors start at $1,000, and the average value of those who are retained increases by 10% each campaign.

Table 8 shows how improved performance in donor retention can increase income by more than 500% in only five renewal campaigns. This calculation assumes an average increase in gift value of 25% for all retained donors in each campaign (a figure that is considerably more conservative than the 39% increase achieved in the Paraplegic Association test) plus the movement of 4% of retained donors to the major gifts program.

The most dramatic example of the difference between typical and donor-centered fundraising appears in Table 9 below. Given the compound effect of donor attrition, I wondered how many donors would be required in each campaign and over a five-campaign period in a typical fundraising program just to keep pace with the revenue acquired through donor-centered fundraising. As before, this calculation starts with the same number of donors contributing the same average gift in the acquisition campaign. It takes *9,030 more donors* to raise the same $625,601. No wonder donors are over-solicited and fundraisers are so exhausted!

Table 9 – Number of Donors Required in Typical Fundraising to Keep Pace with Donor-Centered Fundraising

Campaign	Revenue per Campaign with DCF	Total Revenue per Campaign without DCF	Annual Deficit	New Donors Required to Overcome Deficit	Cumulative Total
Initial Acquisition	$25,000	$25,000	$0	0	0
Campaign 1	$52,500	$19,231	$33,269	1,331	1,331
Campaign 2	$82,967	$17,940	$65,036	1,577	2,908
Campaign 3	$117,530	$17,601	$99,929	1,825	4,733
Campaign 4	$153,592	$16,055	$137,537	2,029	6,762
Campaign 5	$194,012	$15,869	$178,143	2,268	9,030

MARKETING

When charities invest in discrete marketing, they raise more money. This is not a contradiction; it is a fact.

One of the most vibrant examples of this I have seen was a wonderfully creative print media campaign designed by an advertising agency providing pro bono services to Oxfam. It was in the mid-nineties during one of the horrendous famines in Rwanda and also when the OJ Simpson saga was in full swing. At the point when the beleaguered public had had just about enough of the trial, a print ad appeared that read something like this:

OJ Simpson restricted to 10 visitors a day

In other news . . . 6 million Rwandans die of starvation

Oxfam

It was the right ad at the right time, and because it was so creative, it was inserted free in dozens of newspapers and magazines. A separate fundraising drive was launched following this marketing program which was, not surprising, very successful. The ad won many industry awards and showed what can be achieved when real marketing professionals sink their creative teeth into an organization with a fabulous mandate.

Charities should be allocating a minimum of 10% of their budgets to marketing; they should have a strategic marketing plan; and they should resource their departments with qualified marketing professionals including, of course, excellent writers.

Marketing that looks and is professional should not be seen as something that only national charities need to have. There was a trend among individual donors in our study to favor charities in their own communities, especially when economic pressures cause them to cut back on the number of organizations they support. Small or local charities should not overlook strategic marketing nor be afraid to hire a professional agency to help with these things (and others) that influence fundraising success:

- Creating an integrated look including logo/mark, design theme, color, and font on all printed and electronic materials. This builds an image that will be reinforced at every opportunity so that eventually there is an immediate connection between the image, the organization and its important mission.

- Defining key messages in terms that catch the attention of the general public.
- Using their influence with the media to get more and better ad placements, stories, public service announcements.
- Integrating marketing and fundraising activities for maximum exposure and effect.

A Donor-Centered Look at Fundraising Expense

Embracing professional and strategic marketing and implementing donor-centered communication will cost money. Together they are investments that will propel your organization into a new standard in fundraising. With the cost and responsibility for acquisition in marketing where it belongs, professional fundraisers and volunteers will be able to put their other talents to work keeping the donors they have already acquired. Loyal donors give more money.[17] Donor-centered fundraising and communication will give donors what they need to become loyal to your cause.

You can expect to make an investment in donor-centered fundraising before you can reap the benefits. You will probably continue carrying the costs of your current fundraising activities as you take on this additional expense. Chapter 12 argues for investment in donor-centered fundraising and a more realistic approach to the testy issue of spending money to make money.

Partnering . . . and really meaning it

Wouldn't it be interesting to attend a conference in which half the delegates were fundraisers and the other half were donors, especially individual donors? How do you think presenters would alter the content of their speeches and their language if they knew that every second seat was occupied by the "target?"

People want to give and they care deeply about the work that charities do. It won't hurt philanthropy to discuss the deficiencies of fundraising methodology

At the community hospital where I worked one physician had been instrumental in not only starting the hospital but also keeping it afloat during difficult years. As time went on, he disclosed that he had also left a substantial gift to our institution in his will. In honor of his efforts, we decided to name the newly remodeled Education Center after him in a special ceremony.

Our physician/donor was also a survivor of the Bataan Death March and had written a book about his experiences as a doctor to the prisoners during the march. Realizing how important his service to the country was to him, we got in touch with the Library of Congress to pursue a listing for him.

On the night of the event, our local Congressman read out loud the inscription on a plaque from the Library of Congress about our donor's life of dedicated service. There were many wet eyes in the audience that night. I will never forget how much it meant to him to be recognized in that special way.

---

[17] The Canadian Centre for Philanthropy's survey on Giving, Volunteering and Participating found that 44% of donors gave to certain organizations regularly but they accounted for 65% of all donations. A similar question has not been posed to respondents in recent American studies.

After giving once we hear from a charity relentlessly even when we've only contributed an in memoriam gift.

Fundraising is in a rut; everyone is doing the same thing.

Someone who works for my wife said she saw her name on a donor wall at the zoo. It was put up there without our knowledge.

The staff time spent getting donors to approve names and messages on donor walls or plaques is a significant concern.

What bothers me about fundraising is that it is never over.

openly with donors. Maybe we should adopt the model of the trucking companies that share the road with the rest of us drivers. "How's my fundraising?" should be printed on the back of every solicitation and communication piece.

It all comes down to you. Donor-centered fundraising is not an "if only" fantasy; it is a bonafide solution to the chronic under-funding of charitable organizations. As the professional fundraiser, you are the one who is closest to the donor most often. When you allow yourself the privilege of seeing your donors as people and not as file numbers, a donor-centered approach to fundraising is the natural next step.

12
Coming Clean on Cost

I'm a big fan of public radio. A few years ago I enthusiastically responded to my local station's on air pledge drive. Awhile later I received an acknowledgment of my contribution on a postcard with the gift amount clearly visible to anyone who cared to look. This made me uncomfortable so I wrote a letter to the development director asking that the station consider sending acknowledgments out to donors in envelopes in the future. I never heard from her. So, two or three months later I decided to renew my concern in a letter to the general manager and, once again, I never received a response. I'm still a devoted listener . . . but I'm not a donor to my public radio station anymore.

We asked donors in the study about their views on cost per dollar raised in fundraising. 27% were unable to offer an opinion. Of those who did, 32% felt that it should cost no more than 10% to raise money, with 26% of this group feeling that fundraising should not exceed 5%. 14% of donors felt that a 15% cost per dollar raised was acceptable; another 10% felt 25% was OK. Only 3% would accept a 35% cost. In a related question that is actually more revealing, we asked donors about the importance that cost per dollar raised plays in their decision-making about the charities they support. Only 12% said that it plays a primary role in their decision making; 24% said that it was not a factor; and 64% said that it was one of several things they considered.

Cost per dollar raised is definitely a reason why donors *stop* giving, however. 12% of study respondents would cease supporting a charity if they felt it was spending too much on fundraising or administration; 33% would discontinue support for mismanagement of funds, which includes but is not limited to spending too much donated revenue on fundraising. It seems that, currently, the majority of donors do not thoroughly investigate cost per dollar raised prior to deciding to support a charity but zero in on that issue as a reason to discontinue giving if a perceived high cost becomes public. However, this may change in the future. Online information that rates charities according to several criteria including cost per dollar raised, is becoming increasingly accessible, and several study donors reported turning to these sources prior to making their giving choices.

What donors feel is an acceptable cost per dollar raised

no opinion **27%**

5 cents or less **8%**

10 cents or less **24%**

15 cents **14%**

20 cents **15%**

25 cents **10%**

35 cents **3%**

Cost per dollar raised plays a primary role in the decision-making of only **12%** of respondents; **24%** do not consider cost per dollar raised at all when making a decision; **64%** say that this is one of several factors they consider.

Charities feel that donors are satisfied with a fundraising cost of **20%**.

We're concerned about the cost of plaques that some charities produce. We don't want it to be obvious that donors' contributions are being spent on gifts back to donors. That's not why we gave them the money.

WHAT ATTRACTS DONORS' ATTENTION TO FUNDRAISING COST?

Most donors react negatively to receiving gifts in recognition of their philanthropy because they are a reminder that you did not spend all their money on its intended purpose. Even if you obtain recognition gifts for free, donors perceive that money has been wasted and staff's valuable time has been diverted from the core work of the organization. Particularly effective at irritating donors are token gifts like address labels or fridge magnets, whether sent in direct marketing solicitations as incentives to give or provided as thank you's after the fact. 82% of opinions from donors on this issue were negative, including observations that token gifts do not influence them to give, they waste charities' scarce resources, they send the wrong message to donors, and they cause donors not to give or to stop giving. Though this issue has a relatively modest impact on budget, it generates a strong negative reaction from donors. Giving gifts in return for the gifts that donors give you is like waving a red flag in front of a bull.

At the other end of the scale is an issue with a significant impact on budget and that is fundraising program configuration. An imbalanced portfolio weighted heavily in fundraising events and direct marketing programs condemns charities to raising money at very high cost. These programs are not designed to hold onto donors long term or maximize their giving, yet they require a significant investment relative to the revenue they generate. The most extreme examples of this emerge when charities relinquish direct responsibility for fundraising and focus only on the net amount of money they receive through supplier agreements. Most suppliers are honorable and just as concerned as their clients about cost containment, but a few are not. When one example of excessive cost gets the attention of the media, all charities and the reputable suppliers are hurt.

HOW MUCH FUNDRAISING COST IS TOO MUCH?

10%, the maximum cost ratio preferred by most donors, has been the standard in fundraising for as long as I can remember. In the 1970's and 80's it was promoted heavily by a small number of charitable organizations who were able to operate fundraising at or below this level and who could position their cost per dollar raised as a marketing advantage. Charities that supported a 10% ceiling had a lock on unique, low cost workplace fundraising, had endowment funds established generations earlier, or were lucky enough to have their fundraising expenses specifically underwritten by a donor.

The vast majority of charities do not run their fundraising operations on anywhere near 10%; in fact, charities in our study averaged 21% cost per dollar raised. The concern that charities have about how fundraising cost is positioned to donors is evident. When asked to indicate their *published* cost per dollar raised, the figure dropped from 21% to 16.6% with 34% of respondents feeling that they had to move some fundraising expenses to other departments in order to demonstrate a more attractive expense ratio.

This sticky issue can make charities feel they are playing a shell game with donors. And, without mandatory reporting of fundraising expenses based on a common set of criteria, donors cannot be sure that they are supporting a charity with a cost-effective fundraising operation.

Consider these examples:

• Universities and colleges have alumni affairs departments where former students are tracked from the day they graduate until (and after) they are ready to give. That could be ten, twenty or more years after they have earned their degree. Not only are their whereabouts kept current, but they are supplied regularly with information about their university and its work. Is the alumni affairs department budget a fundraising expense? In many organizations it is not, including 39% of the educational institutions who took part in this study. In others, the onus is entirely on the fundraiser (and her budget) to find, keep track of, and cultivate donors.

• Many charitable organizations include the salary costs of permanent fundraising staff in some budget other than fundraising, usually administration. As personnel is the single largest part of any department's budget, removing some or all salary and benefits costs from the fundraising budget changes the cost per dollar raised dramatically. Is the remainder a true reflection of what it takes to raise money? No.

We can move figures around and re-label costs in any budget to make it appear as if less money is being spent, but who does that help? No one. It serves only to further ingrain an unrealistic view of what it takes to raise money within the current fundraising structure. The happy news, though, is that

69% of individual donors and **71%** of corporate donors felt that donor recognition should be restricted to **5%** or less of fundraising expenditures. An additional **10%** of individual donors and **14%** of corporate donors said that charities should not spend any money recognizing their donors.

Of the charities in the study with alumni, **37%** maintain a discrete budget for alumni affairs; **47%** include all costs for alumni affairs within the fundraising budget.

Provide a pragmatic accounting of what happened to the money; be very open about what you are doing with the funds you receive and about how much is being spent on fundraising. Donors like honesty and openness more than recognition.

Charities spend approximately **30%** of their fundraising budget on costs related to communicating with or recognizing donors, two thirds of which is devoted to newsletters, other information mailings, staff salaries, training, and volunteer support.

I've always been a supporter of investing to make more money. As a Board member, I once advocated for a doubling of the development staff which put us in deficit. It paid off handsomely.

because donor-centered fundraising retains more donors longer and maximizes their giving potential sooner, it has the ability to reduce cost per dollar raised to a level that satisfies donors. It simply requires charities to invest differently in their fundraising operations.

Investment, not Expense

The moment a donor's first gift is received is the moment that the process of gift renewal begins. This means that everything you do with that donor is an investment in the next gift; it is not "paying for" the last one. The cost of thank you letters to donors in your December acquisition campaign is attributable to your April renewal campaign because thank you letters play their part in influencing donors to give again. Yes, you need to send the donor a written acknowledgment and this is an extension of the gift he already gave, but a thank you letter is more than just a piece of paper that satisfies the IRS requirements. It has an independent function—to reassure the donor that he made the right decision and to begin establishing the desire to give once again.

If charities think of money in the fundraising budget as intelligent investment in future growth instead of regrettable expense, they can begin to alter their behavior from apologetic to confident when reporting cost. Development professionals need to be advocates for sensible investment in fundraising both to their donors and to their Boards of Directors. Given how frugal the fundraising industry and the not for profit sector are, charities shouldn't be ashamed to invest in order to find and keep their donors.

There can be no single formula for establishing a fair cost per dollar raised across the industry because there are simply too many variables. (There are built-in cost efficiencies for organizations representing highly popular or compelling causes or for charities that have been in business for a long time.) There are, however, two meaningful cost ratios in the fundraising budget, and focusing on them will enable you to monitor change and assess overall performance. Each cost ratio is significant to different people in your organization.

The cost per dollar raised across the whole development department is a figure that employers and Boards should be monitoring. By assessing the cost of the collective fundraising activities (fundraising programs, donor communication, testing, and other related fundraising activities) against overall fundraising revenue, the Board of Directors and CEO can determine whether the development department is doing a cost-effective job. It is possible that investing in donor-centered fundraising today may increase your cost per dollar raised temporarily. (It is also possible that it will not because of expenses that will no longer need to be incurred.) However, if you find you do have to invest in donor-centered fundraising at first, your investment/earnings ratio will improve with the next and every subsequent solicitation. Investing in additional donor-centered fundraising and communication strategies as results begin to show will mean better return in the long run, but not at the same moment the investment is made. Just as in any other business or in retirement planning, you must invest first in order to realize a return. The challenge is to make smart investments.

The second cost ratio relates to the individual fundraising programs in use in your organization. The cost per dollar raised per program is of keen interest to the development director, but the expense ratio varies from program to program. In the case of direct marketing programs, cost per dollar raised may rise and fall within a single program year after year and this does not mean that these programs are being poorly managed. (See "Silos are for Farmers, not Fundraisers" in Chapter 13.) The development director, or the person responsible for overall fundraising performance, needs to have the freedom to shift investment priorities among programs or within program segments to anticipate donor trends and capitalize on opportunity. While the development director shapes and budgets individual fundraising programs, the CEO and Board monitor overall performance. That double-check system works and keeps everyone focused on their respective responsibilities.

DONOR-CENTERED INVESTMENT IN FUNDRAISING

Every donor wishes that one hundred cents of every dollar contributed would go directly to the end purpose; but it is a wish and not an expectation. Donors need information, and information can only be transmitted by people. In order to communicate more effectively with your donors, you may decide to increase your investment in personnel or adjust work priorities within your existing staff contingent. At the same time, you will be able to reduce or eliminate other costs that you now incur for commodities or activities that are not as effective at influencing donors' loyalty and future giving. Table 10 provides some examples of worthwhile investments and possible savings.

On average, charities in the study spend 21 cents to raise a dollar. Their published average cost per dollar raised, however, is 17 cents. Charities feel they need to spend **22%** of funds raised in order to be progressively successful in fundraising.

We are more likely to attribute a cost to the marketing budget than to the fundraising budget. This is because the public/donors are more readily accepting of brand building costs than fundraising costs, and marketing can impact the effectiveness of fundraising, but the reverse is not generally true.

Corporations, foundations, and donors fail to see that fundraising/administrative costs are necessary for raising more money. They expect so much from organizations but give so little to help us do the things they expect.

Table 10 – How Donor-Centered Fundraising Affects Fundraising Investment and Generates Cost Savings

Item	Investment	Increased income and/or cost savings	
Newsletter	copywriters/reporters — to gather news as it happens, to spend time with service providers, researchers, artists, etc.	**distribution:** **production cost:** **design/printing:** **development staff time:**	introduce electronic newsletters for those who want it (ask permission first) reduce multi-page, quarterly newsletter to single page bulletin; produce one comprehensive newsletter a year instead, including the annual report use in-house publishing for bulletin reduced
Donor Recognition Event	hire someone to develop an event concept that reflects the organization and is wholly original	hall rentals, big dinners, gifts for donors	
Prompt Thanks	data input personnel and software, as gifts will need to be recorded as they arrive, even in peak flow periods	higher rate of renewal and higher gift average value in next solicitation without increasing renewal program costs	
Personal Thanks by Board Members	time from development staff to manage this activity, assist and support volunteers	major donor acquisition	
Golf Tournament	development staff time to organize a volunteer post-game personal thank you call to players and sponsors the day after the event	higher percentage of repeat registrations made earlier for next year's event which saves marketing/advertising costs	
Donor Acquisition	marketing professional and marketing budget	higher acquisition, higher average gift, higher rate of return without a proportionate increase in acquisition program cost	
Donor Recognition Commodities	framed photo of "gifts at work"	save money on expensive plaques, gifts, pins, and other commodities	

Because improved communication leads to a dramatic increase in giving, cost per dollar raised will become increasingly attractive the longer a donor-centered approach is employed. Tables 11 to 15 compare the gross and net performance of a donor-centered fundraising operation against traditional fundraising for the same period. Even with the cost of additional personnel for donor relations and additional production and distribution costs for communication materials factored into the donor-centered example, the ratio of revenue to expense in the fundraising budget quickly exceeds traditional fundraising performance.

A prominent donor/alumnus was a spokesperson on a campaign video we recently produced. While filming in the president's office, he noticed a topographical map of our state that had been done in 1919. Delighted, he told us that his father had worked on the map and then used the proceeds of the job to buy an engagement ring for the donor's mother.

As a thank you for his contribution to the video, we gave our donor a framed photo of the map and a description of its history. Although he has been one of our state's longest serving and most respected senators, and has received innumerable awards and recognitions, he was very moved by this small gesture.

Table 11 – Revenue Implications Over Five Campaigns Using a Traditional Fundraising Approach

Campaign	Attrition Rate	# Retained Donors	Average Gift	Revenue by Gift Type	Total Revenue per Campaign	Accumulated Revenue
Initial Acquisition	n/a	1,000	$25	$25,000	$25,000	$25,000
1 – Direct Marketing		495	$28.75	$14,231		
– Major Gifts	50% (500)	5	$1,000.00	$5,000	$19,231	$44,231
2 – Direct Marketing		343	$33.06	$11,340		
– Major Gifts	30% (347)	6	$1,100.00	$6,600	$17,940	$62,171
3 – Direct Marketing		272	$38.02	$10,341		
– Major Gifts	20% (274)	6	$1,210.00	$7,260	$17,601	$79,772
4 – Direct Marketing		215	$43.72	$9,400		
– Major Gifts	20% (217)	5	$1,331.00	$6,655	$16,055	$95,827
5 – Direct Marketing		170	$50.28	$8,548		
– Major Gifts	20% (172)	5	$1,464.10	$7,321	$15,869	$111,696

Table 12 – Cost / Revenue Implications Over Five Campaigns Using a Traditional Fundraising Approach

	Total Donations (DM only)	Cost per Donor	Accumulated Cost	Accumulated Revenue
Accumulated Gross Revenue				$111,696
Renewal Costs	2,495	$0.50	($1,248)*	$110,448

* rounded to the nearest whole dollar

Table 13 – Revenue Implications Over Five Campaigns Using a Donor-Centered Fundraising Approach

Campaign	Attrition Rate	# Retained Donors	Average Gift	Revenue by Gift Type	Total Revenue per Campaign	Accumulated Revenue
Initial Acquisition	n/a	1,000	$25	$25,000	$25,000	$25,000
1 – Direct Marketing		720	$31.25	$22,500	$52,500	$77,500
– Major Gifts	25% (750)	30	$1,000	$30,000		
2 – Direct Marketing		588	$39.06	$22,967	$82,967	$160,467
– Major Gifts	15% (612)	48	$1,250	$60,000		
3 – Direct Marketing		508	$46.87	$23,810	$117,530	$277,997
– Major Gifts	10% (529)	60	$1,562	$93,720		
4 – Direct Marketing		439	$56.25	$24,694	$153,592	$431,589
– Major Gifts	10% (457)	66	$1,953	$128,898		
5 – Direct Marketing		379	$67.50	$25,583	$194,012	$625,601
– Major Gifts	10% (395)	69	$2,441	$168,429		
– Total		3,634				
		273				

Table 14 – Cost Implications Over Five Campaigns Using a Donor-Centered Fundraising Approach

	Total Donations (DM only)	Cost per Donor	Accumulated Cost	Accumulated Revenue
Gross Revenue from Table 13				$625,601
DM Renewal Costs[18]	3,634	$48.50	($176,249)	$449,352
MG Renewal[19]	273	$75.00	($20,475)	$428,877

[18] Includes costs over and above those incurred in traditional fundraising. This calculation allows for 0.2 hours additional time per donor for data entry; 0.6 hours per donor for stewardship, and an additional $20 per donor for costs of communication materials' production and distribution per campaign.

[19] Assumed average cost of major gifts stewardship set at $75 per donor per solicitation in both donor-centered and traditional fundraising methodologies.

Table 15 – Comparison of Net Revenue: Traditional Fundraising versus Donor-Centered Fundraising

	Gross Revenue (DM & MG)	Total Donations Direct Marketing Major Gifts	Average cost per donor[20]	Accumulated Cost	Accumulated Revenue (DM & MG)
Donor-Centered Fundraising	$625,601	3634/	$48.50	($176,249)*	$428,877
		273	$75.00	($20,475)	
Traditional Fundraising	$111,696	2495/	$0.50	($1,248)*	$111,696
		27	$75.00	($2,025)	
Performance of DCF over Traditional Approach	$513,905	1139/	$48.00	($175,001)*	$317,181
		246	$75.00	($18,450)	

*rounded to nearest whole dollar

Table 15 shows that even though the cost of stewardship is higher in donor-centered than in traditional fundraising, the donor-centered approach raised well over $300,000 more in net revenue in the same period of time. But this is not the whole picture. If we look again at gross revenue performance (Table 13), donor-centered fundraising raised $625,000 against $112,000 through a traditional fundraising methodology (Table 11). If traditional fundraising were to attempt to catch up with donor-centered, it would require an additional 9,030 donors to overcome the higher attrition rates and lower gift values. Table 16 illustrates.

Table 16 – Number of Donors Required in Traditional Fundraising to Keep Pace with the Gross Revenue Raised Through Donor-Centered Fundraising

Campaign #	Revenue per Campaign with DCF	Total Revenue per Campaign without DCF	Annual Deficit	New Donors Required to Overcome Deficit	Cumulative Total
Initial Acquisition	$25,000	$25,000	$0	0	0
Campaign 1	$52,500	$19,231	$33,269	1,331	1,331
Campaign 2	$82,967	$17,940	$65,036	1,577	2,908
Campaign 3	$117,530	$17,601	$99,929	1,825	4,733
Campaign 4	$153,592	$16,055	$137,537	2,029	6,762
Campaign 5	$194,012	$15,869	$178,143	2,268	9,030
Total			$513,905		9,030

[20] Costs to steward major gift donors are the same for both traditional and donor-centered fundraising.

Some charities are very creative about involving donors in their work. For example, Sloan Kettering is working on pain management in cancer and they have held several seminars on the subject designed especially for donors.

9,030 more donors will make gross revenue in traditional fundraising equal to that of the donor-centered alternative. However, when the objective is to match donor-centered fundraising's *net* revenue performance, even more donors are required in traditional fundraising.

If we estimate a 2% performance in acquisition, traditional fundraising would need 451,500 prospect names in order to realize the required 9,030 extra donors offering 15,157 donations over the five campaigns. This will require an investment of $225,750 at an assumed 50 cents per prospect, plus an additional $13,464 for major gift stewardship and direct mail renewal campaigns to existing donors, reducing the total net revenue to $275,000.

A donor-centered approach to fundraising raised $429,000 net through 3,907 donations from the retained portion of 1,000 donors acquired in the initial acquisition campaign. Performance exceeded traditional fundraising by 56%. (See Table 15.)

Finally, if we leave off major gift donors and look only at the 3,634 donors who gave initially and continue to give through direct marketing, donor-centered fundraising raises $145,000 from these donors but spends $176,000 on solicitation and enhanced stewardship. Most charities would balk at this performance and, in so doing, relegate themselves to endless, expensive, and time-consuming acquisition in the hope that they will get ahead. But, of course, they never will. By the second or third campaign, traditional fundraising can never catch up because donor-centered methodology is producing many more major gift donors whose performance is much more lucrative.

SHOULD INVESTMENT EVER EXCEED RETURN?

Fundraising is a specialized form of sales, and fundraisers can learn a valuable lesson about customer (donor) development from salespeople. In sales, customers fall into one of four groups:

Group 1: These are the customers who can be counted on to buy whenever a new product comes out. They are the salesperson's current high return on investment not only because they buy but because they need little encouragement (investment) to do so.

Group 2: Still excellent customers, those in Group 2 buy often but not at the same level of dependability as Group 1 customers. They need more attention (investment) but they are still very profitable.

Group 3: These are potential customers who have not yet become purchasers. They are going to buy but not before they learn how the product can help them and why they should buy from this company rather than from the competition. To get them to that point, they will require more of the salesman's attention (investment) than Group 2. The salesman knows the investment is worthwhile because they will eventually move into either Group 1 or 2 and this early investment will pay off in the long term.

Group 4: These are also potential customers who have not yet become purchasers. They are not going to buy. Investment in this group will be time and money wasted.

The parallels between the salesperson's customer profiles and our donor profiles are obvious. Group 1 donors are our "resilient philanthropists" referenced in Chapter 3—those loyal donors who keep giving and give increasingly generous gifts. Group 2 donors are also significant donors but require a greater effort from fundraisers in order to retain their loyalty and increase their level of generosity over time.

But, what is the difference between Group 3 and Group 4? Neither customer group has yet purchased the product, so how does the salesperson know who is going to buy and who is not? By communicating with them. That's why there are sales territories; that's why salespeople make personal visits and calls; in fact, that is why there are salespeople period. Only by getting to know the potential customer is a salesperson able to develop an educated opinion about his likelihood of buying and whether or not time and money should continue to be invested in that relationship.

The slight difference in fundraising is that Group 3 and Group 4 members have all given at least one gift. They are identified as donors (customers) but their future is very unpredictable and they are not yet profitable for the charity. Apart from a few exceptional examples of donors who make substantial contributions the first time they give, most donors begin to support a charity with low average contributions through high cost fundraising programs. The only way to determine which of these donors belong in Group 3 or Group 4 is to communicate with them. And, the sooner you do, the sooner you will be able to move Group 3 donors out of high cost fundraising programs and into high revenue, cost effective alternatives. Group 4 donors will then move on to another charity where the fit may be better able to inspire their generosity.

Investment of time and money cannot be measured on the head of a single donor. Sometimes you are investing more per prospect or even per donor than

---

47% of individual donors and **67%** of corporate donors would be willing to see more money spent on fundraising if it meant that donors would be provided with more useful information on their gifts at work, especially measurable results. Of the donors who would not be in favor of this, most indicated that this information should already be available and ensuring its ready access is a management issue which should not be an additional responsibility of fundraisers.

Having eight hospitals in our system and being a fairly young organization, it is expensive and time consuming to inventory all donor walls and give them a consistent format without alienating donors from the individual hospitals.

It is best to spend on marketing early in the year because it is always the first thing to go as the year progresses and the CEO starts cutting the budget.

We've been managing a $3 million Capital Campaign with existing staff, a volunteer management group, and one ten-hour per week staff person. It has left very little time for non-soliciting communication with donors. We deeply regret that.

The XX Society is notorious for sending multiple mailings. I supported them once and became so frustrated by this that I called them up and said, "I bet the money I gave you this year has done nothing but pay for the huge number of solicitations." It didn't do any good because they're still sending them...but I'm not giving to them anymore.

you are getting in return. But that's why it's called investment, not expense. When you know your donors, you know which ones warrant your continuing confidence and investment in their future return.

Selling Your Donor-Centered Budget Internally

Testing is your key to success. If you want your CEO and your Board to approve a budget that increases investment in fundraising personnel, you must prove to them that it will result in significantly more revenue. Fundraisers have an obligation to bring decision-makers the facts and to create forecasts that are based on statistical evidence. (See Chapter 7.)

Donors as Capital Assets in Fundraising

When we think of capital assets, we think of property or goods with an economic value. In accounting terms, we also think of depreciating the value of capital assets over a number of years. Donors are a development department's capital assets, with a twist. They are the equivalent of the office furnishings that never wear out, the computer that never needs upgrading, the photocopier that never needs repair. They are the fundamental capital asset in fundraising that never depreciates—except through neglect. Just as a business includes both assets and income, so too does fundraising with the donors themselves as the assets and their gifts the income. Assets and income combined are required to get the job done.

The newly acquired donor, not the acquisition process, is the starting point for fundraising. If charities thought about donors in terms of capital assets, it would eliminate the stress over cost of acquisition, while putting the onus squarely on fundraisers' shoulders to keep donors giving for much longer.

It's time to break out of the old way of thinking which assumes that any money spent on fundraising is distasteful. To sustain fundraising growth, charities must utilize the best available professional expertise and fundraising tools at their disposal. What should not be tolerated is increasing cost without a healthy return. Investment in donor-centered fundraising will be justified by its dramatic return on that investment.

13
Managing a Donor-Centered Charity

While compiling our first directory, we took the opportunity to conduct a direct mail appeal to 22,000 alumni. Among the contributions we received was a check for $1,000. We issued a prompt thank you letter and a few weeks later called the donor to invite her to a small celebration we were holding at the college.

During our conversation, she asked us how she might help us further. I suggested an endowed scholarship but cautioned that it required a $5,000 contribution which could, however, be paid over time. She told me that she would check with her husband and get back to me.

At the event a few weeks later, our alumna/donor and her husband said they were interested in the scholarship but they had one problem. They wanted to establish a $25,000, not a $5,000 endowment. "Would that be OK?"

Shortly thereafter, our alumna's husband was nominated to serve on our Board of Directors and asked to chair our next golf tournament. Three months after he joined the Board, we announced our capital campaign. The top gift, $500,000, named the building. Twenty-four hours later he called to say that he would like to name the building for his recently deceased father.

Our wonderful donors progressed from acquisition through direct mail to campaign lead donors in about a year.

This story is a great example of everyone pulling together to maximize fundraising potential. The college's direct mail firm suggested the initial appeal that acquired the donor; fundraising staff were on the ball in making prompt and personal contact with the new donor; a successful event with gracious hosts made it easy for the donor and her husband to offer more; and the Board of Directors saw an opportunity for both the college and the donor/volunteer that led to the campaign lead gift.

We won't be able to simply layer donor-centered fundraising over what we already do. A new approach to communicating with donors will require us to rethink how we ask for money, how we process gifts, how we work with external suppliers, what we ask of our volunteers, how we structure job descriptions and set goals, and how we run development departments.

One person needs to be accountable for stewardship, but donor
relations should be included in
everyone's job description, from
administrative staff to the CEO.

The greatest challenges in donor
relations are consistency and time-
liness. Having someone focused
solely on this function would mean
that donors would get the individual attention they deserve.

THE DEVELOPMENT DEPARTMENT

Silos Are for Farmers, not Fundraisers

The way development departments are structured and managed works against the principles of donor-centered fundraising.

Practitioners learn about fundraising by studying its money-raising programs as isolated entities. Development departments are run in the same way with fundraising programs managed and executed as if each one were independent of the next. Personnel are hired to oversee individual fundraising programs and are separated from the managers of other programs. (The planned giving office is to your right; the direct mail operation is down the hall.) Focused on fundraising as only the raising of money, staff are directed to maximize each program's revenue in isolation. By taking this approach, fundraising "silos" are created, and by insisting that every silo make a profit, the opportunity to make much more money is forfeited.

To understand the impact of a silo approach on fundraising, consider the first lesson you ever learned in the business—the lesson of the donor pyramid. The donor pyramid recognizes that the donor himself is at the core of fundraising. The fundraiser's job is to design programs and communication strategies around the donor that capture his initial interest and, over time, facilitate his increasing generosity. A typical donor pyramid has direct marketing programs at the bottom. Moving up the pyramid, a donor has the option of participating in fundraising events, contributing major gifts, and committing a planned gift. A well constructed donor pyramid also acknowledges that communication is required to move donors from one level of the pyramid to the next. The donor pyramid is shaped like a triangle and not like a ladder because fewer and fewer donors make more generous gifts as they progress upward. That is true; but in a donor-centered environment, the pyramid becomes an isosceles trapezoid[21] as a greater percentage of donors occupies the space at the top.

A silo approach to fundraising is one that increases the likelihood that donors will stay in the lower tiers of the pyramid. Silo fundraising exerts artificial control over donors' own decision-making process, resulting in too few donors moving into higher level fundraising programs at the time they are actually ready to do so. This is why:

---

[21] I had to go back to grade school for a couple of weeks to figure this one out.

1. *Limited product choice*

Any organization that decides against or defers the introduction of a major gifts or planned gifts program is limiting donors' options and, by default, limiting its own ability to make money. This is a basic tenet of doing business—if you don't offer the product, you can't compete in the marketplace. Along with offering the product comes the expectation that you can stand behind it. If you say you offer a planned gifts program but do not put appropriately trained staff in the job or promote your program sufficiently, your donors will "buy the product" elsewhere. *Justifies B. Hoffman*

2. *Losing too many donors too early*

Early donor attrition is directly related to lack of effective communication, and this is supported by the research findings that are explored in this book. If your attention and your budget are diverted into recouping donors because of high attrition (see Chapter 11), you are forced into putting the majority of your effort and your investment funds into programs at the bottom of the pyramid.

3. *Managing to the bottom line by program instead of by the entire development department*

If your development department includes one or more program managers, such as coordinator of direct mail or canvassing program manager, and if you are responsible for supervising those staff, how do you evaluate performance? You probably take into account gross and net revenue, number of active donors, average gift value, and other important considerations such as how they get along with colleagues. However, your most important consideration should be the number of donors who move up and out of direct marketing into higher level fundraising programs.

Donors give at different levels within single programs as they do across the spectrum of all fundraising programs. Often, though not always, donors who continue to give also continue to increase their gift size, so by the time a donor is ready to move out of your direct mail program she may be giving at the top of the range. If you are evaluating your staff against gross to net revenue in a single fundraising program, then the direct mail manager is motivated to keep that top performing donor in the direct mail program. These examples illustrate:

There is so much turnover in fundraising departments that stewardship of our grant goes by the wayside. Development departments need succession planning.

Our agency has one full time development director and a part time receptionist who does data entry for donations and generates thank you letters. The development director writes all newsletters, annual appeals, annual report, runs special events, handles volunteer management, researches and writes operating grants, etc., etc. There is no time left over for donor relations.

How the Direct Mail Manager Thinks and Acts in a Department of Fundraising Program Silos

- The development director wants me to assign my twenty-five top level donors to the major gifts program. They give an average of $500 each per year, or $12,500 total. This represents 5% of my gross revenue.
- I have to show an increase in gross and net return each year; otherwise the development director gives me a poor evaluation.
- To make up for the loss of $12,500 from my top donors, I would have to acquire over 350 new donors at our average entry level of $35.
- To acquire that many new donors in direct mail, I will need to expand the acquisition program by about 35,000 prospect names.
- Assuming I can even find that many suitable prospects, it will cost $17,500 to solicit them.
- My immediate net loss for forfeiting my top donors to the major gifts officer is $30,000. Plus it will take me several more years to build the replacement donors up into more profitable giving patterns.
- Everybody hates me. My development director is an idiot.

How the Direct Mail Manager Thinks and Acts in a Donor-Centered Department

- I have twenty-five donors at the top of my direct mail program who are giving an average of $500 each annually. They have been in the program for an average of three years and I am very concerned that they may soon tire of the arm's length relationship they have with our organization through direct mail. Even though I and my Board members are doing our best to communicate with them from time to time, it is risky to let them languish any longer in the direct mail program.
- I am going to suggest to the major gifts manager that we work together to create a bridge between my program and hers. I'm setting a meeting for next Wednesday where we will develop strategies to move these donors up.
- If only 60% of these donors give a major gift sometime in the next year at the average entry level value of $5,000, that would realize $75,000, or five times what they give us now and considerably more than it will cost me to rebuild my numbers in

the direct mail program. We can increase their likelihood of giving by making these asks in cooperation with the Board members who have been communicating with them.

- Everybody will love me. I'll be promoted into my development director's job.

Taking a broader view of bottom line performance serves donors better and makes more money. This means that the gross to net revenue of the collective department is what really matters. Real performance increase across the whole department is impacted most dramatically by real performance improvement at the top of the giving pyramid; that is, in your major gifts programs. So, if the first responsibility of all staff is movement of donors upward and not making more money in the "feeder" programs, a whole lot will change for the better.

Working in and Managing a Donor-Centered Development Department

As long as the focus is on fundraising programs and not on helping donors find their optimum giving level, each charity will have to carry far more donors than it really needs. Every development office will spend too much time and far too much money on donor acquisition as fundraisers try desperately to compensate for losing too many donors who languish in inappropriate fundraising programs.

Eliminating the silos will change how staff work, how they interact with each other, how they are motivated for success, how staff meetings are run, and, most important, how they think about and interact with donors.

In a donor-centered development office, every employee needs to see the whole picture. Though each may be a specialist in his particular fundraising program, it is the "connection" between programs that matters the most. A donor-centered fundraising plan is essential. This is a plan that focuses on movement through programs and maximizing gift potential and it is certainly a plan that puts donors first. To ensure its effectiveness, the fundraising plan should be created by the entire development department staff; everyone from the receptionist to the CEO has a part to play in getting and keeping your donors.

Staff meetings should also be donor-centered. Reporting on individual fundraising programs is rather meaningless in the context of donor-centered fundraising, but reporting on the movement of donors is incredibly productive. An emphasis on the connections between the fundraising programs will automatically create a new way of working among development staff. They will need each other more. Cooperation rather than isolation will become the norm

33% of charities in the study have staff dedicated to donor relations.

Most common duties of dedicated donor relations staff:
composing thank you letters **88%**
communicating individually with donors **70%**
planning donor recognition events **68%**
writing newsletters **61%**
managing giving levels/honor rolls **58%**
dealing with donor walls **57%**
calling donors to thank them for gifts **56%**
visiting donors **51%**

Most common duties by time spent:
administrative activities **33%**
writing reports for donors **25%**
planning donor recognition events **15%**
composing thank you letters **14%**
visiting donors **13%**

53% of donor relations staff are employed at the management level; **26%** are senior staff reporting directly to management; **19%** are mid level staff; **2%** are junior.

Where charities have hired one or more staff whose time is wholly dedicated to donor relations, the stewardship work of other staff has been affected in different ways. For **37%** of charities, other staff are just as involved in donor relations; other staff are no longer involved in stewardship in **24%** of charities; and for **34%**, donor relations staff have alleviated some of the work, allowing other staff to become involved in new stewardship activities.

In our organization, all development staff are involved in donor relations, including the executive director. Therefore, all of us have a relationship with our donors. A dedicated staff person would be a detriment as it would create a department where one staff member always did the asking and another one did the thanking. It would also mean that only one staff member had an in-depth knowledge of the donor.

and staff will become more innovative. A top down style of management will not be necessary; in fact, it will be counter-productive.

Evaluations will become more interesting and meaningful. I am reminded of a situation that a former client and colleague found herself in a few years ago. As development director, she had increased department revenue by 75% in one year by focusing in the major gifts area. During her annual evaluation, she was criticized for failing to maintain revenue in the direct mail renewal program, though overall performance of the department had been outstanding. She left that organization and the charitable sector soon after. What a loss. Managing staff in a donor-centered department means changing supervision and evaluation criteria to suit the new environment.

So much more is possible and work is more enjoyable when you step out of the fundraising program silos. Imagine the weekly staff meeting as a strategic discussion about the readiness of individual donors for new fundraising approaches. Imagine a meeting where revenue and expense is reported on the department as a whole, and not by program, and where everyone on staff feels responsible for that success or for that under-performance. Imagine a staff structure that includes a few direct marketing program specialists plus several relationship specialists who are each assigned a contingent of donors. Imagine that those relationship specialists can call upon a roster of internal or external consultants who assist them in strategizing approaches to donors and configuring creative gift options.

Donor Relations Staff

30% of the charities in this study have staff dedicated to the job of donor relations, with over 80% positioned at the level of either management or senior staff reporting directly to management. Introducing the position of donor relations has, in the majority of cases, enhanced rather than replaced the work being done in this area by other staff. This is appropriate for two reasons. First, the job is simply too big to be handled by one donor relations staff member except for charities with a small number of donors. Second, charities will be more successful in making the transition to a customer service model in fundraising if everyone understands what it takes to communicate effectively and plays an active role in the stewardship process.

70% of charities in the study do not have anyone employed exclusively in donor relations; rather stewardship duties are shared among all or most fundraising staff.

Either way works. The key to success lies in managing for results. A competent donor relations professional can design a stewardship program that provides donors with relevant information about their gifts at work and appropriate and timely acknowledgment of their support. If hired at a sufficiently senior level, a donor relations manager can make sure that the program gets implemented. In the absence of a dedicated stewardship position, the responsibility for program design and delivery falls to the development director or CEO. Because donor-centered fundraising is bucking the trend, it will be hard to resist the pressure to bypass communication in favor of more solicitation. So, endorsement of good customer service in fundraising and constant reinforcement of its benefits are required—and that needs to come from the very top of the fundraising operation.

Even with dedicated donor relations staff, charities can get bogged down with activities that do not draw donors closer and which are, in fact, administrative support. Though some administration is essential, charities in the study typically reported 40% or more of donor relations staff time was spent in activities that did not involve communicating information to donors or acknowledging their support. A strategic plan for donor communication will help keep all staff on track and focused on the really important work.

DONOR-CENTERED FUNDRAISING INVOLVES EVERYONE

In a charity that operates on donor-centered principles, everyone contributes to fundraising success, not just development office staff.

The Role of the Executive Director or CEO in Donor-Centered Fundraising

Planning
The charity's executive director or CEO has the most far-reaching impact on donor-centered fundraising. She, more than anyone, has the power to sanction or impede the creation and adoption of a strategic plan for programs and services. Although the Board of Directors is the ultimate authority on this matter, it cannot introduce a strategic, results-based plan without the full cooperation and leadership of the executive director.

If you are an executive director working without a plan that includes specific, measurable results, it may be because you feel such a plan limits your options and stifles creativity. But, in reality, you are making your job harder. As long as specific targets are not defined, there is no way of objectively measuring

At work we hold an auction every year and proceeds go to the United Way. Their executive director comes every time and really participates. This is a very nice gesture and makes the event much more fun.

All staff have a role to play in donor relations and should receive formal training in it. Everybody sells. Everybody sells all the time.

Having a separate recognition program for sponsors really helps alleviate confusion and disgruntled corporate donors.

Too much effort is spent asking; far too little is spent acknowledging.

the performance of your staff or, for that matter, your own performance. This is a less satisfying way to work, though it is sometimes seen as "safe" by people new to management and less confident about their own abilities (see Chapter 8, pages 90–93).

In fact, a results-based strategic plan is an invaluable aide for all executive directors whether they are highly skilled practitioners in people management or just learning the art. A strategic plan creates excitement and unites the entire staff behind a common purpose. On a practical level, a plan has the power to focus and shorten staff meetings, and to be an objective and useful gauge of staff performance.

By articulating the charity's purpose and long term goals, and by further stating its present and near future objectives in measurable terms, the strategic plan provides the basis for designated giving. As designated giving is the key to improved donor acquisition and loyalty, a strategic plan is directly related to improved gross and net performance in fundraising.

Managing for Results

Effective management of the development department and its director in donor-centered fundraising means managing for overall results in donor retention, donor movement, and growth in gross and net revenue across the collective fundraising portfolio. Regular reporting on donor attrition, with a view to minimizing the loss of donors in all fundraising programs over time, is a priority; so is reporting on the number of donors who move up from direct marketing programs. Rate of attrition should continue to diminish over time until it levels off. At this point, your organization will be able to determine the rate of annual acquisition required to replenish lost donors. Until then, you may be in a building mode, investing in acquisition, creating new ways of communicating with donors, and refining your direct marketing programs. If you are showing results in reduced attrition plus movement of more donors up to major giving more quickly, then your investment is paying off. If not, a review of the fundraising plan and the internal management of development department programs and personnel is warranted.

Donor Recognition and Communication

The executive director has a unique role to play in communicating with donors. Donors appreciate receiving contact from different people inside the charities they support. They also assess the importance that charities place on their giving, in part, by the person and the position with whom they communicate. Donors feel that fundraising staff's job centers around solicitation, supplying information on gifts at work, and dealing with day-to-day matters concerning donors' relationships with the charities they support. Although a fundraiser who is also a highly skilled communicator can certainly impress a donor, he cannot represent the highest level of authority of the charity or institution. The CEO and the Board play that role.

There are times outside the asking process when the CEO is certainly the best person to be communicating with a donor. The CEO sees the big picture more clearly than do specialized staff, and he has a grasp on the details better than do Board members. When talking about connecting a donor's money to the long term goals of the organization in a pragmatic way, no one does it better than the chief executive officer.

The Board of Directors

Planning and Monitoring

If you remember attending your first Board meeting and feeling disconnected from the discussion and decision-making, imagine how your donors must feel. As the body of leadership volunteers ultimately responsible for the charity's success, the Board of Directors has a special connection to the donors who make that success possible.

Along with the CEO, the Board of Directors is in the driver's seat when it comes to strategic planning. It is difficult to make critical decisions when you are not involved day-to-day in an organization's work. Frankly, it is impossible to set policy and monitor for results when you don't know what you are trying to achieve. For more than anyone else in the organization, a strategic plan makes it possible for the Board of Directors to do its job.

A good plan states clear objectives in measurable terms. The Board is ultimately responsible for seeing that those objectives are met. In fundraising, monitoring only the money puts Boards and CEOs in the weak position of commenting on current performance or, worse, playing Monday morning quarterback. For Boards to stay ahead of the game and to really fulfill their role as the guardians of their charities' *future* financial health, they need to concentrate on these evaluation measures when assessing fundraising performance:

- The rate of donor retention across the entire fundraising portfolio. This figure should always be going up; the level at which it should be rising should reflect the requirements of the strategic plan. (Donor retention in individual fundraising programs is monitored by the director of development.)

- The rate of movement of retained donors from lower to higher level fundraising programs. Retaining donors is important; but the objective is not to retain them in the direct marketing programs. Leaders should insist on an increasing number of donors graduating into top tier fundraising programs. They should also be confident that the staffing contingent is sufficient in both number and capability to make that happen.
- Increasing control over donor acquisition. Improved retention and upward movement of donors will be a welcome replacement for prolific, high cost donor acquisition. Once other measures are in place to hold on to donors more effectively, acquisition will be required only to replace the diminishing percentage of donors who lapse. It is important to remember that more donors do not mean more revenue. More donors mean more cost, more expensive staff time wasted, and a fundraising operation that is running at an unnecessarily high level of risk.

Boards and CEOs should not entertain new fundraising concepts, even donor-centered ones, without prior testing. And, performance statistics from controlled testing should be the basis of any fundraising forecast or budget requiring Board approval.

Donor Relations

Along with the CEO, the Board focuses on the long range goals of the organization while staff work to realize its current objectives. As such, the charity's Board and donors collectively represent its future. When donors are introduced to the future dreams of an organization as well as to its present need, their dreams for their own philanthropy expand. That is why it is so important for volunteers to interact directly with donors. Both speak the same language.

This study shows, in dramatic terms, how much weight donors place on personal contact with members of the Board. 95% of respondents said that they would be very impressed if a member of the Board thanked them promptly and personally for a gift. But the way they answered this question also revealed how under-impressed they are now with the absence of meaningful contact. When asked specifically, "What would you think if a member of the Board of Directors called you within a day or two of receiving your gift just to say thank you?" donors were more likely to say that they would be impressed but that they would also be extremely surprised if it happened (see sidebar, page 76). The test of personal thank you calls conducted with the Paraplegic Association demonstrates how pleasurable personal contact with donors is for both contributors and Board members. Donors hold leadership volunteers in very high esteem. If for no other reason than experiencing the joy of spending time with someone who appreciates you for the volunteer work you do, call a donor today!

If you like everything about being on the Board of Directors except having to ask for money, then donor-centered fundraising is for you. When communication with and recognition of donors is the priority, asking for money becomes simply a natural extension of the relationship. It is much easier to ask a donor for a gift if you have been in contact with that person or company before. If the last contact you had with a donor was to thank him for his generosity and to talk about what the organization was going to do with his money, don't you think the donor would be eager to hear from you again? If you are then able to report measurable results, the donor is likely to offer another gift before you muster up the courage to ask for it. Donor-centered fundraising creates a seamless relationship with donors and turns the job of asking for money from a nightmare into something quite bearable.

According to our study, most of the time spent in donor recognition and communication is contributed by staff. A more equitable balance needs to be struck between staff and volunteer participation in donor communication. Donors are sensitive to the seniority and authority grid inside charitable organizations. If they never hear from leadership volunteers, it says to them that their financial support is not important. I have never known a volunteer who really thinks this. Workloads and priorities need to be adjusted to put the emphasis on the things that matter most.

Where Should Leadership Volunteers' Time and Attention Be Applied?

This research study provides evidence that communication is a prime motivator of fundraising success. Typical fundraising practice, however, positions communication as a reaction to past giving rather than as a strategy to boost fundraising performance. This is especially true when it comes to communication between members of the Board and donors. Leadership volunteers have the ability to influence retention and the upward movement of donors more than anyone else. But most members of the Board interact only with donors who have already made gifts of significant value. While these donors definitely need and deserve acknowledgment from the top of the organization, reserving leadership volunteers' influence for these donors severely limits Board members' ability to impact overall fundraising performance.

59% of charities are dissatisfied with their volunteers' contributions to donor relations.

Sometimes Boards get too inward looking and think their way of doing things is the only way. If they spent more time communicating with their donors, their frame of reference would expand.

I'm on the Board of a local hospital which is in the midst of a capital campaign. One of my fellow Board members recently secured a ten million dollar gift. I ran into him at a business meeting and thanked him personally for his work. Then I thanked him again when I saw him later on. He was very appreciative. Never underestimate or take for granted the work of other volunteers, even when you are the chairman of the campaign.

Board members should be open to questions from donors and be well informed. Also, being clear about why they volunteer on the Board is helpful to donors as it adds to the argument about why we should support them.

Early communication by leadership volunteers secures loyalty and triggers higher level giving. Therefore, charities who want their Board members to influence giving will be asking them to interact with donors who have made smaller contributions. These questions will arise and they should be discussed openly:

Will the donor who gave a modest gift be embarrassed that he was called by a member of the Board?

No. Our testing shows that this doesn't seem to be the case. First, charities make judgment calls when they compare the gift sizes of all contributors to a campaign, ranking them by amount and labeling the smaller gifts as less generous. But donors aren't comparing their gift size with anyone else's at the time they are writing a check. Though *you* may think a donor's contribution is insignificant, *he* doesn't. Second, meaningful contact focuses on the importance of the *donor* to the organization, not the donor's gift. This is the beginning of a relationship, or at least that is what the contact is trying to achieve.

Are Board members too important for this task?

This is a perfectly legitimate question. It is the responsibility of staff to make sure that leadership volunteers are directing their time and effort to the work that will most significantly impact fundraising success. Here is where testing comes into play. Conduct a test; evaluate test results; let the test results guide your long-term decisions.

If the majority of your charity's Board members live a privileged lifestyle and/or occupy the leadership positions in industry, then they may be more comfortable communicating with "one of their own." But, the mark of a real leader and a skilled communicator is that he is as comfortable interacting with a blue collar worker as with a CEO. This is what defines communication as an art form and not just an activity. The fact remains that philanthropy is only partially tied to wealth. Thousands of regular folk only realize their philanthropic potential in death because they weren't provided with the welcoming attention and reinforcement that would have spawned their largess in life. We never really know how much a person is worth, no matter how clever our research is. And, we definitely don't know what motivates someone to support one charity over another . . . unless of course we give them an opportunity to tell us.

We are not the philanthropy police. Our job is to encourage the generosity of all who want to give. A Board of Directors that demonstrates that it is genuinely interested in all donors, no matter what their giving capacity, is a Board with its priorities straight and a Board that can't help but convey its own decency. That, in itself, will make donors want to give as generously as they can.

No Board or charity wants to send the message: "Only the rich need apply," so let's not limit our fundraising potential by deciding that certain people are philanthropists and others are not.

Managing External Suppliers That Communicate Directly with Your Donors

If you contract with an external direct mail, canvassing, or telemarketing company, you might wish to assess your relationship by making a prioritized list of the reasons why you prefer to work with an outside supplier. If your reasons are negative: "To get the work off my shoulders," or "Because I don't have time," you may not be getting all you can from your supplier relationship. The best reasons to engage an outside firm for direct marketing programs are positive ones such as:

- "To apply high level expertise and greater breadth of experience to our direct mail program."
- "To improve donor acquisition or retention beyond our own level of capability in our canvassing program."

When you work with a service provider for positive reasons, you have the makings of a real partnership. In typical fundraising, though, it comes down to money. The supplier with the lowest bid is the supplier that gets the contract. But the more important issue is determining which supplier could build the number of donors and make more money *if* investment were adequate. Here is a particularly good opportunity for controlled testing.

If you want your external suppliers to treat your donors and prospects as the precious commodities they are, you the client need to make the supplier contract worthwhile and you need to insist on improved performance. You aren't selling carpet cleaning here. You, and they, are creating philanthropists.

To facilitate a true partnership with service providers in which both parties work together to maximize donor satisfaction and giving, charities need to:

1. Award contracts based on more than just bottom line cost.

Hire a direct marketing firm that understands the entire continuum of fundraising and the role that direct mail, telemarketing, or canvassing plays in readying donors for major gifts. Be confident that your supplier can recognize a donor who may be ready to move to a higher level of giving.

88% of individual donors who are called by telemarketers say they do not give over the phone but would like to have information forwarded to them by mail. **78%** of donors who ask this never or hardly ever receive the requested information.

In focusing on recruiting new donors, it is too easy to cut back on the time dedicated to current donors. Even more contact with existing donors through phone calls and personal letters would improve our relations.

I don't want to be recognized just for being a donor. I don't mind so much about being recognized for the volunteer efforts I make.

2. Hire firms whose respect for donors is reflected in their work.

This is a bigger issue than you might think. I have dealt with both direct marketing program managers and suppliers that think donors who give through these fundraising programs are less well educated and less intelligent than major gift donors. Of course, this is not so. According to a 2003 North American survey conducted by Lang Research for the FLA Group and Mal Warwick & Associates, 67% of direct mail donors have university education and 46% have professional or graduate degrees. Though almost all individual donors in our study had a history of contributing gifts at the leadership and major gift levels, 47% also gave regularly through direct marketing programs.

When staff and suppliers make inaccurate assumptions about donors and prospects, it shows in the letter copy they write, the telemarketing scripts they prepare, and in their demeanor at the door.

3. Work with your supplier.

Develop a process together for immediate response to special requests from donors and potential donors. Design a cooperative system for transferring information from supplier to client and test it to be sure it achieves desired results, taking donor sensibilities into account.

4. Monitor performance.

If your reason for hiring an external supplier is to get the workload off your shoulders, you are less likely to monitor your service provider's work as closely as you should. And, if your external call center or the canvassing route is at the other end of town, you will find that you just don't get around to spending time tracking their performance. Expert or not, your service provider is going to respond to the clients who set and monitor standards, so it is in your best interests to stay on top of your own program. It will be too late to make changes or introduce innovations when the campaign is over. Do yourself and your supplier a favor by evaluating performance for optimum quality. You may be paying for the service but you still need to be visible, involved, and proactive in order to maximize your investment.

5. Encourage suppliers to move donors up and out of their own direct marketing programs.

Whether your supplier is compensated on a commission or a flat fee basis, contract renewal is based largely on previous gross and net performance. So, just like your internal staff, your external supplier is motivated to keep as many donors as possible within the direct marketing program. Losing the top 10% of donors to the major gifts program could mean an actual loss of 30% or more of the revenue. Suppliers need to be encouraged to work with you to identify donors who are ready for other higher level fundraising programs. Your agreements with supplier companies should reflect your first priority, which is donor movement, and your second priority, optimum donor retention.

6. Fulfill your end of the fundraising bargain.

Increased success in donor renewal by external suppliers will depend on the combined performance of the supplier firm and the charity. Fulfilling your end of the partnership means providing donors with the three things they need after their gifts have been secured. Telemarketing, canvassing, and direct mail companies are justified when they complain about being in a constant state of acquisition, regardless of whether they are conducting an acquisition or a renewal campaign. Supplier staff who are in direct contact with your donors or communicating with them by letter, inspire giving by talking about the future, a future that depends upon the generosity of donors. If donors never learn the results of their efforts before the next solicitation call, it puts suppliers in a defensive position. Callers, canvassers, and copywriters are trained to make asks and secure gifts. Don't waste their expertise by turning them into excuse-makers. If you fulfill your end of the bargain, these experts will deliver better results with each successive campaign. Donor-centered fundraising means never having to say you're sorry! (I can't believe I said this.)

7. Contract out work but retain responsibility.

In a donor-centered fundraising context, charities have a right to expect consistently excellent performance from suppliers. But expecting it and getting it are two different things. Suppliers are not charitable organizations; they are profit-making companies, so as long as they are making a profit and staying ahead of their competition, they are not likely to challenge the status quo. But the people they interact with are *your* donors, not theirs, so the responsibility for your donors' welfare and your own fundraising success will always rest with you.

Because you vest your most precious renewable resource in your contract suppliers, you must stay in control of your direct marketing programs. In today's fundraising industry, suppliers have a huge influence in shaping Americans' opinions about the business of fundraising and in introducing them to or furthering their philanthropy. The talents of both charity-based fundraising practitioners and suppliers are needed for donor-centered fundraising.

So many development staff; so little communication. In some cases a single donor will get several calls from different people in our organization on the same day because we don't take the time to manage our internal communication about our donors in an effective way.

Our capital campaign spends too much time and attention on process and too little on personal contact and stewardship.

Sponsors should share in the recognition. . . . The big disease charities give much more exposure to the national sponsors than the local ones. This is a problem for us. We give more money every year but we're still not getting our logo on the T-shirt.

The one thing charities would do if they had more time/money

spend more time communicating with donors **49%**

thank donors for gifts in more personal ways **15%**

improve/increase electronic communication **9%**

increase donor recognition events **8%**

With staff dedicated to donor relations, management can accurately identify the separate costs of stewardship and active fundraising.

I think the responsibility of having one person generating all of the acknowledgments is a tremendous help to the development officers. They know that their gifts are being acknowledged appropriately and in a timely manner.

"EVERYTHING IS CONNECTED TO EVERYTHING ELSE"

In addition to serving as executive director of a non-profit land trust, I happen to work as a writer, editor and activist on environmental and social justice issues.

One December a call came through to me from a woman who said, "I want to give $5,000 right now; and next spring I want to do a $15,000 challenge grant. And if you have any trouble paying off the bank by the end of next year, I want to make a bridge loan." I expressed increasing wonder and gratitude at each interval in that statement until we both lapsed into silence. Then she said, "I followed your column in the Times twenty years ago and I read your books."

What this story means to me is this: Everything we do is preparation for a future we can't foresee. Who we are and how we live our lives as individuals is part of the success or failure of the organizations we build together. It's important to do the best we can as we go along.

"Everything is connected to everything else" is an old aboriginal saying that describes the environment as a product of an infinite number of interdependencies. It applies as much to the inside workings of charitable organizations as it does to the environment. Fundraising depends on people and departments outside the development office for its success as well as on the skillful execution of fundraising programs. Prompt gift acknowledgment cannot be achieved if receipting takes place in a finance office that sees no reason to adjust its one month turnaround time. Gift designation cannot happen if the programmers, researchers, artistic directors, and educators cannot or will not clearly articulate the work they do and the things they are trying to achieve. Results cannot be measured if decision-makers and policy-setters are not working to an objectives-based plan.

Working in isolation to avoid impacting others actually impedes others more than does working cooperatively. It is only through cooperation that independent action can happen effectively. Allowing process to triumph over purpose is a victory for small-mindedness over innovation.

It takes the whole organization to achieve fundraising success. When volunteers, managers, staff, and suppliers are pulling together, and when donor-centered fundraising and communication are the framework for your efforts, donors will respond and you will raise more money.

14
The Professional Fundraiser in a Donor-Centered Environment

THE OLD-STYLE FUNDRAISER

We all know at least one old style fundraiser—the ones who raise money in the way they used to in the "good old days." They are consummate "people persons" who exude a special warmth in their dealings with donors, displaying a genuine interest in them as individuals first and as donors second. Today, these fundraisers are admired on the one hand for the connection they are able to make with others, but sometimes seen as less than major players in the business. They are often passed over for promotion or, when they retire, are replaced by more modern day fundraising pros who came up through our programs-based system.

I know many, but I always think of one particular person with great fondness. Until she retired a few years ago, she was the director of development of a vibrant theater company. Her personal touch, focusing on one donor at a time, was responsible for growing the organization's subscriber base to its highest level ever. When she thought a patron was a little slow in renewing his annual subscription, she would call and find out why. The check would come the next day, often delivered in person. When attendance was down for a particular production, she would call her contacts in the media, negotiating half page ads for a fraction of their value and endless free radio spots.

She knew everyone by name and they knew her. It was an amazing experience to attend a performance with her because in the course of one fifteen minute intermission, she would talk to at least twenty theatergoers. She addressed them by first name, asked about their children/mother/spouse (whose first names she also knew) and made them feel wonderful. And, these weren't one-way conversations. People were just as interested in her as she was in them because of her many interests outside her work in fundraising.

When she retired, the theater hired a fundraiser with professional training and the right credentials to take her place. Over the next few years, subscriptions declined by 50%.

There is a serious shortage of trained, experienced professional fundraisers. Donor-centered fundraising, which advocates a more regular and meaningful flow of information to donors as well as more personalized gift acknowledgment, will put additional pressure on a system that cannot find and keep enough people now. Significant progress has been made in the last decade by membership and advocacy organizations and by senior practitioners in improving fundraising education and introducing professional accreditation. But if we are going to move as an industry into a new standard of donor relations and fundraising, we need to introduce strategies that train junior professionals more quickly and thoroughly in the basics of fundraising. We also need to find ways to encourage more fundraisers to stay in the business as a lifetime career.

QUALITIES AND QUALIFICATIONS

Professional fundraisers need to master the technical and analytical aspects of the development industry and have a tremendous flair for interacting with people. This includes superior communication and relationship-building skills with donors and volunteers as well as inspired leadership ability with staff.

Interpersonal skills emerge in childhood, are largely influenced by parenting, and mature as integrated parts of our personalities. How people interact with others is increasingly difficult to influence the older we become. Because donor-centered fundraising places a high premium on people skills, a superior ability to communicate and a genuine interest in people should be coveted as core talents when hiring fundraising staff. If need be, new staff can learn the technicalities of the job while on the job.

The following skills, accomplishments, and characteristics position someone as a serious candidate for donor-centered fundraising:

1. A broad-based college education.
A university level education in any discipline says that the candidate for a position in fundraising set out to accomplish something challenging and succeeded. Sustaining donor-centered fundraising in a development department is definitely a challenge that will take perseverance, so the discipline of higher level education is a decided asset.

2. An ability to communicate in a compelling fashion, both orally and in writing.

This is the essence of fundraising—to be able to put your organization's ambitions and dreams before a donor and convince him to support your cause.

3. A background of varied interests and accomplishments.

A fundraiser who is an accomplished individual is a more interesting person and lives in a broader sphere, which enhances opportunities to connect with donors on another level. For instance, if a fundraiser has her private pilot's license, or is an off-road cyclist, or has an interest in medieval history, she is going to connect with donors with similar or related interests.

4. A keen understanding of human psychology.

A good fundraiser can put himself in the donor's shoes. By fully understanding and appreciating what the donor feels about and needs from the organization, a fundraiser can write a more compelling letter, structure a more appealing event, and communicate progress in a more meaningful way.

5. An ingrained curiosity with an innovative streak.

People with the least experience in a subject sometimes have the greatest insights. They ask questions and make observations because they don't know enough to realize that what they are thinking may be outside accepted practice in the business. Being a really successful fundraiser means acquiring and using all the inside expertise without losing the outside point of view; it means staying curious; it means having out-of-the-ordinary ideas and being willing to try new things.

6. A willingness to challenge the status quo.

This is necessary to see the business in another way, to be able to use accepted standards and methodologies while, at the same time, not be constricted by them.

7. An analytical predisposition.

Analytical capability saves time and money. Knowing what to look for, how to interpret comparative reports, why and how to test potential, how to forecast from existing data, and simply how to extract meaningful information from a database, is fundamental technical know-how that is essential to all fundraisers. The answers to almost all the questions and problems that fundraisers face today are contained

We wanted to do something very special for the chair of our building campaign. Staff knew she had a passion for collecting quilts so we decided to commission a small pillow quilted in an unusual origami style and done in the colors that matched her living room decor. It's been almost two years now since we gave her this gift at the campaign donor recognition ceremony, but whenever we visit, this simple, cotton pillow in the colors she loves can be seen propped up in one of the oriental chairs in her elegantly appointed living room.

Ballet Arizona has been very nice. When I was in the hospital, the Ballet's director sent me flowers.

Our donor recognition event is built around an art show featuring work from blind or visually impaired artists.

A few years ago, I agreed to canvass a few blocks in my neighborhood for contributions for a well-known healthcare charity. I received a packet of information containing contribution forms, instructions and my fundraising goal. I exceeded the fundraising goal that was assigned to me and returned all contributions as instructed to the organization. I never received a thank you call or letter from the organization or any type of acknowledgment of my efforts or the results of the campaign overall. I did, however, receive a call the next year asking me to volunteer to raise funds again. I explained my experience and disappointment in never being acknowledged or updated on the outcome of the campaign and declined to participate again.

A simple letter or call would have made me a lifelong canvasser for this organization, but since I was treated so poorly, you can be sure I'll never volunteer for them again! I can only assume that all my fellow neighborhood canvassers were treated the same.

in the data that is right under their noses; but because practitioners' knowledge is too limited in the area of data interpretation and systems control, the data and systems tend to control the practitioners. A senior programmer for Raiser's Edge, the leading fundraising software system in North America, says that, on average, industry professionals use only about 20% of the software's available functions.

8. Physical stamina.

It is physically draining to work in fundraising. Convincing someone to pay for a product or service that will then be consumed by someone else, takes both talent and unwavering perseverance. Working through a group of volunteers to achieve that end is doubly challenging, requiring humility, patience, and superior teaching skills. People simply have to have stamina to work in this business.

9. An ability to manage for results.

Managing for results demands an unwavering focus on the end goals, a deep interest in what the organization is mandated to achieve, and confidence in how those goals will be met. It's like keeping a running report card in your head at all times, constantly monitoring the state of affairs and comparing today's reality with yesterday's performance and tomorrow's intentions. Someone who manages for results thinks in the future but acts in the present in order to get to the future.

10. Experience living and working in different cities, countries, or cultures.

American cities, states, and regions all have characteristics that make them as different from each other as night is from day. For instance, raising money poses unique challenges in Boston, Detroit, or Los Angeles. Fundraisers with work experience or just life experience in other cities or cultures can be a boon in donor relations and in developing fundraising strategies that address the individual challenges of diverse communities.

A rare commodity, fundraisers from America's minority groups possess language skills and cultural knowledge that are fundraising assets so precious, they cannot be measured.

Interestingly, proficiency in specific types of fundraising programs does not make it to this "top ten list," though it is important. Fundraising programs can be learned on the job or in specialized courses, but there is actually a better way to gain this knowledge more quickly and in greater depth that would be a boon to the industry at the same time.

TRAINING NEW PROFESSIONAL FUNDRAISERS

The fundraising industry needs a formal, well organized, national apprentice-ship system for new fundraisers.

An intelligent person can learn in a matter of hours what a direct mail program is, how it works, what it is intended to achieve, and its relationship to other fundraising programs. In three months, he can experience the planning, development, execution, and reporting of a single direct marketing campaign. In a year he might experience three or four similar campaigns. However, the person who is especially valuable is the one who is hired into the charity with a volume of experience behind him—experience gained from working campaigns for different causes and under different conditions. This is a person who knows that a single approach or technique does not work for all situations, who has experienced a variety of problems and learned to resolve them quickly, and who has learned to produce results within tight deadlines. This is a person who learned the business inside other charities or while employed by supplier companies.

There is a supply and demand problem throughout the fundraising industry, but nowhere more intense than in the direct mail, telemarketing, canvassing, and capital campaign companies. Why? The work is limited in scope and compensation is less than offered by the larger charities. But the intensity of training and experience is incomparable. For my colleagues who own and run direct marketing or capital campaign companies, this turnover of personnel must be frustrating; however, they cannot operate profit-making companies without accepting high turnover as a price they pay for success.

If high turnover is a fact of life in service supplier companies, but training within those companies is vigorous and superior, then perhaps the industry should use this to their advantage. A pool of better trained personnel can be developed more quickly with private companies as the starting point for an organized, national apprenticeship system in fundraising.

Consider this illustration: After graduating from a university or college and spending a short period of time (say three months) in a fundraising overview course, a student earns apprentice status. She then works for limited periods of time in companies specializing in direct mail, capital campaigns, and the like, where she experiences five to ten times the number of charities and campaigns than she would have been exposed to if employed in a single charity. She is paid for this work, of course. She "graduates" to other forms of fundraising with other companies. After working through the apprenticeship placements, she is ready for another course (maybe six months in duration this time) designed in a case study format. It deals with donor communication, relationships between fundraising personnel and other departments and personnel inside charitable organizations, volunteer leadership support, multi-disciplinary fundraising departments (inter-relationship of different kinds of fundraising programs), etc. Then, she becomes a full fledged, accredited fundraising professional.

Is an organized apprenticeship program better than the present system for training student fundraisers? In conjunction with some classroom learning, yes. Though there is value in learning in a classroom setting about the individual fundraising programs and how they work, this isolated environment does not bring students into contact with donors and prospects and cannot provide the depth of training needed by today's entry level professionals. Development directors and CEOs should be able to hire fundraisers who can hit the ground running in one or more kinds of fundraising programs. They should come into a charity having already learned that every organization, every fundraising program, and every donor has some common characteristics, but also that every charitable organization is different. Then managers could put their supervisory and training energy into the more intangible learning sphere that is donor relations, donor communication, and negotiation. With an undergraduate or graduate degree in any field of particular interest to the student, followed by a period of apprenticeship within the industry that includes focused classroom learning, a new fundraising professional will quickly rise to the top.

The supply/demand problem inside companies offering specialized services will never be completely eliminated; most fundraisers will eventually want to work directly for a charity so they can experience the satisfaction of making a difference for a single cause. However, in a training environment where apprenticeship is the norm, at least a greater number of developing fundraisers would be available to the private companies for a pre-determined period of time, and while they are there, they would be highly motivated to do well on the job.

CONTINUING EDUCATION

Introducing the CFRE and ACFRE[22] accreditation programs for professional fundraisers was an important step in the right direction in the effort to build expertise and bolster credibility in the fundraising profession. Becoming a CFRE requires

[22] Certified Fund Raising Executive designation, offered by CFRE International and Advanced Certified Fund Raising Executive designation, administered by the ACFRE Certification Board

meeting education, employment, achievement, and continuing education criteria, and staying current with trends and practices through regular re-certification.

Investing in continuing education is essential, not optional. Education budgets are frighteningly thin in the third sector and always in jeopardy of being suspended or eliminated in times of constraint. The short shrift given to continuing education makes a strong negative comment about the not for profit sector concerning its attitude toward professional fundraising staff. Charities must invest in the continuing education of fundraisers so that they can avail themselves of the knowledge within the industry that will help them raise more money.

It is not only the corporate sector that has changed shape in the last twenty years. While manufacturing and communication have been undergoing a complete rebirth, so too has the business of raising money. Fundraising is no longer a job that one falls into or is coerced into; it is a full-fledged profession that has seen the introduction of specialized fundraising programs such as planned giving and sponsorship. It is supported by sophisticated technology and strategies for gift management. It is innovative and leading edge.

Fundraising success is directly related to ability; ability is measured by education and experience. Not for profit organizations need to allocate a minimum of 5% of the value of gross salaries to continuing education annually, and they need to insist that fundraising staff build the time for upgrading their skills into their work schedules. Staff are as notorious as employers in the not for profit sector for seeing budget as cost and not as investment. They are likely to turn down opportunities for continuing education as a heroic, cost-saving gesture. This hurts everyone.

Conferences

As professionals leading a vital industry, fundraisers need the time and the forum to delve into complex issues such as donor attrition. The AFP, AHP[23] and other national and international conferences are a boon to continuing education for professional fundraisers. Thanks to the diligent and almost entirely volunteer efforts of professional fundraisers who established and sustain these associations, these learning forums improve in quality every year.

Fundraising conferences suffer, however, from having to fulfill the dual role of basic trainer for junior fundraisers as well as discussion forum for more experienced practitioners. If they were relieved of their obligation to provide

We hold our events in unique venues. Our last one was held at the Museum of the New South which had been recently renovated. Everyone was excited to see the new space which added to the caché of the event.

Our donor recognition event which is twenty-five years old, has become more popular with age. It is a black tie affair and people start calling me in the early spring to find out the date so they can mark it on their calendar.

Several years ago, an elderly widow called one of our Board members and proudly reported she had received a "special" valentine from our organization. Later in the conversation, she revealed why it was special: it was the ONLY valentine she had received. A few months later, she contacted our organization to find out our legal name for her will. Needless to say, to this day, we continue to send these holiday postcards.

[23] Association of Fundraising Professionals and Association for Healthcare Philanthropy

elementary training by vesting that responsibility in universities, colleges, and private sector fundraising companies, conferences would become even more exciting and enticing experiences. This would also serve to re-engage more senior practitioners, many of whom do not find enough to satisfy themselves within the typical conference agenda.

Junior, intermediate, and senior practitioners need to mix with each other more in conference sessions that are issues-oriented. Though senior fundraisers have accumulated knowledge and wisdom as their advantage, less experienced professionals see the business in a fresh light and are more likely to challenge the status quo. For this reason, I am not a proponent of "streaming," a process that directs conference delegates into sessions according to years of experience. Allowing all delegates to determine for themselves what they want to learn at any point in time makes sense because the charitable sector is so large and so varied. So many professional fundraisers work in one person or small staff shops and have to handle complex situations from their first day on the job. They need greater access to training sessions, forums, conferences, and courses structured at a higher level. They also need free rein to make their own decisions about continuing education, regardless of the number of years they have been practicing in the business.

I can clearly remember the moment many years ago when I learned the most in a fundraising conference workshop. It was the day I slipped into an advanced session on planned giving led by Frank Minton.[24] There were twelve other people in a room that held three hundred. They were all crowded around Frank at the front, nodding and interjecting with questions. Having never attended a planned giving seminar before, I had the good sense to hang back a few rows. For two hours, I listened to what Frank had to say or, more accurately, watched his lips move and wondered if he was really speaking English. I didn't understand a word he was saying. But when I left that session, laden down with a pile of intimidating position statements, I knew that I had a great deal to learn and that I'd better get at it. This day marked the beginning of my education in planned giving and I'm very glad that no one was at the door to tell me that the course was too advanced for me. What we don't know in this business can definitely hurt us.

Though conference organizers want to focus on quality, their desire to chart new waters is frustrated by format. Conferences (not just fundraising conferences but all of them) are too often a series of predictable overview sessions instead of forums for innovation and debate. They also bear witness to an overemphasis on minimizing cost, something that is understandably habit-forming

[24] President, Planned Giving Services, Seattle

for people in fundraising. Many national and international conferences make eyebrow-raising profits instead of ensuring that delegates' registration fees go entirely to the educational purposes intended. New energy could be injected into conferences by diversifying the speakers' rosters, incorporating innovative learning techniques, and varying session formats to a greater extent. Length of individual sessions should take a back seat to content; importance of topic should take precedence over volume of sessions. More people as presenters from outside the industry would be a welcome addition to the roster of senior fundraising practitioners and consultants, who are highly qualified but limited in their point of view. More donors and corporate executives leading sessions as well as receiving awards would be an exciting thing to see and hear.

Finally, there is no need to be concerned about convening a forum or conference that is too high level. Delegates, like all students, will rise to the challenge. Expect brilliance and you will get it.

SENIOR FUNDRAISING PROFESSIONALS NEED ATTENTION TOO

The supply and demand problem in professional fundraising means that practitioners are moving around and up in the industry very fast. This is great for the resumé but very hard on the individual and on the organizations that are hiring. The skills that experienced fundraisers and charities need the most are embodied in the senior people at the top of the business, but there are too few of them to meet the needs of the not for profit industry. Just as entry level fundraisers need a private industry apprenticeship system to accelerate their training, more experienced fundraisers need opportunities for learning that speak to their and their organizations' complex needs.

There is a dearth of advanced education opportunities for senior fundraising professionals. This is not for lack of trying by organizations like the Association of Fundraising Professionals that works diligently every year to create appealing Masters Tracks in their annual conferences. However, it is very difficult to satisfy seniors' varied and specialized needs within a general conference setting. As well, very few professionals at the top of the business can take the time to enroll in the few available graduate programs.

Senior practitioners need periodic paid sabbaticals. Ensuring income during sabbatical years can be achieved by withholding and investing a portion of an employee's wages each year. A sabbatical could be taken to write a professional publication, teach at a university or college, or become the interim CEO or development director for an emerging organization otherwise unable to

> We sent a memorial donation to Rice University, Houston. They sent us a very modest letter, not fancy, but extremely well written. And, they have not put us on a solicitation list. I really appreciate the way they conduct themselves with donors.

afford someone of this caliber. Or, the exhausted fundraiser could pursue a personal dream. Sabbatical placements could be international; a senior fundraisers' speakers bureau could be developed; a group of senior practitioners on sabbatical could organize the educational content of an international fundraising conference. The possibilities are limitless.

A NEW LOOK AT THE JOB DESCRIPTION FOR PROFESSIONAL FUNDRAISERS

In the context of donor-centered fundraising, professional fundraisers have three responsibilities, but at the moment, all the focus is on only the third one. In order of priority, they are:

- To cultivate the philanthropic spirit and encourage giving, not to a single organization but to the charitable sector, for the benefit of society as a whole.
- To be an advocate for donors, no matter which charities they are supporting.
- To raise money for one's own organization.

This is not some lofty moral code for fundraisers, but a pragmatic three-tiered job description that will help all practitioners achieve their objectives more easily, position the profession of fundraising in a better light, and increase charities' ability to provide more and better programs and services. Professional fundraisers are already performing admirably in the third area. Following the principles of donor-centered fundraising will realize the second responsibility. But it is the first one that matters the most because it affects the industry as a whole. A more successful global fundraising industry will influence the performance of each fundraising organization and each professional fundraiser.

The Professional Fundraiser's Role in Furthering Philanthropy

Giving and volunteering are directly linked. 93% of individual donors in the study are volunteers and 95% of those donors give financial contributions to the organizations in which they volunteer their time, as well as to other charities. Any influence that charities exert on someone to become either a donor or a volunteer has a good chance of impacting the contribution of money, time, and expertise.

Philanthropy is a learned behavior and not everyone is lucky enough to learn it at home. Professional fundraisers need to be facilitators of the philanthropic spirit, finding ways to help more people introduce themselves to the joy and privilege of giving. And, they need to spend some of their professional time doing this unconditionally. Although donor attrition is high, people with a philanthropic spirit tend to keep giving in spite of poor donor relations or disappointment over the end use of funds. The philanthropic spirit seems to breed resiliency . . . and loyalty. If a fundraiser spends time with a non-donor or a discouraged donor helping her gain or regain her commitment to giving, should he only do so on condition that the donor support the fundraiser's own organization? Will putting a condition on her philanthropy at this sensitive time risk losing the donor completely?

The Ultimate Investment

If one day per month of every professional fundraiser's time were devoted to the global issue of furthering the spirit of giving, there would be no stopping the growth of philanthropy. Could it be possible for fundraisers to invest in both their own efforts and the collective advancement of philanthropy simultaneously? Yes, and it would have important ancillary benefits for fundraisers themselves. First, it would expand everyone's horizon. Working every day for a single organization narrows one's point of reference and ability to see the bigger picture, which is the donor's environment.

Second, major challenges in the industry can only be addressed by focusing on the detail while keeping the global issues of philanthropy in sight. Working for a single organization most of the time and contributing to the broader picture some of the time would educate and re-energize fundraisers quickly and cost-effectively. Third, it would increase opportunities to learn from others while contributing to a fundamentally important cause. Lending their fundraising professionals for one day a month to the global issue of encouraging philanthropy is a pragmatic investment by any charity in its own future.

The direct involvement of all professional fundraisers in the broad issue of philanthropy must not be an afterthought or something that practitioners do on their day off. In order to make a measurable difference, the global industry must become everyone's core concern.

Visiting a donor without asking for another gift contributes a great deal to future gift increases. The donor does not feel pressured and often increases his gift size because of that.

Our theater has a lobby wall with donors' names on huge stars. Most donors are companies and they see this as advertising. It's OK, I guess, but as an individual donor, I like to be as private as I can. I know that this kind of recognition does work but it's not important for me.

Our local education foundation mails holiday postcards to our donors. For Valentine's Day, the postcards are inscribed with a large heart and the message "We love our donors." Elementary-age students color and/or decorate the postcards, many adding their own special messages.

At their own initiative, the National Crime Prevention Council got a local counselor to recognize us in the Congressional Record.

One great benefit of being a member of our Art Gallery is that I can buy artworks but I can also sell them through the gift shop on consignment. Terrific!

A DONOR-CENTERED FUNDRAISING APPROACH TO JOB HUNTING

Since fundraising requires such a high level of skill and stamina, and since so few people are in the business relative to need, charities are having to compete aggressively for skilled and experienced professionals. Not for profit organizations that advocate a donor-centered approach to fundraising will be more attractive to professional fundraisers and more successful in hiring.

If you are a charity seeking a fundraiser or a fundraiser looking for a new job, these questions will help you determine whether your organization, or the organization you are considering, would be open to a donor-centered approach to fundraising:

- Do you have a multi-year strategic plan for programs and services delivery? If so, does your plan include specific, measurable objectives to be reached each year? What was your track record relative to achieving your strategic plan's objectives last year?
- For what purposes are donated funds used in your organization? What is your position on the designation of donors' gifts to specific programs or services?
- What role do you expect/want your senior development staff to play in long term planning? As major gift fundraising is focused on selling your future dreams, it is important that the senior fundraiser be fully informed of long range plans as they are being developed. Is that individual part of the strategic planning team?
- In specific terms, how is your Board of Directors currently engaged in fundraising? What does your Board feel is its role in and responsibility for fundraising? How does the Board interact directly with donors at the present time? Is the Board open to changing its role relative to donor recognition and communication, even if it means putting more time and effort into this work?
- How is your organization currently communicating with donors when you are not asking them for money? What is your position on communicating information in specific and measurable terms concerning the use of donated funds?
- How much money has your organization raised in the last year? What was your cost per dollar raised? How much do

you plan to raise in the next twelve months? What is your position on investment now in fundraising for future return?

- Is there a budget for continuing education and training of fundraising staff? What percentage of overall salaries is allocated to training?

If you pose these questions as a job applicant, and the organization you are considering does not come through with flying colors, this is not necessarily a signal to get up and run. If the charity is willing to challenge its own beliefs about fundraising and consider new ideas, this is a hopeful sign. You can tell by the tenor of the discussion whether a potential employer is paying lip service to your issues or is genuinely looking for new ways of approaching the business of raising money. Similarly, charities should look for flexibility in the applicant, willingness to try new strategies for overcoming old problems, and non-conformist thinking.

DECIDING TO MOVE ON

If you are less than fulfilled in your current position, considering the above questions may illuminate the cause of your dissatisfaction. If the conditions seem to be right but fundraising is underperforming, then perhaps you need advice, additional training, or a mentor. If your dissatisfaction stems from working under the conditions and limitations that these questions imply, however, you may need to assess whether things can change or whether it is time to move on.

Of the three elements of a fundraiser's job description, only the obligation to raise money for your own organization is affixed to the charity that employs you. The more important and more universal responsibilities in your role as a professional fundraiser include furthering the philanthropic spirit and advocating for donors. These remain constant no matter where you are employed. For your own sake, for the sake of all donors, and for the sake of the growth of philanthropy, work where you have the best possible chance for success. The not for profit sector cannot afford to lose its dedicated and experienced practitioners.

At the end of a delightful visit with an elderly donor, I wrapped up my conversation and materials and said, "Thank you for visiting with me and letting me share with you some stories about the children. Is there anything I can do for you before I leave?"

"As a matter of fact, there is," my donor replied. "I am really having trouble getting around lately. Could you go upstairs and clean out my bathtub?"

15
Becoming Donor-Centered

Soon after I hired our first fundraising associate, I asked him to make some personal visits to out-of-town donors. I requested that he simply thank the donors for their past support and not ask for another contribution or, indeed, make any reference to the possibility of a future gift.

My new staff person didn't believe that making calls on donors without a tangible fundraising objective was a worthwhile allocation of his time, so he was somewhat dubious as he set off for three days on the road. But by the time he returned to the office, two donors had already sent in another contribution. He was amazed . . . and convinced!

Donor-centered fundraising is not a program or even a strategy; it is a fundraising philosophy that extols specialized and superior customer service. Donor-centered fundraising influences the shape and improves the outcomes of fundraising programs but it does not replace them.

Donor-centered fundraising cannot be layered on top of what you are doing now. Repositioning donors as customers and partners means re-engineering how money is raised. Donor-centered fundraising cannot be implemented all at once; it requires a lot of thinking before acting and a lot of discussion among colleagues and employers. Donor-centered concepts must be tested first and then implemented in controlled, deliberate steps. If you try to transform your organization into a donor-centered state overnight, you will experience an initial rush of enthusiastic activity, and then you will quickly fall back into the old way of doing things.

In 2001, $212 billion was contributed to charitable causes, representing 2.1% of gross domestic product.[25] That is a lot of money given by generous donors and raised by hard-working fundraisers. So why would you go to the trouble of changing methodology if fundraising already works? Because donor-centered fundraising raises so much more. **Of the donors in our study who felt there was room for improvement, 70% would definitely or probably increase their overall philanthropic giving if charities improved the quality of their communication.** If charities need more money in order to save more people's lives and

[25] Giving USA 2002, AAFRC Trust for Philanthropy, Inc., 2002

improve the quality of life for others, and if donors say they have more money to give, then it is incumbent on the fundraising industry to find new ways to maximize their philanthropy.

Change in fundraising methodology is warranted for another reason. A wealth transfer is underway from a generation of donors who trusted charities to use their contributions wisely to a generation of donors who demand accountability. Donor-centered fundraising is the right fundraising philosophy for the times.

EVERY FUNDRAISING PROGRAM CAN BE DONOR-CENTERED

Major and planned gifts are already donor-centered, defined by the one-on-one relationships that are established through cultivation and negotiation. Direct marketing programs and the people who run them can be donor-centered, too.

Direct marketing staff and suppliers deal every day with frustrated donors who are over-solicited and under-informed. Though they are part of the system that causes donors' irritation and attrition, they are also its victims. Direct mail staff and suppliers work in a doubly difficult environment because they are not directly interacting with donors. They are not there seeing the body language or hearing the objections when a prospect or renewing donor is reading their letter.

Whether direct mail, canvassing, or telemarketing, direct marketing programs can enhance their productivity by incorporating donor-centered techniques.

Canvassing

The Donor-Centered Canvasser

The other day a canvasser rang my doorbell. I had seen him coming up my walk so I made sure I had an armload of papers and a harried look on my face when I answered the door. (This is usually all it takes for a quick dismissal, no matter what the person is selling.) I opened the door and waited for the first few words of the inevitable sales pitch. There stood a thirty-something, casually dressed fellow, head cocked to one side, his own file of papers under one arm. He said nothing; he just stood there sizing me up. I did the same. "Two can play this game," I thought to myself.

Eventually he said: "I'm with Greenpeace and I'd like to tell you about the two most significant accomplishments we have made over the past year. I hope you will give me a moment because it's important information that directly affects you."

Taken aback with the direct but effective approach, all I could say was, "OK." He then succinctly summarized his charity's work and accomplishments in genetically modified foods and coal-burning plants. As he began highlighting the work that Greenpeace was planning to do this year with the money they were now trying to raise, I noticed my purse was sitting on the floor right by the door. (Note to self: don't leave your purse by the door.) I picked it up, found my wallet, pulled out all the cash I had and handed it to him. (Note 2: don't carry so much cash in your wallet.)

He hesitated for a moment, probably because not too many people hand him money before he actually asks for it, then took the contribution with a pleasant "thank you." "Here is a one-page fact sheet on our progress on coal-burning plants," he said, handing it to me. "Can I give you three more copies to pass on to others who might be interested in this issue?" "Don't press your luck," I replied. He smiled. I smiled back.

I asked his name and how he came to be so well versed on these complex environmental issues. He talked about the charity's training program for canvassers and his dedication to the cause. I told him it showed. When he's on the job, David talks face-to-face with about thirty donors every night. "Do you work for this charity all the time?" I asked. "Only when their canvassing program is on," he replied. "What do you do the rest of the time?" "I get by," was all he said.

We said our goodbyes and I watched him head down my walk. Fifteen minutes later the bell rang again. I opened the door and on the other side stood a very well dressed middle aged woman with a clip board in her hand. "I'm collecting for X Charity," she said and waited for my response.

I felt that old familiar irritation well up inside me. "Sorry," I replied, "I just gave to the canvasser from Greenpeace." "Oh, you mean someone else is canvassing on this street?" she asked with alarm. "Yes," I replied, "and he's good!" "Well, can I leave this with you?" she asked, as she handed me something. "OK," I replied unenthusiastically. It was a pledge card with an envelope—nothing else. As she walked away we both knew I would never send it in. Too bad she didn't know why.

In a donor-centered environment, the canvasser isn't just someone who rings bells and collects money; he is the most important person in the fundraising operation because he is the one communicating measurable results to donors. If you want to maximize performance in your door-to-door fundraising program, make sure your canvassers are very well informed and passionate about the cause. And, give them time to do their job well.

Money is not the issue. My greatest challenge is convincing key staff and volunteers that honest and well conceived communication with donors is essential to developing strong relationships. They talk about "working the donor" which suggests manipulation rather than clear and open communication. A healthy donor program cannot be developed within this kind of philosophy.

Philanthropy is "paying rent for living on this planet" and "putting my money where my mouth is."

There are post-gift opportunities in a donor-centered canvassing program. Even if a tax receipt is provided at the door, a thank you call from someone at the office the next day reminds canvassed donors that this charity is on the ball. If, down the road, you follow up with a one-page newsletter summarizing your achievements, you can be confident that you have done everything possible to renew this person's support. The best situation of all would be to have the same canvasser revisit the donor to renew his gift, supplied with appropriate information so that he can acknowledge the donor's previous contribution.

Many charities try to renew canvassed donors through their direct mail program, with limited success. This is not surprising when donors are asked to keep giving while being sent two rungs down the fundraising ladder (from face-to-face solicitation to appeal by letter). Donor-centered communication bridges the gap between solicitations. Renewing canvassed donors through the solicitation strategy that won their support in the first place only makes sense.

Telemarketing

The Telemarketing Call

Parent   Hello.

Caller   Hello, I'm calling from the Faculty of Engineering at your daughter's University. Is this Kelly's mother?

Parent   Yes it is.

Caller   I'm calling because a package was sent to you in the mail about two weeks ago containing information about our engineering program. Did you receive it?

Parent   No, I don't recall getting that. How can I help you?

Caller   Oh. We did send it out to all parents of first year students, so you should have received it.

Parent   I didn't.

Caller   Well, anyway, maybe I could just summarize briefly over the phone.

Parent   OK.

Caller   We conduct a Parents' Campaign every year to raise funds for specific program enhancements for engineering students. This year, the monies we raise will go to improving curriculum services such as increased library resources and upgraded equipment in the labs. Would you consider a gift of two hundred dollars to this campaign?

Parent   I would certainly give the University and the Faculty of Engineering serious consideration for a gift, especially because the Dean went out *of his way to accept Kelly as a transfer student. However, I tend not to give over the phone. Would you mind re-sending the package and I'll be sure to look out for it.*

Caller I can't do that.

Parent Why not?

Caller This is the last day of the campaign and the package would get to you too late.

Parent That's all right. I'll mail in a contribution.

Caller No, you don't understand. This is the last day.

Parent Do you mean that if I send you money next week and the campaign is over, you won't accept it? That's a first.

Caller I don't know. I don't make those decisions.

Parent Look, I don't usually give this out, but since it's the University, I'll give you my home fax number so you can send me the information right now.

Caller No, I'm afraid I can't do that.

Parent Why not?

Caller Because I'm not authorized to send you anything.

Parent (exasperated sigh)

Caller Well, thank you for your time. I'm sorry you're unable to contribute at this particular time, but maybe you will consider supporting the Faculty of Engineering at a future date.

Parent Huh?

Caller Good evening. (hangs up)

This is an example of a disconnection among donor, charity, and supplier. Callers working in external or in-house call centers quickly learn to read the signals and play the odds. Experience tells them that potential donors who ask for written information and say they don't give over the phone are using a stalling tactic. Statistically, they don't give. Besides, if they did give by mail at a later date, the successful ask would not be credited to the call center. So, there is no benefit in pursuing this potential donor further. She won't be giving; time is ticking away; time is money.

In a donor-centered environment, no one would risk dismissing a potential donor in this manner. What if she were telling the truth? The signals were certainly there. "I would certainly give the University and the Faculty of Engineering serious consideration for a gift, especially because the Dean went out of his way to accept Kelly as a transfer student." What if your call center

Charities should invest in relationship management. That's what it's all about. There is lots of training out there. It is a real weakness . . . but there's always hope!

I understand why charities are calling . . . but consider me in all this.

Appreciate your donors! Recognize that donors are giving of their free will and their gestures are valuable. Nothing can happen without donors' support and all they want in return is for charities to recognize (not publicly, but personally) what they do.

Dalhousie University completed an ambitious campaign recently. Because everyone was asked to go that "extra mile," there were several major donors who told us quite emphatically that this would be their last major gift to our university. Now that our president and Board members have turned their attention to other fundraising needs, I have been suggesting that they visit some of our campaign donors when traveling to their cities. It's been a hard sell on my part. Several Board members have said, "That donor said he would never give us another gift, so why should we visit?" However, I stood my ground and our president and volunteers made those stewardship calls. So far, three donors who insisted that their last gift was definitely their last gift, have made new contributions that average 100% more than the value of their gifts to the campaign.

made that extra effort to provide the requested information to that donor, and then she didn't give? Would the world come to an end, or would this call become part of your prospect cultivation efforts?

88% of donors in our study who are called by telemarketers say they don't give over the phone but they would be willing to receive information in the mail. 78% of donors who request information by mail never or hardly ever receive anything. Several study donors said they ask for written information so that they can differentiate between legitimate and fraudulent charities or telemarketers. Not one donor said that he asks for information in the mail as a means of ending the call.

Charities and their internal or external call centers are missing an opportunity here. So focused on getting the gift right now, they are missing real opportunities to prove to potential donors that they are listening and not just following a script, and that they are willing to follow through on requests. If a donor or prospective donor asks for information and you provide it promptly, he is already part way along the road to saying yes. When you call him later, you will be able to remind him of the package he requested. You have done your part and now it will be easier for your donor to do his.

Telemarketing companies and in-house call centers have a golden opportunity to become communicators as well as solicitors. What if call centers took responsibility for communicating measurable results to donors, using the same callers where possible for sharing information as were used in the initial fundraising call? This would have many benefits:

- It would deepen the relationship between the caller and the donor.
- It would make the subsequent renewal solicitation so much easier, increasing the rate of successful asks.
- It would lead to more satisfied employees who stay in their jobs longer.
- It would, by default, reduce the volume of solicitations in cases where donors are currently being called many times a year. If a call to convey results takes place between solicitations, then sufficient time must pass for the charity to achieve something worth reporting.

These two tables illustrate that the cost of an informative follow-up call will easily be absorbed by a renewal campaign that increases retention and average gift value. Table 17 follows attrition and revenue from retained donors over five renewal campaigns. Table 18 shows improved performance in donor retention through a follow up phone call in which measurable results were communicated to donors. Even when taking the cost of communication calls into account, $155,000 more is raised through this donor-centered approach than would have been raised through traditional fundraising—a 48% improvement. This calculation does not take into account the real possibility that a small percentage of retained donors will be willing and ready to offer a major gift and the communication call will be the opportunity for that to happen. This concept is definitely worth testing.

Table 17 – Accumulated Revenue Over Five Solicitations in Typical Fundraising

Campaign #	Attrition Rate	# Retained Donors	Average Gift	Campaign Revenue	Accumulated Revenue
0–Acquisition	n/a	1,000	$100.00	$ 100,000	$ 100,000
1	50%	500	$115.00	$ 57,500	$ 157,500
2	30%	350	$132.25	$ 46,287	$ 203,787
3	20%	280	$152.09	$ 42,585	$ 246,372
4	20%	224	$174.90	$ 39,177	$ 285,549
5	20%	179	$201.14	$ 36,004	$ 321,553

Table 18 – Accumulated Revenue Net of Communication Call Between Solicitations in Telemarketing Program

Campaign #	Communication Call Expense[26]	Attrition Rate	# Retained Donors	Average Gift	Campaign Revenue	Accumulated Net Revenue
Initial Acquisition	n/a	n/a	1,000	$100.00	$ 100,000	$ 100,000
Renewal 1	$3,200	35%	650	$140.00	$ 91,000	$ 187,800
Renewal 2	$2,100	25%	488	$160.00	$ 78,080	$ 263,800
Renewal 3	$1,600	18%	400	$185.00	$ 74,000	$ 336,200
Renewal 4	$1,300	12%	352	$200.00	$ 70,400	$ 405,300
Renewal 5	$1,120	8%	324	$225.00	$ 72,900	$ 477,080
Total	$9,320					$ 477,080

One day I received a letter from someone whom I had never met informing me that, in lieu of gifts for her approaching 50th birthday, she would be requesting friends and relatives to direct donations to our agency. We had never heard of this person so we checked with all our Board members, volunteers, etc., but no one knew who she was. Soon the donations started to pour in, eventually totalling over $100,000, including contributions from wealthy and famous people from all over the United States. Several times we tried to contact this person and invite her to our agency, but she never responded. We never found out why she picked our agency or how she knew about us.

[26] based on $32 per calling hour @ 10 calls/hour

The de Tocqueville Society, which includes donors who contribute ten thousand dollars a year or more, selects an annual philanthropist of the year. This year we were lucky enough to win this special award. We received a beautiful crystal award and a dinner to which many members of our family were invited. Someone from the Society came to our house a few weeks prior to the event to get to know us better and ask us what kind of food we like. We were very pleased.

Direct Mail

My Dog, Chloe

When my dog, Chloe, died, I sent an in memoriam gift to my local animal shelter and received a thoughtful acknowledgment card in return.

Four months later, I got a letter in the mail from them which started, "Dear Animal Lover." I guess it had been issued by another department at the shelter because the letter suggested that I might like to have information about their in memoriam program. It must be hard to keep track of all the people who send in gifts to memorialize their pets. I guess I shouldn't expect them to remember.

But . . . if they had sent a letter addressed to me by name, and including something like, "I know it's been only a few months since Chloe died, etc.," I would have written them a check immediately—and sent them more money than I did the last time.

As direct mail is the direct marketing program of choice for most charities, adapting it to be donor-centered will have a marked influence on fundraising success. It is worth noting that 88% of charities in the study solicit donors through direct mail. As well, even though the majority of study donors made gifts of significant value and served on Boards of Directors, direct mail was still the fundraising program through which they were most likely to contribute to charitable organizations.

The following issues require new thinking in light of donors' need for better information and improved customer service:

- The number one complaint from donors about fundraising is over-solicitation and, as direct mail is the most common fundraising methodology, charities need to urgently address the volume of direct mail requests they make in a single year. The prolific number of solicitations is made to seem even more excessive by some charities who include outright or veiled requests for another gift within their thank you letter copy.
- While the high rate of donor attrition in direct mail programs is partly attributable to over-solicitation, it can also be traced back to lack of meaningful information on gifts at work. Generalized appeals and lack of information on the intended use of funds also limit acquisition and renewal success.

- Appeal copy often attempts to compensate for lack of specifics by driving the general message home more forcefully. Lengthy letters with repetitive copy and bolded or underlined statements meant to grab the reader's attention are the literary equivalent of jumping up and down and flailing arms wildly. They are an insult to intelligent donors and a frustration to skilled copywriters who could do so much more if they were working with compelling information.

Reducing solicitations and upping the bar on letter content is a good first step. Tying the solicitation theme to results achieved in another letter sent to donors later on will close the information loop. Direct mail staff and external suppliers who are experts in communicating in written form could take responsibility for the one-page bulletin that contains those measurable results. This opens up a new area of business for suppliers who may see fewer solicitations as a threat to their livelihood. Donor-centered fundraising does not spell the end of any fundraising program. It suggests another way to maximize each one's productivity.

The talent is already in the industry but it needs to be redirected into activities that speak to donors' bottom line requirements. Let's give our direct mail copywriters something to sink their teeth into; and let's give our solicitors the tools they need to renew every possible donor.

Fundraising Drives

The Food Bank

As a single mom with three children, my salary as a contract physiotherapist has to stretch a long way, so I have to be really frugal. There simply isn't money for extras. But, I was quick to respond when my eldest daughter wanted us to 'help the poor children who don't have as much as we do.' Thanksgiving was approaching so our local food bank was fresh in our minds. We decided that we would add a few items to our grocery cart each Saturday until the last food drive just prior to Christmas.

I was amazed at the commitment my children showed over the following weeks. They contributed part of their allowance, did chores for the neighbors to earn extra money and really pulled together to make a difference. By the Saturday before Christmas, we had amassed quite a supply of groceries.

We had the option of depositing the groceries in a very large box at the

> *Communication should be continuing, personal contact between the donor and someone inside the charity. Personal touch is everything. It's not the amount that is being requested; it's the person who is doing the asking that generates the decision.*

> *The giving habits of older people are quite different from younger donors. Many young donors coming out of school don't have a giving philosophy. Charities have to figure out how to involve youth in giving and help them develop a philanthropic spirit.*

I think there's a whole group of people who haven't yet made up their minds about how they are going to express their philanthropy and they have a lot of money to give.

We can't seem to figure out how to move donors who are in a lower giving level into a higher one.

entrance to our neighborhood grocery store or taking our 'loot' to the local fire hall. Needless to say, the kids chose the latter. So, I piled bags and children into the car and off we went. At the station, the children could barely contain themselves, each weighed down with groceries and trying to peek over the top of the bags as they made their way to the entrance. Once inside, we waited in the reception area for someone to come along . . . and we waited, and waited. I suggested that maybe all the fire fighters were off fighting a fire but we could clearly see both gleaming red trucks through the glass partition.

I looked around for a bell and that's when I noticed a handwritten sign taped to the wall over in the corner of the room. It said . . . Leave food bank donations here . . . thanks . . . followed by a roughly drawn arrow pointing down to the floor where a couple of other lonely bags of groceries sat. Something from the way the sign was written also told me that it meant 'don't bother us.'

As gently as I could, I told the kids that the fire fighters probably had to stay in a certain place in the station so that they could hear the alarm calls and get down the pole quickly and that's why they wanted us to leave the groceries over there.

So, we did as we were instructed; we put down the groceries and left. It was a pretty quiet ride home. I couldn't sleep very well that night, thinking about the children and how disappointed they had been. It's hard to be that selfless when you're only four or six or nine. I don't think we'll do this next year. I don't want my children to be hurt again.

If a positive early experience can set a young person on the road to lifelong philanthropy, then it stands to reason that a negative one can turn someone off.

Fundraising programs that involve donors directly in providing a charity's core product or service (food banks and used clothing collection agencies are good examples) need to be especially careful about how their donor programs are designed. In the story above, using fire halls as product drop-off locations for food banks seemed like a good idea; however, it also created an expectation for donors that fire fighters could not satisfy. Though transportation of goods from point of purchase to food bank is definitely important, donor sensibility is the more urgent consideration.

A re-allocation of human resources might fix the problem in this situation. For example, many people volunteer their services to sort goods at the food bank. As these goods are non-perishable and will be allocated to people in need over a period of several weeks or months, it is perhaps less urgent to have a concentration of volunteers at the depot during peak holiday times. More important, perhaps, is to have them located at the drop off points. If volunteers were stationed where donors make their contributions, there would be an opportunity for meaningful and personal thanks, and volunteers could provide interested donors with more information about food bank operations. Personal contact inspires donors to offer more and more significant gifts as well as their volunteer service.

Fundraising Events

A common complaint of donors in this and other studies is that they do not hear about the fundraising results of campaigns and events. Donors who participate in events suffer from the same combination of too little information and too much solicitation as do donors in direct marketing programs.

One way to solve this problem is to communicate with participants immediately after the event. At the time the fundraising event is planned, the organizing committee should also plan post-event communication. A phone call to attendees the next day to say thank you and to tell them how much you raised the night before will be very much appreciated. You will see the benefit in increased early registrations for the following year's event leading to quicker and easier sell-outs. Sold-out events quickly develop a caché which makes them even more popular (everyone wants to go when they think they can't get in). Then you can raise the ticket price and make even more money.

Pre-planning that call is a must. Even more than other fundraising programs, events demand increasing commitment up to and on "the night." Anyone who has been responsible for running an event knows how hard it is to re-energize volunteers and staff after the event is over. Asking Board members to make thank you calls to participants within a day or two of a draining event may not be met with enthusiasm, especially if the calling is not pre-planned. When trying this for the first time, test a manageable number of calls across a combination of first time and repeat attendees. Using controlled testing, you will gather valuable information such as whether a larger percentage of the test group buys tickets to next year's event, whether they buy earlier, whether more of them become sponsors, contribute in-kind commodities, buy higher priced tables or more tickets, etc. Most important, you will want to follow this test group for longer than the span of time between one event and the next to see how many move into the realm of philanthropic giving, something that you are aspiring to achieve with all your event-based donors.

A call from a member of the Board can start event participants on the road to philanthropy where the net return on investment for the charity is higher. A

We have found that a number of our donors don't like to be in the limelight and therefore do not attend our recognition events.

We're often concerned about planning events that offer food and drink for fear we are "devaluing" our donors' gifts.

Membership is critical for us—it builds loyalty. However, members see their membership gift as their donation and seldom give extra unless it's for a capital campaign.

fifty cent cost per dollar raised is common in fundraising events, and many events rise and fall in popularity. They are great marketing and acquisition tools but less effective as dependable, long term fundraisers. Moving donors out of fundraising events and into major giving should be part of your growth strategy. Personal thank you calls can mark the beginning of that migration.

Even pledge-per-point fundraisers like run-a-thons can be donor-centered for thousands or even tens of thousands of donors if donors are pledging online. Race results and fundraising goals achieved can be communicated to contributors the next morning via broadcast email. Here's another opportunity to make the most out of modern technology's ability to enhance donor communication.

BARRIERS TO CHANGE

As you change to a more donor-centered way of doing business, you may come up against the following barriers. Some are common to all workplaces; others are unique to the fundraising business. They can all be overcome, however, through honest self-assessment and consistently supportive management.

1. Fear of losing one's job.

This will be the number one concern of non-management staff, especially people in direct marketing programs. To people in this part of the business, fewer solicitations and smaller acquisition programs add up to layoffs. In fact, donor-centered fundraising is likely to need at least your current staffing contingent but some staff time may be redeployed to donor communication.

Suppliers will also fear losing a contract or having the value of their contracts reduced. Chapters 12, 13 and this chapter provide information about how suppliers can enhance their value to clients in a donor-centered culture.

2. Fear of communicating with donors.

This is more widespread than you might think given the nature of the business. In fact, the majority of people working in fundraising do not actually interact with donors, except incidentally. The exceptions are planned and major gifts professionals who, according to our study, spend about 40% of their time in direct communication with donors. The people who interact with donors far more than anyone else are telemarketers and canvassers who are employed at the very bottom of the staffing grid, their working conditions are the worst, and they are paid the least!

You should look at your own staff contingent and calculate the overall percentage of time being devoted now to direct interaction with donors. You will probably be surprised at how small it is.

Fear of communicating with donors is real. The way to overcome it is to make donor communication everyone's job. Try having all staff, regardless of their position, call one donor in the morning before they start anything else, and one more before they go home at night. I know several charities that have implemented this suggestion and it has completely changed the cultural mindset in the development office. Not only that, it has been directly responsible for raising more money.

Your staff may actually become the greatest beneficiaries of communicating with donors. They won't be able to help feeling great because they made a donor feel important. What a wonderful way to start and end the day.

3. Getting bogged down with the volume of donors.

Direct marketing programs rely on volume to make money. Donor-centered fundraising does not. However, here you are with a whole lot of donors, wondering how you will ever communicate with them all individually. Well, you won't.

For instance, you do not have to call all your donors after a single campaign; as a matter of fact, you shouldn't. It is important to start with a test to gather financial and other data. The size of your test should be determined, in part, by the time you can devote to the test and the availability of volunteers to make the calls. If even a test is out of reach at this time, start with a call to one donor, then another, then another. No matter when you decide to stop momentarily and look back at your performance, you will find that you are ahead of where you were when you started. That is progress.

Thank-a-thons are not the solution. A thank you calling binge designed to get through as many donors as possible in as short a period of time as possible is just another mass marketing program and donors will see it as such. Don't get caught up in the number of donors you haven't yet called; concentrate on the future benefit of what you have already done. Volunteers will soon tire of "thank-a-thons" so it's better that you help them and paid staff learn that communicating one-on-one with donors is part of the year-round job of being a fundraiser. In that context, you want to encourage consistent, yet manageable attention to this work.

Donor-centered communication includes more than calling donors personally to thank them for their gifts, of course. Chapters 9 and 10 dealt with other communication and recognition activities that are all part of donor-centered

I consider giving has nothing to do with amount, and everything to do with the willingness to do so.

Let donors know that you truly appreciate them, regardless of how you choose to do it.

fundraising. Determine where you can make improvements now within your existing workload. Working differently while fulfilling existing expectations is part of becoming donor-centered. Every step you take counts.

4. Lacking an analytical culture.

Fundraisers purchase incredibly sophisticated software, then relegate it to running the most banal and predictable reports. True to the industry's preoccupation with the money and not the donor, reports are largely income-based. How much money came in this month? How does that compare with last month and last year at the same time?

Without knowing what is transpiring with the donors themselves, fundraisers cannot do anything but mull over current and past performance and hope for the best in the future. Donor analysis, however, is revealing and gives you information for long range planning and forecasting.

5. Failing to test.

Controlled testing is essential in order to apply your organization's real numbers to the issues explored in this book. It also provides the evidence that you must present to decision-makers in order to adequately resource donor-centered fundraising. (See Chapter 7.)

6. Failing to acknowledge that donor attrition is a problem.

In a recent wide-ranging fundraising conference, not one of over one hundred eighty training sessions and panel discussions tackled the issue of excessive donor attrition. High attrition seems to be accepted by the fundraising industry as a price of doing business when it is actually a symptom of a business in trouble. Excessive attrition and the things that cause it need to be discussed more openly by senior practitioners and institutions that represent fundraising. This problem needs to be solved.

7. Prioritizing short term fundraising over more lucrative long term strategies.

Pressure is always intense to raise the money right now; but any success (or lack of it) in the short term is attributable to what you did or did not do six to twenty-four months ago. There are only two ways to get your hands on fast money and I wouldn't recommend either of them:

- Rely on untested fundraising events to raise current
  year revenue (if they do, you just got lucky this time).

- Rely on third parties to raise your money for you for a percentage of gross receipts. (You must be willing to relinquish almost all the money they raise using your good name and you may not get the donor list at the end of the campaign.)

If you succumb to the pressure to focus entirely on short term fundraising, you will always be looking over your shoulder. With no long term or progressive strategies in place, your energy will be devoted to fending off short term crises rather than building progressive relationships with donors. But, like the boy who cried wolf, your increasingly urgent cries for help will cause donors to become indifferent and to seek out more stable partnerships.

8. Anticipating disinterest or lack of cooperation from employers.

The only way to convince yourself that donor-centered fundraising works is to try it. But, to try it, you need the cooperation of your CEO and your Board of Directors. The toughest pitch you will ever make in fundraising is not to donors but to your own colleagues and your boss. It is worth the time and effort to do it right if it means moving your organization to a much higher level of fundraising success. You must speak their language if you want your message heard. Focus on results; show your Board and CEO the cost/benefit of raising money differently, backed up with evidence from testing. Give them a sound business reason to adopt donor-centered fundraising.

Donor-centered fundraising will benefit leadership volunteers just as much as paid staff. With more and more predictable resources at hand, planning will be easier and much more enjoyable. Time spent by Board members in dealing with financial problems will lessen, allowing more time for considering innovative and progressive ideas and for communicating with donors.

9. Anticipating lack of cooperation from non-fundraising colleagues.

Unless you are a one-person shop, it will take more than the development office to make donor-centered fundraising work. If gifts are receipted in the finance office, if the incoming mail is opened by the receptionist, if the data input assistant is shared with another department—changes that affect people other than fundraisers may have to be made in order to implement donor-centered fundraising.

Reminding yourself and others of the reasons why change is necessary will help. These should ring true for *all* personnel, not just fundraisers:

I think that people are very concerned about the future world and how it's going to look. Charities have to make a strong case that their work is going to have an impact on the world that they are creating for tomorrow. If it isn't doing that, they have to rethink their direction and their priorities. In a global environment, we must be much more involved in what our future is going to look like. For example, in New York and other big cities, how is my charity affecting the quality of life in my community? We must be very astute about what that means. It's a whole new world with shifting economy and shifting power and we must be prepared for those shifts.

- Donor-centered fundraising is designed to make more money so that programs and services can be expanded and improved.
- Donor-centered fundraising minimizes risk and expense while maximizing revenue.
- Donor-centered fundraising creates a more financially stable organization with a predictable financial future.

Focusing your colleagues as well as yourself on "one step at a time" will also help. (See Chapter 7, *Test Everything*.)

IF IT'S RIGHT FOR DONORS, IT'S RIGHT FOR FUNDRAISING

For a long time, questionable fundraising methodologies and tactics have had a free ride on the coattails of the charitable sector's good name. Aggressive and invasive appeals, rampant over-solicitation, trading and selling private information—have been endured by donors who were determined to be philanthropic. But it seems that donors have now reached the limit of their patience and they are beginning to take action. Donors are demanding greater protection of their privacy and better controls on how money is raised, and they are insisting on measurable results from the charities they support. Lawsuits concerning fundraising practice, which would have been unthinkable only a few years ago, are working their way through the courts. Legislators are drafting protective measures.

The fundraising industry needs to get out in front of the logistical and ethical issues that donors are having to confront on a daily basis. We need to see our business from our customers' point of view, make changes that work better for donors, and stand behind those changes with progressive policies. The image will not be good if the industry has to be dragged, kicking and screaming, into a better way of doing business.

Though the language of fundraising tells another story, donors are not targets, hits, or a commodity that can be overlooked or easily replaced. They are people, customers, partners . . . and vital to the survival of the entire not for profit sector. The third sector can enter a whole new era by showing the world that it can take the high road, opt for the ethical alternative, and still make money. In fact by doing the right thing, charities can make much *more* money. It is possible. Sometimes the good guys win.

16
The Policy

This is my tribute to donors and the philosophy I hope you will adopt in your organization.

DONOR-CENTERED FUNDRAISING POLICY

Donors and Philanthropy

We recognize that a philanthropic spirit is the common characteristic of all donors.

We recognize that a philanthropic gift is one whose worth is relative to means and that only the donor can define generosity. It is the act of giving and not the size of any donation that underlies our donor communication philosophy and our actions.

We recognize that our organization and its volunteer leaders and professional staff play an important role in introducing Americans to the privilege and opportunity of giving, whether their giving is directed to our organization or not.

We recognize that we have the capacity to influence giving to our own as well as to other not for profit organizations through how we communicate with our donors.

The Donor-Centered Philosophy

We practice an approach to communication and recognition that is donor-centered. This means that the fundamental interests and sensibilities of donors are paramount in the design and delivery of all aspects of our fundraising program. We adhere to the following principles:

- Our donors can expect to receive prompt, personalized acknowledgment of the gifts they make to our organization.
- Our donors can expect to be informed of the specific designation of their gifts.

- Our donors can expect to receive meaningful and measurable information on their gifts at work prior to being asked to give again.
- Our donors do not receive gift acknowledgments or information about their gifts and solicitations simultaneously.

Donor-Centered Principles in Action

We agree to:
- Work at all times within a three (or more) year Strategic Plan which defines our long term goals, describes the specific programs and services that will reach these goals, and includes measurable objectives, both qualitative and quantitative, for each program.
- Welcome designated giving to specific programs or services.
- Issue personalized thank you letters to donors within two working days of receipt of their gifts.
- Acknowledge donors' generosity from time to time through personal calls and visits from members of the Board of Directors and other organization leaders.
- Design and execute donor recognition events that showcase donors' gifts at work as a priority, that adhere to a stringent budget to avoid real or perceived criticisms about cost and that, in tone and delivery, acknowledge the collective generosity and importance of all our donors.
- Communicate information on their gifts at work to all our donors as effectively as possible, and do so before asking donors for another gift.
- Refrain from providing or withholding information based on individual gift value, in the belief that generosity can only be defined by the donor, and that all donors need and deserve information on their gifts at work.

Our Active Role in Expanding Philanthropy

Though not limitless, donors' generosity can be far-reaching. Donors do not seem to adopt an either/or position when it comes to making giving decisions; rather, they are influenced to give more to our organization as well as to others if they feel their efforts are appreciated and measurably worthwhile. We have a vested interest, therefore, in playing an active role in expanding Americans' interest in philanthropy, whether or not they choose to give to our organization initially, by:

1. Introducing more people to philanthropy.
Each staff person employed in the development office and each member of the Board of Directors encourages people within his or her sphere of influence to give or volunteer, whether it be to our own organization or to other charities.

2. Reducing donor attrition.

We acknowledge that the longer a donor gives, the more likely he is to keep giving. We also acknowledge that too many willing donors stop giving after a poor experience, which is related to lack of information on their gifts at work and under-appreciation. We apply the principles of donor-centered fundraising and communication to all donors regardless of their longevity, both in consideration of the investment that was made initially to acquire them and in the knowledge that their future giving potential is incalculable.

> Philanthropy is a heart size, not a gift size.

17

Living the Definition of Donor-Centered Fundraising

Awhile ago, I had the good fortune of working as a volunteer on a capital campaign which was chaired by the president of a national division of a large international company. To minimize the demands on his time, campaign meetings were held at his office.

Even on days when there was evidently something urgent transpiring and his executive assistant was fielding requests for his time, the president remained focused on the task at hand and on us. At the end of each meeting, he always took the time to see us to the door. Since his office was as far as you can get from the entrance, the trip to the elevator took a few minutes. Once in the lobby he would always wait with us until the elevator arrived and he would still be there, smiling at us and not moving, as the elevator doors closed between us.

Recently, he was promoted to the position of worldwide president. Everyone in the industry said that it was because of his outstanding track record, his creativity, the way he anticipates new business trends, his early rise to the position of president of the national division—and all those things and more are true. But I know why he really got the top job—it's because he has a way with people. It's because when you are with him you have his full attention no matter what else may be happening around him. It's because he walks his guests to the elevator.

No matter who you are—professional fundraiser, executive director, member of the Board, or fundraising volunteer—you are at this moment the sum of everything that you have learned and that you have experienced. Success in fundraising, like success in all business and in life itself, demands a high level of acquired skill in partnership with the ability and desire to interact with people. Do not be defeated by the numbers—whether numbers of donors, amounts of money, or quantity of work that lies ahead of you. In the end, it all comes down to one: the single donor fulfilling her philanthropic objective with you, the skilled catalyst, there in the right place at the right time, doing the right thing. Your consistent focus on one, who at that moment in time receives your undivided attention, will add up without you ever having to worry about the math. One day, as you are walking another donor to the elevator, it will simply occur to you that you have succeeded.

That is donor-centered fundraising.

Acknowledgments

This research study would have been impossible without the two hundred sixty-seven charitable organizations that participated in this project. I am sincerely grateful to staff members of the following organizations for completing an on-line survey that investigated how they interact with donors and recognize contributors for their support. Their information and advice were vital in bringing depth and perspective to this project. My sincere thanks go, as well, to charities that chose to participate anonymously:

200 Women's Initiative for Self Employment
Abramson Center for Jewish Life
Adolescent Pregnancy Prevention Coalition
    of North Carolina
Advocate Health Care Charitable Foundation
Advocates for Children & Youth
Alive
Alliance of Artists Communities
American Health Information
    Management Association
American Red Cross
American Red Cross, Rio Hondo Chapter
Animal Protection Society of Durham
Anza-Borrego Foundation
Arizona Humane Society
Assistance League of Southern California
Association of New Jersey
    Environmental Commissions
Ballet Arizona
Ballet Tech Foundation
Bank Street College of Education
Baptist Children's Services
Barnes-Jewish Hospital Foundation
Bayfront Health Foundation
Bergen Community College Foundation

Blodgett Butterworth Health Care & DeVos
    Children's Hospital Foundation
Bowdoin College
Boys & Girls Clubs of Las Vegas Foundation
Boys & Girls Clubs of Metro Atlanta
Boys & Girls Clubs of Middle Tennessee
Brandeis University
Bread for the World
Breast Cancer Family Foundation
Burleigh-Morton Red Cross
Cannon School
Carnegie Mellon University
Casa El Dorado
Catalina Island Conservancy
Catholic Guild for the Blind
Catholic Social Services
The Center for a New American Dream
The Center for Development & Population Activities
Charlotte Repertory Theatre
Child Abuse & Neglect Council of Saginaw County
Children's Safety Center
Christ Lutheran Academy
Christian Legal Services of Cleveland
Cincinnati Country Day School
Claremont University Consortium

Claremore Public Schools Foundation
College of Saint Benedict
Colorado Energy Assistance Foundation
Community Child Care Center
Congregation of Benedictine Sisters
The Connecticut Forum
Contemporary Museum
Correctional Association of NY
COSAC
The Cove Schools
The Cultural Landscape Foundation
Da Camera of Houston
Defiance Regional Medical Center
Delta Delta Delta Foundation
Detroit Medical Center
Development Workshop Foundation
Dillon International
Diocese of Lansing
Diocese of Tulsa
Doheny Eye Institute
Eagle Mount Billings
Easter Seals of Arizona
The Eastern Baptist Theological Seminary
Elijah House
EMQ Children & Family Services
Family Literacy Foundation
First Presbyterian Day School
FOCUS St. Louis
Foundation for North American Wild Sheep
Frank Lloyd Wright Foundation
Genesis School
Girl Scouts of Black Hawk Council
Green River Community College
HALT -- An Organization of Americans for
    Legal Reform
Hannah More School
Harbor Branch Oceanographic Institution
Harry Hynes Memorial Hospice

Hazelden Foundation
Healing the Children, Northeast
Henry W. Grady Foundation
Heritage Harbor Museum
Hesston College
Homewood Retirement Centers Foundation
Hope (HIV Outreach, Programs & Education)
Hospice Hawaii
Housatonic Valley Association
I Have a Dream - Houston
Idaho Law Foundation
International Baccalaureate Organization
Island Moving Co., Arts & Cultural
    Alliance of Newport County
IT Resource Center
Jesuits of the Missouri Province
The Joffrey Ballet of Chicago
KAET-TV Channel 8 -- Arizona State University
Kemmerer Village
Kid One Transport
Lake Forest Open Lands Association
Laurel School
Lawrence Arts Center
Lincoln Medical Education Foundation
Linfield Christian School Foundation
Literacy Chicago
Loon Echo Land Trust
Lupus Foundation of Northern California
Lutheran Community Foundation
Marian Clinic
Marie Selby Botanical Gardens
Massachusetts College of Liberal Arts
Mayo Clinic Foundation
McLeod Medical Center Foundation
Medical University of South Carolina
Mercy Medical Center
Methodist Children's Home
Metropolitan Ministries

Michigan's Children
Mid-Island Y JCC
Midwest Whole Child Development Group
Mississippi Valley Regional Blood Center
Mitchell Area Adjustment Training Center Foundation
Monterey Jazz Festival
Mount Mary College
Moveable Feast
Mujeres Latinas en Accion
Music Academy of the West
The Music Hall
Mystic Valley Elder Services
New Haven Home Recovery
New York Foundation for the Arts
North Shore Senior Center
North Suffolk Mental Health Association
Northwestern University Settlement Association
Oakland Public Library Foundation
Ogden Nature Center
Ohio Academy of Family Physicians Foundation
OMNI Youth Services
Opera Roanoke
Orangewood Children's Foundation
Pace Center for Girls
Park Slope Geriatric Day Center
Paws With A Cause
PCC Farmland Fund
Pennsylvania Horticultural Society
Physician Assistant Foundation
Pitt Academy
Polish American Association
Pratt Area Community Council
Predator Conservation Alliance
Presbyterian Children's Services
Professional Convention Management
    Association Foundation
Progressive Agriculture Foundation
Project Angel Heart

Providence Child Center Foundation
Rehabilitation Opportunities, Inc.
Ronald McDonald House at Stanford
Ronald McDonald House Charities
    of Greater Cincinnati
St. Catherine's Village
St. Joseph Institute for the Deaf
The Salvation Army Massachusetts Division
Samford University
Search Native Seeds
Set of Colorado Springs
Share Self-Help for Women with Breast or
    Ovarian Cancer
Small World Ministries
Southern California College of Optometry
Southwest Center for the Performing Arts
Spaulding for Children
Springfield Victory Mission
Tabitha Foundation
Teaching Company
Theater Works
Topeka Civic Theater & Academy
TROA Scholarship Fund
Tulane University
Turning Point for Families
United Way of Greater Toledo
United Way of Jackson County
United Way of Norwalk & Wilfox
University at Buffalo
University of Idaho
University of Maryland School of Medicine
University of Miami
University of North Carolina at Greensboro
Upper Valley Land Trust
Ursinus College
Volunteer Center of Rhode Island
The West Side Catholic Center
West Virginia University Foundation

Western Washington University Foundation
Westside Children's Center
Wheaton College
Wildlife Heritage Foundation of Wyoming
William Temple House
Wisconsin Lutheran Child & Family Service

Wistar Institute
Woodmere Art Museum
World Neighbors
YMCA of Dane County
Youth Horizons
Youth Outreach Services

Most charity respondents provided this study with samples of their gift acknowledgment correspondence, and many went out of their way to recount creative, humorous, and often poignant stories about their donor communication experiences. Though space prevented me from including every story in the book, I would like to acknowledge each respondent who took the time to put his/her experience on paper and who did it so well. My appreciation goes to:

Association of New Jersey
   Environmental Commissions
Bergen Community College Foundation
Bowdoin College
Claremore Public Schools Foundation
College of Saint Benedict
Detroit Medical Center
Dillon International
Elijah House
EMQ Children & Family Services
Family Literacy Foundation
Hannah More School
I Have a Dream – Houston
Idaho Law Foundation
Island Moving Co., Arts & Cultural
   Alliance of Newport County
Lawrence Arts Center
Marian Clinic
Mid-Island Y JCC

Midwest Wholechild Development Group
Monterey Jazz Festival
North Shore Senior Center
North Suffolk Mental Health Association
Northwestern University Settlement Association
Ogden Nature Center
Pennsylvania Horticultural Society
Predator Conservation Alliance
Presbyterian Children's Services
Search Native Seeds
Turning Point for Families
University at Buffalo
University of Idaho
Upper Valley Land Trust
Westside Children's Center
Wisconsin Lutheran Child & Family Service
Woodmere Art Museum
YMCA of Dane County
Youth Horizons

Several Canadian charities that participated in the first study published in 2000 provided information on their experiences with donor-centered fundraising that have informed this book. My thanks to:

BC Cancer Foundation
Calgary Health Region
Campbell River Hospital Foundation
Dalhousie University

Hospitals of Regina Foundation
Parkwood Hospital Foundation
Queen of the Valley Hospital Foundation
University of Saskatchewan

Special thanks go to the **Ontario Division of the Canadian Paraplegic Association**. The test of personal thank you calls managed by its staff and conducted by members of the Board of Directors is an important example of the power of personal communication.

These gracious individuals, companies, and foundations, who do so much for the charitable sector already, took the time to participate in lengthy interviews, offering valuable insights on donor communication and recognition, and providing anecdotes on their relationships with the charities they support. I am so appreciative of these donors and the many people who chose to participate anonymously in this study for their thoughtful contributions. Donor respondents clearly articulated a common sense solution to attrition and other fundraising problems, and their contributions literally shaped this book. My gratitude goes to:

The Allstate Foundation
Charlotte Barrett
Kate R. Barrett
Maria Bechily
Diana Behm
Adelaide Benjamin
Roger Berle
Doris Brackney
Rich Braugh
Ann Brown
Christa Burke
Chris Burkett
Florence Canter
Al Carlson
John Celick
Janet Christensen
Bob Colosimo
Timothy A. Crummy
Charles H. Dana

The Dana Corporation
Evon Dean
Dr. Karen Dees
Michael Devorkin
Robert Dill
Joe W. Dobbs
Harrison Drinkwater
Myra Duvally
Howard L. Ewart
Roberta Ezell
Fairfield County Savings Bank
Christine Farrington
Anne Faulkner
J. Michael Fay
Doris M. Fell
Robert Fiorani
Valerie Fisher
Kay Folan
Lynda Foote

Linda Foss
Sulma Gandhi
Patricia H. Garman
NaDean Garrett
John Gibbons, Jr.
Eileen Goldblatt
Sally Graham
Lynn Green
Kathleen Grewe
Dr. William T. Griffin
Lavina Guertin
Hallmark Cards
Harper Industries
Hershey Foods Corporation
Phebe Holcombe
Suzie Horst
Howard S. Wright Construction Co.
Betty Hughes
Becky Janzen
Bernie Jeifa
John H. Johl
Kaiser Permanente
Dr. John Kelsey
Laurie Kennedy
Mary Kinsell
Roberta Krull
Stephen A. Kula
Bonnie Lau
Pat Lightfoot
Lincoln Financial Group
Anne Livingston
Massachusetts Mutual Life
Frank McGuire
Thomas J. P. McHenry
Jane McKay Morrell
Kinnaird McQuade
Allen Model
Jack Natterman

Carol Nelson
Betsy O. Chandler
Tim O'Malley
Dr. & Mrs. Robert Osborne
David Ott
Pride Mortgage
Public Service Electric & Gas Company
Jim Putnam
Patricia Relfe
Perry Relfe
Debbie Reynolds
Priscilla Richardson
Gloria Robinson
Nancy Roering
Sharon Rydel
Susie Schechter
Scripps Howard Foundation
Stephen Seibert
Kathryn H. Sheehy
Jan M. Smith
Stuart V. Smith, Jr.
Jack Smither
Lisa Stauffer
Marilyn L. Steinbright
Janet Stockhausen
Michael Stromberg
Stryker Howmedica Osteonics
Talking Rain Co., Inc.
Anne Thompson
Sara Vance
Beth Vandenberg
George Webb
Frankie Wellins
Linda Wishard
Mary T. Wolfe
Joe Wolking
Michael N. Wood
Sherley Young
John C. Zimdars, Jr.

And thanks to...

Brian P. Twohey and **Annabelle Bennetts** retired earlier this year from long careers in the financial services and management consulting industries respectively...or at least they thought they retired. With much good humor and professionalism, they came out of retirement to assist with this project. Thanks to both of you for devoting so much time to conducting interviews with donor respondents. Thanks as well to **Graham Hallward** and **Laurie Francis** who led us to several study donors.

Many other research studies on philanthropy and fundraising were very important to me as I wrote this book. My appreciation goes to these fine organizations whose work is so important to the charitable sector and whose research is referenced in this book:

AAFRC Trust for Philanthropy for *Giving USA 2002* – the annual report on philanthropy for 2001, Indianapolis, IN, 2002
Canadian Centre for Philanthropy, for *Caring Canadians, Involved Canadians: Highlights from the 2000 Survey of Giving, Volunteering and Participating*, August 2001
Independent Sector for *Giving & Volunteering in the United States*, 2001 edition, Washington, DC, 2002
Lang Research, Mal Warwick & Associates, and The FLA Group for *Surveys of Charitable Donors in the United States and Canada*, March 2003
Princeton Survey Research Associates, Inc., *BBB Wise Giving Alliance – Donor Expectations Survey, Princeton, NJ*, September, 2001

Also very helpful in identifying research sources, offering industry statistics, and providing professional advice were the **Association of Fundraising Professionals**, especially Cathlene Williams, Ph.D., CAE and Joyce O'Brien, the **University at Buffalo, Karen Cairney, Legacy Leaders, Inc.** and **Artsmarketing Services, Inc.**

The emails that introduce Chapter 2 and which really were the catalysts to my writing this book were submitted by **Diane Hinrichs**, Director of Donor Relations at KSU Foundation and **Debbie Meyers**, Stewardship and Donor Relations, University of Florida Foundation, Inc. There were days when I wished I had never seen those emails, but now that the book is written...thank you.

I first encountered **Marion K. Ringe**, M.A., CFRE (Grants and Publications Director, Detroit Medical Center) when she reviewed the Canadian edition of this book for *Advancing Philanthropy* (May/June, 2001). I asked her to look at just a few pages of the first draft of *Donor-Centered Fundraising* and, before you knew it, she had edited the entire book. Marion, I cannot thank you enough for your perseverance, your grace, good humor, and your terrific grasp of language and grammar.

The beautiful cover design, company logo, and design and layout of *Donor-Centered Fundraising* are the work of **Mark Narsansky, RBA Advertising Ltd.** Thank you, Mark, for your incredible talent and for managing this end of the project. **Valerie Appleby** and **Rana Chow** worked with Mark to bring the book to fruition. **Friesen's Corporation**, our amazing printer, produced the final product. **Deborah Greenfield Findlay** energetically assists our company in marketing the book and our associated seminars and speaking engagements. Thank you, Deb.

As always, my gratitude extends to my incredible family – especially my mother, **Jean Burk** and late father, **Bill**, for instilling in me a love of ideas, an insatiable curiosity, and a sense of humor. The environment that they created in our home taught my five siblings and me to bring something interesting to the dinner table if we wanted to participate in the discussion. We also learned to back up our claims if we wanted to avoid being served up with the meat and vegetables. Thanks for such a great beginning.

To my children **Jeffrey, Jonathan,** and **Jason** go my adoration…and my gratitude for your patience.

My final acknowledgment goes to **Jeff Dubberley, B.A., M.A.,** who, more than anyone else, made *Donor-Centered Fundraising* possible. For six years he guided the research for both the Canadian and American studies that shaped the concept of donor-centered fundraising. He is responsible for securing the charities and donors that participated in the US study, for analyzing all the data, for managing our website, and for our online and print marketing strategies. His value to Burk & Associates Ltd. and Cygnus Applied Research, Inc. is immeasurable. Jeff, thank you so very much for all you have done to bring this idea to life.

About the Author

Penelope Burk, author, trainer, and President of Cygnus Applied Research, Inc. and Burk & Associates Ltd., has over 30 years' experience in not for profit management, fundraising, marketing, and research. A native of Montreal, Canada, she began her career in public relations with leading arts organizations followed by senior positions with social service and recreation charities including Big Brothers/Big Sisters. Her in-depth and varied career established her as a senior professional advocating innovative approaches to fundraising and marketing. Burk & Associates has been serving clients, conducting unique training programs and industry research for fifteen years. The company has offices in Chicago, Toronto, Vancouver, and the United Kingdom.

Penelope is an accomplished writer who has authored dozens of seminars, most of which feature scenes and short plays about real life fundraising situations portrayed by *The Burk & Associates Players*, a lively troup of professional actors who perform to the delight and amazement of delegates. Burk & Associates' seminars have been acclaimed as unique, engaging, and among the most effective training programs in the not for profit sector today. Penelope is also the author of *The Philanthropist*, a play about a reclusive entrepreneur, his evolution into a significant community donor, and the professional fundraiser who encouraged him.

Penelope is especially well known for her leading edge research in donor communication. Author of two major North American studies on the subject, Penelope's work is the only statistically-based research ever published on the effect of communication on donor retention and gift value. Her first research study on the subject was published in Canada in 2000. It garnered unreserved accolades from critics and readers and has become a best seller.

CYGNUS APPLIED RESEARCH, INC. /
BURK & ASSOCIATES LTD.

Cygnus Applied Research, Inc. conducts innovative research and training programs in and for the not for profit sector. Burk & Associates Ltd. manages related client consulting services. With offices in the US (Chicago), Canada (Toronto, Vancouver), and the United Kingdom (York), the firms include senior management, fundraising, and communication consultants who provide strategic advice to clients, and conduct leading edge training programs.

The core services of the company include:

Donor-Centered Fundraising and Communication - consultation, planning, testing, and training

Research and Analysis - fundraising program and development department audits, marketing assessments, donor giving and psychology studies, pre-campaign assessments

Strategic Planning - strategic plans for development departments, fundraising programs, organizational programs and services, marketing plans

Training and Seminars - seminars, training programs, and keynote addresses on more than forty topics and varying in length from one hour to three days, including a one-day introduction to donor-centered fundraising and a three-day donor-centered institute (the latter to be inaugurated in 2004)

For a complete list of currently available seminars and more information on the company's consulting services, visit our website at **www.donorcentered.com** or call (800) 263-0267.